Zhou

Group Process and Productivity

SOCIAL PSYCHOLOGY

A series of monographs, treatises, and texts

EDITORS

LEON FESTINGER AND STANLEY SCHACHTER

Jack W. Brehm, A Theory of Psychological Reactance. 1966

Ralph L. Rosnow and Edward J. Robinson (Eds.), Experiments in Persuasion. 1967

Jonathan L. Freedman and Anthony N. Doob,
Deviancy: The Psychology of Being Different. 1968

Paul G. Swingle (Ed.), Experiments in Social Psychology. 1968, 1969

E. Earl Baughman and W. Grant Dahlstrom, Negro and White Children:
A Psychological Study in the Rural South. 1968

Anthony G. Greenwald, Timothy C. Brock, and Thomas M. Ostrom (Eds.),
Psychological Foundations of Attitudes. 1968

Robert Rosenthal and Ralph Rosnow (Eds.), Artifact in Behavioral Research. 1969

R. A. Hoppe, E. C. Simmel, and G. A. Milton (Eds.), Early Experiences
and the Processes of Socialization. 1970

Richard Christie and Florence Geis, Studies in Machiavellianism. 1970

Paul G. Swingle (Ed.), The Structure of Conflict. 1970

Alvin Zander, Motives and Goals in Groups. 1971

Stanley Schachter, Emotion, Obesity, and Crime. 1971

Charles A. Kiesler, The Psychology of Commitment:
Experiments Linking Behavior to Belief. 1971

Jacobo A. Varela, Psychological Solutions to Social Problems:
An Introduction to Social Technology. 1971

David C. Glass and Jerome E. Singer, Urban Stress:
Experiments on Noise and Social Stressors. 1972

Ivan D. Steiner, Group Process and Productivity. 1972

Shelley Duval and Robert A. Wicklund, A Theory of Objective Self Awareness. 1972

Alice Ross Gold, Richard Christie, and Lucy Norman Friedman, Fists and Flowers:
A Social Psychological Interpretation of Student Dissent. 1976

GROUP PROCESS AND PRODUCTIVITY

IVAN D. STEINER
University of Massachusetts

ACADEMIC PRESS   New York   San Francisco   London
A Subsidiary of Harcourt Brace Jovanovich, Publishers

ACADEMIC PRESS, INC.
111 Fifth Avenue, New York, New York 10003

United Kingdom Edition published by
ACADEMIC PRESS, INC. (LONDON) LTD.
24/28 Oval Road, London NW1

LIBRARY OF CONGRESS CATALOG CARD NUMBER: 73-182671

PRINTED IN THE UNITED STATES OF AMERICA

Contents

Preface

The group seems to have gone out of fashion. Throughout the first half of the twentieth century social psychologists surveyed its problem-solving capacities, examined its cohesion, and debated its ultimate reality. But by the late fifties interest in the group as a productive unit, a system of interacting parts, had diminished. Attention was turned to the processes that occur within the single individual: attitude change, dissonance arousal, and impression formation. The group, when it was not ignored, became merely the arena in which attitudes were shaped, dissonance was created or reduced, and people inferred one another's motives and intentions. The group as a task-performing system was largely forgotten.

The emergence of new and exciting lines of research was not solely responsible for the social psychologist's flagging interest in groups. By 1950 the empirical investigation of group productivity had outdistanced theory, and each new study tended to stand aloof from others. Literature reviews had become encyclopedic listings of discoveries that appeared somehow to belong in the same abstract category, and one investigation was piled on top of another. In retrospect, it seems clear that this chaotic state of affairs reflected two notable deficiencies in the early work: investigators had tended to pay little attention to the demands that tasks impose upon groups, and they had often attempted to investigate productivity without examining the processes by which groups become productive. In the absence of evidence concerning these two important matters, neither programmatic research nor integrative theory was very feasible.

In this book I have endeavored to combine some very early findings with evidence generated by more recent research, and I have stressed the integrative role of task demands and group process. The resulting theory is modest in scope, and it deals with only a portion of the available literature. My aim has been to inspect a limited number of phenomena in an orderly, systematic fashion, and to describe a small but consistent network of interrelationships. Perhaps even a partial integration will help to dispel the malaise that has fallen over the study of group productivity. Much of the world's work continues to be done in and by groups, and questions raised during the first half of the century continue to deserve answers.

I am indebted to George Levinger, Richard Hackman, and Joan Kerpelman for critical comments concerning several chapters of the book. Many students at the University of Illinois and the University of Massachusetts favored me with their insightful reactions to portions of the manuscript, and psychology classes at both institutions listened with proper impatience to oral drafts of my thoughts.

Chapter 1

Introduction

Living things survive collectively. The tiny clostridium is wedded to bacterial partners which remove the oxygen from its atmosphere, leaving only the nitrogen it needs. Countless generations of protozoa have been sheltered inside the stomachs of termites where they perform functions their hosts cannot manage for themselves. There are tree roots that ally themselves with fungi, and algae and fungi that combine to accomplish the joint colonization of bare rock. Ants exchange hospitality for the milk of the aphid, and the plover flies into the open mouth of the crocodile to eat the blood-sucking leeches from its gums.

Mutual assistance by members of different species is only one aspect of the process by which living things achieve collective survival. Cooperation by members of the *same* species is equally common. Although the social insects provide the most obvious examples of this phenomenon, nature is replete with cases in which one individual contributes to the creation of the environment needed by another of the same species. Goldfish in large numbers are better able to resist poisons in their habitat than is the solitary goldfish. A herd of deer can more readily cope with deep snow than can the individual animal, and a flock of birds can survive where a single member of the species cannot. When attacked by wolves, musk oxen assemble themselves into a star-shaped formation with their antlers poised to fend off their assailant; in this fashion, each animal avoids an attack from the rear, against which musk oxen are almost totally helpless.

Man is no exception to the rule. Biologically, he is the least specialized of Earth's creatures, and poorly equipped to survive alone. By comparison with many other species, his body is weak; it is unprotected by hair, scales, or shells; and it lacks claws, tusks, or stingers. Upright posture leaves man's pelvic organs exposed to injury, and his two-legged gait is slower than that of many four-footed animals. He cannot climb, dig, or conceal himself as well as can many of his competitors, and he is equipped with less sensitive organs of sight, hearing, and smell. Nature has left him no alternative; he can combine his efforts with those of his fellows, or he can perish. But man has survived. Indeed, he has achieved "dominion over the fish of the sea, and the fowl of the air, and over every living thing that moveth upon the Earth [Genesis I, 28]."

Social scientists have attributed man's success to a variety of factors that include an opposable thumb, superior cortex, linguistic abilities, and the capacity to develop and transmit cultural solutions to recurring problems. Equally important is the ingenuity with which humans pool their resources to produce outcomes that no single individual can accomplish alone. For, although collective action is found at all levels of biological development, when practiced by man, it assumes a distinctive character. Among lesser creatures, cooperation reflects the push of instinctive tendencies, augmented and tempered by meager learning and limited insight. Musk oxen achieve collective survival because each does what comes naturally, and the same is generally true of infrahuman primates. But nature has failed to equip man with an elaborate repertoire of collective responses. Instead it has endowed him with the intellectual capacity to discover for himself how his interpersonal efforts should be organized, and with communicative abilities that permit him to tell his associates what he believes should be done.

It is obvious that man's approach to collective action can be far more flexible than that of any other creature. Humans can more readily modify their behaviors to meet the changing demands of their environments, and can discard one interpersonal arrangement in favor of another that seems more appropriate. Unlike musk oxen that assume the same star-shaped formation regardless of whether their assailant is a wolf or an armed hunter, humans can adjust their reactions to fit the problem at hand. Man's comparative freedom from instinctual determination and his vastly greater ability to evaluate and plan, permit him to employ collective action in a highly selective, flexible and adaptive manner. His triumph over other creatures has, in large measure, been a consequence of his superior ability to devise new and more effective ways of combining his own efforts with those of his associates.

Man's freedom to decide for himself how he will relate to his fellow men is not an unmixed blessing. Among the many possible patterns of collective action that may be employed to meet a given need, some are likely to be much more productive than others, and a few may be utterly disfunctional. Freedom to choose entails the obligation to choose wisely—at least as wisely as nature has chosen in behalf of its less thoughtful creatures, and as prudently as other human beings. For, having achieved supremacy over other animals, man vies with his kind for prestige, space, and material goods; and the success of his undertakings depends largely upon the quality of the alliances he forms with his associates, and upon the comparative merits of his own and other people's social units. Some groups, organizations, and societies function better than others, and the rewards received by participating members are likely to vary accordingly. Freedom to construct one's own social units implies the right to fail as well as the right to succeed.

Because the satisfaction of human needs is so often contingent upon the kind of collective arrangements people devise, man has shown a continuing concern for the adequacy of his social structures. Some of his oldest written documents offer advice to those who wish to enjoy harmonious family or group relationships, or who seek to establish a just and productive society. However, until very recently, such prescriptions have been based on casual observation rather than upon scientific inquiry. Knowledge about social systems has, on the whole, remained less abundant than knowledge about biological or physical systems. During the 20,000 years since our progenitors emerged from their caves, human curiosity has penetrated the problems of the land and the seas, and even the stars and planets that rise above them. But man himself, and the groups in which he thrives, have yielded their secrets less readily. Although recent decades have brought striking developments in the social sciences, no discipline has succeeded in charting group processes with the precision of a botanist who analyzes the structure of a fallen leaf, or the accuracy of a chemist who evaluates the processes of a hydrocarbon molecule. Moreover, our meager knowledge of human behavior is distressingly uneven. We know more about the individual man, the solitary mortal in the laboratory, than we know about man in his social habitat—the group. The psychology of semi-isolated *homo sapiens* has been more rigorously explored than has the psychology of men in interaction with one another.

To be sure, everyday experience offers valuable lessons concerning the nature and consequences of collective behavior. Insights that are based on informal observation though, are often rather imprecise and even contradictory.

Consider, for example, the following pairs of adages.

> *Two heads are better than one,* but
>   *Too many cooks spoil the broth.*
> *The more the merrier,* but
>   *Three is a crowd.*
> *If you would have a thing well done, do it yourself,* but,
>   *Jack of all trades, master of none.*
> *In unity there is strength,* but
>   *A chain is no stronger than its weakest link.*

Propositions such as these express the wisdom of the ages that has accumulated as people have noticed interesting regularities in human behavior. Undoubtedly, each is correct part of the time, but the circumstances under which any one of them is valid are not specified. Adages permit an observer to "explain" events that have already occurred, but they provide little real understanding of the phenomena with which they deal, and they have very limited predictive value. Understanding, prediction, and control are goals that can be fully realized only when the insights of everyday life are supplemented by the conclusions generated by carefully controlled research.

This book examines empirical literature dealing with the processes and productivity of comparatively small, task-oriented groups. It emphasizes the findings of laboratory investigations, and attempts to assimilate the data of many such studies to a conceptual framework. A major aim is to organize experimental evidence in a way that reveals some of the conditions that determine whether or not common-sense propositions about collective behavior are likely to be correct.

Task Groups

Collective action can involve as few as two persons or as many as a million. In some respects, everyone on earth is probably dependent upon everyone else, though such interdependencies often go unrecognized and are generally too indirect and weak to be of great practical importance. Within a single society, people rely upon one another for the satisfaction of many needs, including military security, protection from disease, and economic stability. However, awareness of such mutual relationships is likely to be intense only when wars, epidemics, or depressions are imminent. On other occasions, the behaviors of members may be so effectively guided by norms and role systems that people scarcely realize they are participating in a nationwide network of cooperative activity. In the case of a specific organization, such as a church, business enterprise, army, or political party, people are likely to be quite aware of their commonality of fate and to recognize the necessity of finding a collective solution to their problems. In smaller units—families, work groups, or committees—mutual interrelationships are even more apparent, and people generally employ direct, face-to-face, communication to harmonize and coordinate their individual efforts. Social aggregations of this kind are the building blocks out of which organizations and societies are constructed. The quality of the collective actions that transpire in such "primitive" social units tends to color the character of the larger units.

It is evident that man's collective behaviors may be examined at any of three levels: the group, the organization, or the society. Conceptual distinctions among these three kinds of social units are often blurred and artificial, but it is helpful to view groups as collections of mutually responsive individuals, to conceive organizations as sets of mutually responsive groups, and to regard societies as clusters of mutually responsive organizations. As attention is shifted upward in the conceptual structure, more and more human beings are implicated, but the immediacy and strength of the influence any one person is likely to exert on another decreases. Although members of a single group can ordinarily communicate directly and frequently with one another, people who are members of the same organization but of different groups generally cannot. Indeed, contacts among members of different groups tend to be routed "through channels," or to be mediated by third parties who function as communication specialists, liaison agents, or leaders. Members of different organizations ordinarily affect one another in an indirect manner either through the somewhat formal and stylized encounters of their elected or appointed representatives, or through the impact of their own organization's activities and products on those of the organization in which the other person functions. Face-to-face interchange among rank-and-file members of different societies tends to be even more rare. Although we may be exaggerating the differences among the three social levels, the units we call groups are the only ones in which all members may easily, rapidly, and effectively exercise deliberate and selective influences on all others.

To say that a group consists of a set of mutually responsive individuals is to provide only a minimal definition of the phenomenon with which this book is concerned. How intense, direct, and persistent must the responsiveness of the members be in order for a collection of individuals to qualify as a group? When the members go their separate ways after a period of interpersonal activity, does the group cease to exist? Is it a new group when members resume their collective actions? By what criteria can one specify who belongs in the group and who does not? Do groups possess attributes that entitle them to be regarded as entities in the sense that separate individuals are deemed to be? Or is it true, as some writers have contended, that groups have no reality apart from that of their individual members, the word "group" being only a convenient label for a class of people who are most accurately viewed as separate and distinct behavioral agents? These and other questions are best deferred until the collective behaviors of group members have been examined in considerable detail. For the present, it is only necessary to establish the fact that we are dealing with small sets of people who influence one another through direct, generally face-to-face, contacts.

Some groups are not much concerned with the performance of a task, or the creation of a product. Thus, intimate friends who assemble at someone's home may have no other aim than to enjoy one another's company, and a meeting of the Ladies Aid Society may be devoted more directly to the satisfaction of sociability needs than to the resolution of community problems or the performance of charitable functions. Groups may be conceived to vary along a continuum that ranges from "complete concern with task performance" to "complete concern with sociability." Perhaps few groups belong at the extreme ends of this continuum, but it is clear that different groups occupy different positions on it. This book is focused primarily on groups that are task-oriented; however, reference will be made to other kinds of groups, and to organizations and societies, when available evidence concerning such social units may contribute to an understanding of task groups.

Determinants of Productivity

How well an individual or group performs a task depends upon three classes of variables: task demands, resources, and process.

Task Demands

A housewife who wishes to bake a cake can consult a book of recipes and find a detailed description of the ingredients she must have, the tools that are required, and the procedures she should follow in transforming the raw materials into a finished product. Somewhat similar "recipes" are available to the man who wants to build a boat or grow a flower garden. In each of these cases, people who are experienced in the performance of the task have analyzed the requirements and written copious instructions for the benefit of the novice. Comparable "job descriptions" are not available for all tasks, but it is difficult to imagine a project for which a rather complete manual could not be prepared. Nobody has yet assembled a single, authoritative guidebook for launching an astronaut into space, but it is obvious that experts can identify the kinds of equipment and skills that are necessary, and can specify the steps that must be taken in order to accomplish the desired end. Indeed, the success with which such launchings have been conducted suggests that very precise job analyses can sometimes be made even before the task has been performed.

Task demands encompass all the prescriptions listed in a complete job-manual. They include the requirements imposed on the individual or group by the task itself, or by the rules under which the task must be performed. Such requirements determine whether a particular resource (knowledge, ability, skill, or tool) is relevant, how much of each kind of resource is needed for optimal performance, and how the various relevant resources must be combined and utilized in order to produce the best possible outcome. A statement of task demands may be likened to a set of building plans that not only describes the house that is to be produced, but also the materials that are to be used, the tools that are to be employed, the order in which various steps in the construction process are to be taken, and the manner in which the total process is to be managed. Needless to say, task demands are seldom specified in such a detailed fashion, but a clear understanding of group process and productivity may require that they be very carefully enumerated. Whether, and how well a group can perform a task depends in part upon the nature of the task it is asked to perform.

Resources

Resources include all the relevant knowledge, abilities, skills, or tools possessed by the individual(s) who is attempting to perform the task. If the actor is a group rather than a single individual, this determinant of productivity also includes the distribution of relevant resources among group members (for example, a pertinent body of knowledge may be possessed by only one member, *or* different bits of knowledge may be possessed by different members). It should be noted that task demands are largely independent of the resources of an individual or group. Task demands specify the kinds and amounts of resources that are *needed,* and the utilization pattern that is required if maximum productivity is to be obtained. The resource variables specify the types and amounts of resources actually possessed by an individual or group.

It is sometimes possible to evaluate task demands and resources even before the individual or group begins its work. In the typical laboratory study of individual or group productivity, these two classes of variables are established at specific (but often unknown) levels by the experimenter, who selects the persons who will participate as subjects, and dictates the characteristics of the task they will perform. A careful job analysis would presumably reveal the task demands which the experimenter is imposing on the individual or group, and an exhaustive battery of tests would indicate the amount and distribution of relevant resources possessed by the subjects.

Together, task demands and participants' resources determine the *maximum* level of productivity that can be achieved. If an individual or group possesses all the needed resources, it has the potential to perform the task in question. If certain resources are lacking, or are possessed in insufficient quantities, the individual or group may still be able to complete the task, but will be unable to do so as rapidly or as satisfactorily as would otherwise be the case. In this book, the expression *potential productivity* will be used to designate the maximum level of productivity that can occur when an individual or group employs its fund of resources to meet the task demands of a work situation. Potential productivity can be inferred from a thorough analysis of task demands and available resources, for it depends only upon these two types of variables.

Process

Actual productivity—what an individual or group does, in fact, accomplish—often fails to equal potential productivity. Lacking a clear and precise recipe for successful action, people are likely to use their resources improperly, to do the right thing at the wrong time, or to take steps that are, at best, a less than maximally effective solution to their problem. Even when previous experience or a written manual has identified the most productive course of behavior, people may pursue a less efficient one that seems more interesting or less effortful. Members of a group may hold different views concerning the proper pattern of collective action, and may be immobilized by their disagreement or end up producing a patchwork of poorly coordinated or even contradictory behaviors.

Process consists of the actual steps taken by an individual or group when confronted by a task. It includes all those intrapersonal and interpersonal actions by which people transform their resources into a product, and all those nonproductive actions that are prompted by frustration, competing motivations, or inadequate understanding. In short, process consists of the individual or collective actions of the people who have been assigned a task. In a productive group, these actions will include the intellective and communicative behaviors by which members evaluate, pool, and assemble their resources; decide who shall do what, when; assign differential weights to one another's contributions; and extoll one another to participate fully in the group's task-oriented activities. In the case of a single individual working alone, process is less complex for it does not involve interpersonal exchange and coordination. Rather, the single person must decide which of his resources are relevant, and in what sequence and combination they should be used.

Unlike task demands and resources, process cannot be measured or evaluated before work begins. Process is a series of behaviors, one following another, each determined to some degree by those that have gone before and each, in turn, influencing those that will come later. To the extent that the total sequence of behaviors corresponds to the pattern demanded by the task, actual productivity will approximate potential productivity. We may anticipate that the degree of correspondence is sometimes not very great.

It is apparent that task demands specify the resources that are needed, and the manner in which they should be employed, in order to generate a good product. The adequacy of the resources available to an individual or group determines its potential productivity; the appropriateness of its processes determines how well its actual productivity approximates its potential productivity.

Actual productivity = potential productivity − losses due to faulty process.

This formulation suggests that one group (or individual) may be more successful than another because it has a better supply of relevant resources (i.e., its potential productivity is higher), or because its processes more fully meet the demands of the task, or both. For the same reasons, a group may be more productive than a single individual, or an individual may be more productive than a group. From this perspective, it is not very meaningful to ask whether groups are more effective than individuals, or whether large groups are more productive than small ones. Answers to these questions may be expected to depend upon the nature of the task, the fund of resources individuals or groups can bring to bear upon it, and the ease and dependability with which they can employ the processes that will transform resources into a product of high quality.

Trends in the Study of Group Process and Productivity

A group may be viewed in either of two very different ways. It may be regarded as a unit in its own right, as an amalgamation of interacting individuals who collectively generate outcomes that are different from those any single member might produce alone. A group may also be seen as a critical aspect of its members' environment, as a social context that exerts powerful effects on its members' behaviors and thoughts. Of course these two perspectives are not necessarily contradictory; a group may be both a functioning unit and a determinant of its members' actions, but scholars generally find it difficult to maintain both views at the same time, or to conduct research that examines simultaneously both aspects of the total picture. Consequently, most of the studies reviewed in this book are focused on one or the other of these two perspectives; they either treat the group as a functioning unit *or* as social context.

Much of the earliest research regarded the group as a setting in which the individual's behaviors might be influenced by subtle social processes. The productivity of individuals when they worked alone was compared with their productivity when other people were doing the same task in their presence or were merely observing their behaviors. In this type of study, individuals were not required, or even permitted, to pool their resources and produce a joint product. The presence of co-workers or spectators was found to influence the speed and accuracy with which subjects performed a variety of judgmental, problem solving, and motor tasks. We shall examine some of the detailed findings in later chapters. Here, it is sufficient to note that research of this kind, though it was focused on individual performance, had implications for group performance as well. Groups are composed of individuals, and anything that influences the manner and effectiveness with which individuals employ their resources is likely to have a bearing on group productivity.

Studies that examined group effects on *individual* productivity flourished from the last quarter of the nineteenth century until the late 1930s. The succeeding decades brought a change in emphasis, which will be described after we have considered early attempts to treat groups as functional units.

During the period preceding World War II, research into the productivity of groups was generally prompted by a desire to demonstrate the superiority of group action over individual action. The usual strategy in such investigations was to bring a number of people together in a room, confront them with a problem or task, and urge them to produce a single solution. The products achieved by such *ad hoc* groups were then compared with those of individuals who worked alone on the same task. Needless to say, studies of this kind yielded a diverse assortment of findings. Groups were sometimes found to be more effective than individuals, but in other cases no significant differences were observed, or individuals seemed to be more productive than groups. As it became increasingly apparent that group performance was not consistently superior to that of individuals, attempts were made to discern the conditions that favored group success. However, data obtained during this period did not provide a very secure basis for identifying the variables that influenced group productivity. Most of the research was focused almost exclusively on productivity, and neglected task demands and process. To be sure, it was sometimes possible to infer the resources and processes required by the tasks experimenters had imposed on their groups, but data concerning the processes that had actually occurred were generally missing and impossible to reconstruct. Consequently, most of the early studies that treated groups as functional units did little to increase our understanding of how groups operate or how their productivity levels are determined.

The period after World War II brought a marked change in research emphasis. Having previously stressed productivity and neglected process, during the postwar decades, investigators reversed the stress, emphasizing process and showing little inclination to examine productivity. This development was most clearly evident in the work of Bales (1950) and others who developed elaborate techniques for observing and recording the interpersonal transactions that occur in groups. Although the groups to which these new methodologies were applied generally were assigned a task to perform, more often than not the task was primarily an excuse for asking people to interact. The interest of the experimenter was centered on what people did when they were asked to produce a joint product; it was a matter of lesser concern whether their actions happened to result in a good product.

The postwar emphasis on process was also manifested in the work of Lewin (1951) and his students. As major contributors to what has come to be called a "group dynamics movement," these investigators often combined an interest in the group as a social context with an interest in the group as a functioning unit. Their research was focused on interacting individuals rather than on passive spectators or co-workers, but the phenomena that were examined rarely included either a group or individual product. The group dynamicist attempted to understand how an individual's decisions, attitudes, aspirations, and satisfactions were influenced by the behaviors of people with whom he participated in face-to-face exchanges. To this end, researchers examined the processes by which interacting individuals became elements in one another's "life spaces," or hindered or facilitated one another's progress toward goals. Lewin and his students did little research in which the quality of a group product was a matter of critical importance, nor were they much inclined to study the effects of group processes on individual productivity.

Several factors were responsible for the reduced concern over productivity. Earlier attempts to investigate group outcomes had not been very successful, and it is understandable that many scholars experienced a feeling of disillusionment. Moreover, there was a growing awareness that productivity depends upon process, and that research into the latter should be accorded high priority. Then too, attention was drawn away from the issue of productivity by the dramatic successes investigators were experiencing in other areas. Sherif's (1936) classic study of conformity was followed by Asch's (1956) demonstration of extreme compliance in social situations. Hovland, Janis, and Kelley (1953) and others were reporting encouraging progress in the study of communication processes that affect attitudes, and Festinger and Thibaut (1951) published interesting findings dealing with informal communication in small groups. Success attracts those who wish to succeed, and the study of group productivity had not contributed many spectacular successes.

The postwar emphasis on process favored other changes. In order to achieve maximum experimental control, and to avoid the intrusion of confounding stimuli, researchers often discarded the *ad hoc* group as a setting in which to examine interpersonal transactions. Sometimes they created "groups" in which all but one of the members were accomplices who had been programmed to behave in specific ways. In other cases, individuals were informed that the tape-recorded messages they heard through earphones were the spontaneous contributions of other members of "their group," or were led to believe that the written messages they received from the experimenter were coming from work partners located in other rooms. Through a variety of clever deceptive practices, investigators created synthetic "groups" which provided individual subjects with a preplanned social environment. In this manner, researchers were able to gain dependable information concerning the responses that individuals are likely to make in specific social situations. However, in their efforts to increase the precision of their investigative techniques, experimenters tended to separate process from the group in which it normally occurs, and to break it into very small segments. The behaviors of subjects in situations of this kind were, at best, only brief and episodic fragments in the continuing chain of events that is ordinarily called process. The other elements in the sequence were supplied by the real or imaginary associates whose behaviors were dictated by the experimenter himself. Moreover, there was little opportunity for *mutual* responsiveness to occur, since the actions of most of the members of such "groups" were determined in advance by the investigator. Needless to say, synthetic groups of this kind are of limited value to anyone who wishes to examine group products. Their popularity as research tools reflects the low level of concern for productivity that has become typical since the 1950s.

However, it should not be concluded that work on group productivity ceased in the late 1940s, or that studies of process have become totally disassociated from the group. These are general trends that characterize recent research; but investigations that deviate from such trends continue to be performed. Furthermore, attempts to analyze task demands, never a favored preoccupation of researchers, have been more numerous during recent years than ever before.

Present knowledge concerning group process and productivity is uneven and poorly integrated. We know a good deal about people's reactions to specific social situations, but know much less about the mechanisms by which two or more people react to one another to produce long sequences of collective action. Data are available indicating the effectiveness with which individuals and groups have been found to perform a number of tasks, but it is not at all clear how task demands, resources, and processes have determined the outcomes represented by those data. In many respects, the study of collective problem solving remains in a primitive stage. In this book, we shall examine some of the available evidence and attempt to organize it into meaningful patterns.

In the chapters that follow, potential and actual productivity will be treated as dependent variables, and attention will be focused on the factors that influence them. Although this approach will lead us to examine a rather broad assortment of concepts and empirical studies, we will not sample the full range of research and theory dealing with interpersonal behavior. We will not, for example, be much concerned with the dynamics of "*T* groups," which are thought by many to be potent instruments for increasing the self-insight or social sensitivity of their members (see the review by Campbell and Dunnette, 1968). Nor will we devote much attention to the extensive literature indicating that groups are powerful determinants of attitudes and beliefs, or that they often serve as vehicles for the satisfaction of sociability needs. Instead, this book concentrates on task performance and asks what groups *can* and *do* accomplish when situations call for the creation of a joint product. Other publications are available to those who wish to view group activities from other perspectives (Cartwright & Zander, 1968; Davis, 1969; Hare, 1962; McGrath & Altman, 1966).

We shall begin our inquiry by examining relatively simple situations, and will delay consideration of troublesome complexities until a frame of reference has been developed.

Chapter 2

Group Performance of Unitary Tasks

How well a group can perform a task depends upon the adequacy of the resources members have at their disposal. How well the group will actually perform depends, in addition, upon the manner in which the available resources are used. The adequacy of available resources determines the group's potential productivity, the maximum level of performance it can possibly attain. To the extent that the process by which members transform their resources into a group product is less than optimally efficient, actual productivity will fall below potential productivity.

Both the adequacy of resources and the efficacy of process depend upon the character of the task that is to be performed. The nature of the task determines whether a particular kind of resource (knowledge, ability, tool, etc.) is relevant, and how much of each kind of resource is needed in order to permit a high level of success. Task demands also specify the processes members of a group are permitted to employ when they attempt to create a group product, and the particular process they must employ if their product is to be the best

14

that can be fashioned from their available resources. Because task demands are critical determinants of both potential and actual productivity, they will receive close attention in the pages that follow. Tasks will be categorized on the basis of the requirements they impose on groups. The success with which groups can and do perform each of several kinds of tasks will then be examined. However, this chapter will deal only with relatively simple cases.

A Partial Typology of Tasks

In everyday speech, the word "task" generally means the work that must be done in order to accomplish some purpose. It refers to a set of behaviors that must be performed or to the actions that someone is required to take. A more useful conception of task, though, focuses upon the end that is to be accomplished and the rules and constraints that govern the manner in which that end can be achieved. There are many legitimate ways of earning a dollar, and for some purposes it is convenient to regard all of them as methods of performing the same task. According to this view, a task is not a specific pattern of behaviors but a "job assignment" that can be fulfilled in one or more ways. It is a set of specifications identifying the goal that is to be achieved and the procedures that an individual or group may employ when attempting to achieve it. In the discussion that follows, tasks are categorized in a manner that reflects this view.

Divisible versus Unitary Tasks

Some tasks are readily divided into subtasks, each of which may be performed by a different individual. If ten arithmetic problems are to be solved, each of ten persons may work on one of them, or if a house is to be built, special functions may be allocated to carpenters, masons, plumbers, and painters. However, many tasks cannot easily or profitably be broken into smaller parts. If the ten arithmetic problems first mentioned are items in a test, academic rules will prohibit a division of labor, and if there is only one problem to be solved, little or nothing will be gained by having one person do the thinking and another the writing. Although it is probably true that any task can be conceived to consist of two or more subtasks, in many cases the conceptually distinguishable parts are so thoroughly interdependent that they cannot profitably be performed by different people. Two persons who read alternate sentences of this paragraph will not gain a better understanding of its content than will a single reader. The weight of a package will not be very accurately estimated if one person does the hefting and another does the deciding. Many of the tasks employed in research on group productivity are of this kind. In order to make a contribution to the group product, it is necessary for the individual to perform all phases of the job. Although the members of a group may sometimes work simultaneously on such a task, and may exhort one another to work hard, no real division of labor is possible. Work assignments that make mutual assistance impracticable will be called *unitary tasks*. Those that make a division of labor feasible will be called *divisible tasks*. This chapter deals only with the former.

Pulling on a rope is a unitary task. To be sure, it can be conceived to involve a number of subtasks such as grasping the rope, bracing one's feet, contracting one's biceps, etc.; but all phases of the total act must be performed by a single individual. Several people may pull simultaneously on the same rope, but when this occurs, we have an instance of parallel performance rather than division of labor.

Maximizing versus Optimizing Tasks

Sometimes the goal that is to be achieved entails doing as much as possible of something, or doing it as rapidly as possible. Thus, if an individual or group is asked to exert a maximum force on a rope, a strong pull is regarded as a more successful performance than a weak pull. If a team of mountain climbers is asked to ascend a cliff as rapidly as possible, maximum speed is the criterion against which performance is evaluated. Tasks that make success a function of how much or how rapidly something is accomplished, may be called *maximizing* tasks.

In other cases, the goal is not to maximize but to produce some specific, most preferred outcome. If individuals or groups are asked to exert a force of exactly 100 pounds on a rope, the quality of their performance is a function of the degree to which the force they exert approximates 100 pounds. If the task is to estimate the temperature of a room, the goal is to agree with the value indicated by a thermometer. Job assignments that make success a function of how closely the individual or group approximates a predetermined "best" or correct outcome may be called *optimizing* tasks.

Permitted Process

When a task is unitary, mutual assistance is not possible. A group's product must therefore be the outcome generated by one of its members (or an outcome that two or more members have independently produced) *or* some combination of the outcomes that have been generated by separate individuals. Tasks differ with respect to the ways they permit members to combine their individual products.

Disjunctive tasks. Imagine a situation in which the members of a group are asked to pull as hard as possible on a rope that is long enough to be grasped by only one person at a time. If the rules governing the performance of the task allow only one "pull" to be counted as the group's product, the success of the group will depend upon which member's performance is selected to represent the group effort. The group product is really an individual product that is sanctioned by the group. The task may be said to be *disjunctive* because it requires an "either-or" decision; the group can accept only one of the available individual contributions as its own, and must reject all others. One member receives total "weight" in determining the group product and others are accorded no weight at all.

Tasks are sometimes made disjunctive by virtue of the fact that groups are required to select one of two or more discretely different options as the group product. This is the case when the job assignment is to answer "yes" or "no" to a question, to determine which of several specified solutions to a problem is correct, or to solve a problem when it is obvious to everyone that the correct solution must be one or another of a few unspecified alternatives. Under circumstances such as these, the only procedure that is both permissible and meaningful is to select somebody's preferred answer as the group's product. One member (or perhaps two or three members who have supplied the same outcome) is given total weight, and others are accorded none.

It should be noted that the rope-pulling example involves a task that is unitary, maximizing, and disjunctive, whereas the judgmental and problem-solving examples involve tasks that are unitary, optimizing, and disjunctive.

Conjunctive tasks. Imagine that the rules governing rope pulling are changed to require that each member of the group take his turn, and that the criterion of group success is the strength of the force exerted by the member who does *least* well. Under these conditions, a single individual's output again becomes the group's product, but the critical individual is selected by the rules rather than by the group. The group resembles a chain that is no stronger than its weakest link, or a team of mountain climbers who can move no faster than the slowest member. When performance is governed by rules of this kind, the task is *conjunctive*, because the group product reflects what members can accomplish when they must operate conjunctively—tied together like mountain climbers. If the group is asked to pull as hard as possible, the task is unitary, maximizing, and conjunctive. If instructions are to pull exactly 100 pounds, and success is measured by the closeness with which the least effective member approximates that value, the task is unitary, optimizing, and conjunctive.

Additive tasks. A different set of rules would require that each member of the group take his turn and make group success depend upon the sum of the individual efforts. Under these circumstances, the group's product is no longer supplied by a single member; it is a summative combination of the outputs contributed by all group members. Consequently, a task of this kind may be said to be *additive*. If success is defined as a function of the magnitude of the total pull, the task is unitary, maximizing, and additive. If success is determined by the degree to which the total pull approximates a specified value, the task is unitary, optimizing, and additive.

Discretionary tasks. Conditions sometimes permit members of a group to combine their individual contributions in any manner they wish. When this is the case, a group can assign total weight to a single member, weight all persons equally, or grant each person a different weight. Moreover, the weighted contributions can be added, divided, multiplied, or subtracted, as the members desire. In situations of this kind, the group chooses its own process and the task may be said to be *discretionary*.

Optimizing tasks sometimes permit such freedom of process. Thus members of a group who are asked to exert a force of exactly 100 pounds on a rope may be allowed to work in either a disjunctive or additive fashion, to average their individual contributions (either with or without unequal weighting), or even to subtract one person's contribution from another's. However, judgmental tasks are more likely to be discretionary than are those that involve motor activities. If a group is required to make the best possible estimate of the temperature of a room, its members are free to combine their individual estimates in any way they prefer. The discussion process by which they reach their decision will ordinarily involve unequal weighting and the "computation" of an average estimate.

Maximizing tasks seem not to allow such discretion. When the goal is to accomplish as much as possible (e.g., to exert maximum force on a rope) members may be allowed to assign differential weights to one another. However, task demands make any "averaging process" seem futile, and neither real-life nor laboratory rules permit members to multiply their individual efforts by some factor in order to achieve a more attractive outcome.

Although we have employed rope pulling to illustrate all types of unitary tasks, it should be evident that a variety of problem-solving and judgmental activities might have been chosen for this purpose. Furthermore, it should be apparent that rules and criteria can be devised to define other kinds of unitary tasks. However, the types considered here are rather commonly encountered both in laboratory and real-life settings.

Prescribed Process

In previous paragraphs, we have examined the kinds of processes that are *permitted* when tasks are disjunctive, conjunctive, additive, or discretionary. However, task demands not only specify what is permitted; they also *prescribe* the process that must be employed if maximum success is to be achieved. For example, a disjunctive task permits the group to allocate total weight to any one of its members, but maximum success can be achieved only if total weight is actually assigned to the most proficient member. It is possible to classify tasks on the basis of prescribed, as well as permitted process, but to do so would make our taxonomy exceedingly complicated. In this chapter, the processes prescribed by various kinds of tasks will be discussed along with the processes that are permitted.

Disjunctive Tasks

In an early study of group performance, Marjorie Shaw (1932) asked individuals and groups to solve the following problem.

On one side of a river are three wives and three husbands. All of the men but none of the women can row. Get them all across the river by means of a boat carrying only three at one time. No man will allow his wife to be in the presence of another man unless he is also there [p. 492].

This is almost certainly a unitary task. The several steps by which the husbands and wives can be transported across the river are conceptually distinguishable, but logically inseparable. Each phase of the solution reflects the previous ones and anticipates those that follow. A mental problem of this kind allows little opportunity for a division of labor. Furthermore, the task is disjunctive. Although different individuals may reach different conclusions, the group must endorse a single solution. There is no meaningful way in which different solutions can be added, averaged, or otherwise blended into a group product that is a composite of the views of all members. It is a unitary, optimizing, disjunctive task.

In Shaw's study, 21 college students attempted to solve the problem individually and 20 others worked on it in 4-person groups. Three of the five groups were successful as were three of the 21 individuals who worked alone. Thus 60 percent of the groups produced the correct solution while only 14 percent of the individuals did so. Shaw concluded that a major factor in the group's superiority was the tendency of members to correct one another's errors.

A quarter of a century after Shaw's findings were published, Marquart (1955) suggested that Shaw's groups were successful if, and only if, they happened to include at least one member who could have solved the problem had he worked alone. According to Marquart's view, it was unnecessary to postulate interaction effects or to invoke the notion of pooled resources. Instead, one might simply assume that any individual who possessed the resources needed to solve the problem would have solved it regardless of whether he worked individually or in a group, and that if any member of a group solved the problem, his solution would have been accepted as the group's selection. In a test of this line of reasoning, Marquart essentially replicated Shaw's study, obtaining very similar findings. She then proceeded to compare the obtained proportion of group successes with the proportion that might have been expected to occur if her theory were correct. There were two ways in which the "expected proportion" could be inferred.

Marquart's procedure for estimating the expected proportion of successful groups involved the creation of *nominal* groups. Individuals who had worked singly on the problem were randomly assigned to be "members" of purely imaginary groups that never actually met or worked together on the task. After the assignment procedure was completed, Marquart determined the proportion of such groups that contained at least one member who had solved the problem while working alone. For both her own study and that by Shaw, it was found that this proportion was quite comparable to the proportion of real groups that had produced correct solutions. On this basis, Marquart argued that the quality of a group's product was a direct consequence of the ability of its most competent member.

Taylor (1954) and Lorge and Solomon (1955) independently reported a procedure that accomplishes the same purpose as does the use of nominal groups. If, in a given population, the proportion of people possessing the ability to solve a problem is P, and the proportion of people not possessing the ability to solve the problem is Q, the probability of drawing at random from the population a single person who will not have the ability to solve the problem is Q. The probability that *nobody* in a randomly assembled group of size n will have the ability to solve the problem is Q^n, and the probability that at least one member of the group will be able to solve it is $1 - Q^n$. Thus, if the presence of at least one competent member is sufficient to guarantee group success, the proportion of successful groups will equal $1 - Q^n$.

When applying this procedure to the data of the Shaw study, $P = .14$ (the proportion of the persons who solved the problem when working alone) and $Q = .86$. Since there were four members in each of Shaw's groups, Q^n becomes $.86^4$, which equals .404. Therefore, the expected proportion of successful groups is $1 - .404$, or .596. It is to be recalled that .60 of Shaw's real groups produced the correct answer. Consequently, it is entirely reasonable to conclude that her groups were successful if they contained a member who could solve the problem, and were unsuccessful if they did not. Of course, the fact that the obtained and expected proportions are almost identical does not prove that Marquart's theory is correct, but it is certainly consistent with that theory.

Marquart's reappraisal of Shaw's data had the merit of suggesting that a group's product is sometimes provided by a single member whose efforts may be comparatively unaffected by the presence of other members. But Marquart's reanalysis, and that of Lorge and Solomon (1955) who reached similar conclusions, had an unfortunate impact on group research. People were sometimes led to conclude that nothing very exciting really happens when groups attack problems. If a group's product is the consequence of a single person's work, why should anyone undertake complicated research to delineate the processes by which people combine their resources to create a joint outcome? Why not concentrate one's attention on the problem-solving behaviors of individuals who, after all, seem to be the critical agents determining group productivity? If groups perform no better than their most competent members would have done alone, what is so remarkable about groups?

Two kinds of responses can be given to these questions. In the first place, the evidence on which Marquart and Lorge and Solomon based their conclusions dealt with a specific kind of group performing a specific kind of task. Neither Marquart nor Lorge and Solomon contended that their findings were applicable to all, or even to most of the situations in which groups perform tasks. It is regrettable that people sometimes generalized their conclusions in a manner that made additional group research seem rather pointless. More importantly, there was no good reason why the Marquart-Lorge-Solomon findings should have discouraged further investigation. Far from stifling group research, the data ought to have stimulated experimenters to ask new questions. The nature of these questions will become apparent when task demands are examined in conjunction with the productivity findings.

As already noted, the task employed in these studies was disjunctive; consequently, a successful performance could occur only if all necessary resources were possessed by at least one member of the group. Although we cannot identify the required intellective resources, it is clear that they were possessed by at least 14 percent of the subjects. In addition to requiring that at least one member have the ability to solve the problem, task demands prescribed the actions members of the group must take if the group were to be successful. Any individual with the necessary resources should proceed to solve the problem and announce his solution to other members of the group. The latter should, in turn, renounce incorrect solutions in favor of the correct one. Only if these procedures were followed would a group containing a sufficiently competent person arrive at the correct solution; and if these procedures were followed, such a group could not fail to be successful. The intriguing aspect of the Shaw and Marquart studies was not so much the fact that groups performed at the level of their most competent members, but the fact that they seem almost invariably to have functioned "perfectly"—actual productivity equaled potential productivity. Group process apparently proceeded exactly as prescribed by the task, resulting in the best possible use of available resources.

Surely, groups do not always function so well. Why, in the case of these particular groups, was there no apparent loss in productivity due to less than maximally effective process? Why were individual members, who possessed the requisite resources, so uniformly willing to use them in behalf of the group? Why, when such individuals announced the correct answer, did other members accept it as the group's decision? Does truth always triumph over untruth, or was there something unusual about these groups, the task they performed, or perhaps both? Answers to these questions will be inferred from other research to be reviewed in this chapter. Examination of studies in which group discussion has not so uniformly generated acceptance of a correct solution will move us in the right direction.

In 1952, Maier and Solem reported a study in which individuals and groups were asked to solve the following problem.

> A man bought a horse for $60 and sold it for $70. Then he bought it back for $80 and again sold it for $90. How much money did he make in the horse business [p. 280]?

Like the task employed by Shaw and Marquart, this one cannot profitably be divided into subtasks and assigned piecemeal to two or more persons. Group success requires that one or more members possess the resources needed to solve the total problem, that such members use their resources for this purpose, that they communicate the correct answer to other members, and that the correct answer be accepted by their associates as the group product. Furthermore, the task does not permit members to average their individual contributions. This is the case because members will almost invariably realize that the correct answer must be $0, $10, or $20, and it is apparent that an averaging process will not produce any of these solutions. The task is unitary, optimizing, and disjunctive.

Maier and Solem took several important steps before they asked anyone to solve their problem. The college students who were to serve as subjects were assembled in groups of five or six persons and were asked to select a representative. About half of the groups were told that their representative would function as an observer and would refrain from expressing any view concerning the problem they were subsequently to discuss. The rest of the groups were informed that their representative would function as a discussion leader who would "encourage the participation of all members and ask questions so as to cause the group to think together rather than as individuals." Discussion leaders were prohibited from expressing their own views, but were instructed to try to obtain group agreement on an answer.

Following these special instructions concerning the role of the observer or leader, the problem was read to the group and members were asked to solve it individually without any discussion. One minute was allowed for this purpose and subjects wrote their answers on cards that had been provided. (Experience with the problem indicates that people almost always produce an answer within 1 min, and that incorrect answers are seldom changed when additional time is allotted for individual work.) After this phase of the experiment had been completed, subjects were asked to begin their discussion of the problem. At the end of 8 min, each person recorded his solution on the answer card. (This could be either the same answer he had given earlier or a different one depending upon whether the individual had changed his mind during the discussion period.)

Approximately 45 percent of the subjects solved the problem correctly during the initial 1-min work period. After the 8-min discussion, 83 percent of those whose group representative had served as a discussion leader, recorded the correct answer on their cards, whereas only 72 percent of those in "observer" groups did so. This difference is statistically significant; it is too large to be attributed to chance factors. Thus, discussion led to a noteworthy improvement in the quality of subjects' answers, and this improvement was especially large when the oral exchange of ideas was supervised by a discussion leader.

Sixty-three of Maier and Solem's 67 groups contained at least one person who had solved the problem correctly while working as an individual. If truth triumphs over untruth, all of the members of these 63 groups should have given the correct solution at the conclusion of the discussion period. Actually, less than 80 percent of them did so. The percentage of subjects shifting from an incorrect to the correct response was especially low when only one or two members of the group had been correct originally, and when the group representative functioned as an observer instead of a discussion leader. Under these circumstances, there were even a few instances in which persons who were initially correct shifted to an incorrect answer following the discussion. It is clear that truth did not always triumph over untruth, even when truth was known to several members of the group, and that truth was less likely to triumph under some conditions than under others.

The contrast between the findings of this study and those of the Shaw and Marquart experiments is rather striking. In the latter investigations, the presence of a single member with the ability to solve a problem was apparently sufficient to guarantee that all members would solve it, but that principle did not hold for the Maier and Solem research. Why not?

For some problems, the correctness of the proper solution is readily apparent or easily demonstrated once that solution has been obtained. Getting the three husbands and three wives across the river is a complicated and rather difficult problem, but an individual who solves it will ordinarily feel quite certain that he is right. Furthermore, he can easily demonstrate the correctness of his solution to anyone else. Problems of this kind are commonly called *eureka* tasks. ("Eureka, I have it!") Certain other tasks, of which the horse-trading problem is a notable example, may be no more difficult to perform but the merit of the correct or best solution is far less apparent and less easily demonstrated. (The reader may test this contention for himself by trying to persuade a friend that the man made a $20.00 profit in the horse-trading business.) As might be expected, truth tended to triumph in the Shaw and Marquart studies that employed a eureka task, but it was less uniformly triumphant in the Maier and Solem research which did not.

The character of the task does not account for certain of Maier and Solem's critical findings. Why was truth more likely to prevail when several members of the group had already solved the problem correctly than when only one or two had done so? Why was truth more persuasive when the group was led by a discussion leader than when it was not? Unfortunately, Maier and Solem did not attempt to observe the processes that occurred in their groups, so we can only speculate concerning answers to these questions. It seems probable that a single individual who had solved the problem correctly may have been reluctant to express his decision when confronted by several others who had reached a different conclusion. He may have doubted his own accuracy or, at least, have felt that he should not attempt to impose his view on others. Even if he tried to defend his solution, it is possible that he was "howled down" by the majority who favored another answer. If he persisted in advancing his own argument, others may not have paid much attention to his minority view. However, when the correct answer was known by at least three members of the group, it should have stood a better chance of being presented, defended, and given serious consideration. In other words, the greater the proportion of members who possessed the necessary resources, the greater the likelihood that the processes required for group success would actually occur within the group.

Why did the presence of a discussion leader facilitate the process? It is to be recalled that the discussion leader was assigned the responsibility for assuring everyone a chance to talk, and was, in fact, told to solicit the views of all members. It is probable that he moderated the inhibiting effect of the majority and created an atmosphere in which a minority with the correct answer felt willing or even obligated to express and defend it. In this connection, it is noteworthy that the discussion leader's salutary effect was limited to situations in which only a minority of the group members had solved the problem when functioning as individuals.

The foregoing discussion suggests that there are several reasons why a group may fail to perform a disjunctive task successfully. (1) The group will fail if none of its members possesses the resources demanded by the task. (2) The group will fail, or will function at a reduced level of effectiveness, if its processes are not in accord with task prescriptions. This will be the case if (a) the member(s) with the necessary resources does not use them to perform the unitary task; or (b) members with the necessary resources use them appropriately, but other members do not accept their contributions as the group's product (i.e., successful members are not accorded total weight). Whenever the task is not of the eureka type, there is an increased possibility that group processes will be less than maximally effective and that actual productivity will be lower than potential productivity.

Torrance (1954) employed the horse-trading problem in an investigation of the conditions under which truth triumphs over untruth. Members of B-26 bomber crews served as experimental subjects. Each crew included a pilot, navigator, and gunner who had served together for several months. After subjects had written their individual answers to the horse-trading problem on a piece of paper, they were assembled into three-man groups, half of which contained the members of a regular crew while the other half were composed of a pilot, a navigator, and a gunner from *different* crews. The former may be regarded as "intact" crews and the latter as *ad hoc* crews. Each group conferred until a single decision had been reached.

Fifty percent of the navigators, 31 percent of the pilots, and 29 percent of the gunners solved the problem correctly before they entered their discussion groups. Although Torrance does not report how many of his three-man groups contained at least one member who had solved the problem correctly, it is apparent that a very large share of them must have met this criterion. In other words, most of the groups should have had the potential ability to solve the horse-trading problem, because most included at least one member who knew the answer before entering the group. However, actual productivity fell below potential productivity. In intact crews, 37 percent of the gunners who knew the correct solution failed to convince their associates they were right. Twenty percent of the navigators and 6 percent of the pilots also failed to induce their crews to accept the correct solution. In the *ad hoc* crews, failure rates were lower, being 12, 10, and 0 percent, respectively. However, in both types of crews the group decision was sometimes inferior to the judgment of the group's most competent member because the person who was most competent to perform the task was not able to override the conflicting opinions of his colleagues.

It should be noted that pilots, whose position in a B-26 crew gives them the highest status, were most successful in getting their opinions accepted, and that gunners, whose status is lowest, were least successful. It is also noteworthy that status was a more important consideration in intact groups than in *ad hoc* groups. In groups with a history and a future, the opinions and suggestions of high status members are likely to be accepted even when they are wrong. When the group has neither a history nor a future, status has less effect on group process, but it may still lead the group to make less than maximal use of its members' resources.

Johnson and Torcivia (1967) carried the investigation of process a step further. College students first solved the horse-trading problem individually and rated their confidence in the answers they had given. Two-person groups were then formed by pairing a person who had solved the problem correctly with one who had not. Each pair was allowed 15 min to decide upon a single solution. Seventy-two percent of the pairs reported the correct answer whereas 100 percent of them would have done so if they had made the best possible use of their resources. In 18 of 36 pairs, the individual with the correct answer had indicated greater confidence than his partner, and 17 of these pairs emerged with the correct solution. In seven pairs, the person who had been wrong had reported greater confidence, and only two of these groups were successful. The remaining 11 pairs contained persons who had been equally confident; seven of these groups decided upon the correct answer.

These data suggest that how well group processes satisfy the demands of the task depends in part upon the confidence that members have in their resources. Actual productivity may fall below potential productivity because members do not weight one another's contributions in a manner that generates the best outcome they are capable of producing.

In none of the preceding studies using the horse-trading problem, was group process actually observed and recorded. Instead, it was inferred from a comparison of members' answers before and after the discussion took place. Data concerning what actually happens in discussion groups were obtained in a study by Thomas and Fink (1961). College students first attempted to solve the horse-trading problem individually and were allowed 1 min to record their answers. Then, they were randomly assembled into groups of two, three, four, or five, and were asked to discuss the issue in order to arrive at a group decision. However, members were told that their final "report" might be either unanimous or divided, and no pressures toward uniformity were applied by the experimenter. Each group was permitted a maximum of 2 min per member to discuss the problem; allotted time was prorated by group size in order that all members of the larger groups would have ample opportunity to speak. As the discussion proceeded, the experimenter marked a tally sheet each time a member (a) stated the correct answer; (b) rejected an incorrect answer; (c) expressed a rationale for the correct answer; (d) stated an incorrect answer; or (e) gave a rationale for an incorrect answer.

Twenty-nine of the 44 groups contained at least one person who had solved the problem correctly before the discussion began, but only 15 groups succeeded in producing a unanimously correct report. Thus, truth did not routinely triumph over untruth. The size of the group did not significantly affect the quality of the decisions rendered following the discussion. However, there was a striking tendency for members of groups to converge on a single (not necessarily correct) answer. Six of the 44 groups were "unanimous" even before they were assembled; after talking about the problem, 28 groups were unanimous. It is clear that the exchange of information and opinion led to a marked increase in agreement, but it did not greatly affect the correctness of members' judgments.

What happened in the successful groups that may explain their high productivity? In 18 groups, only one member was correct at the outset, and six of these groups produced unanimously correct solutions following the discussion. In all six of these successful groups, the person who had solved the problem correctly while working alone talked more often than anyone else in his group. In only one of the 12 groups that failed to produce a unanimously correct answer did the most qualified person dominate the discussion. The effect of talkativeness is also revealed by another comparison. In 19 of the 44 groups, one person talked more than anyone else. Nine of the ten groups in which the most talkative person was correct at the beginning of the session emerged with unanimously correct answers; eight of the eleven groups in which the most talkative person had been incorrect unanimously adopted his incorrect solution. Apparently success requires not only that someone in the group be able to perform the task, but that he be willing and able to press his solution upon other members.

Thomas and Fink described a three-step model which appeared to encompass the critical aspects of group success.

Resources. Can any member solve the problem? How many can solve it?
Input. Does any member actually propose the correct solution? Is the correct solution proposed more often than incorrect ones?
Facilitative processing. Does the correct solution more often elicit supportive statements than do incorrect solutions?

According to this formulation, resources tend to determine input which, in turn, affects facilitative processing and leads eventually to a correct or incorrect solution. Thomas and Fink developed a numerical index for each of these three steps and computed correlation coefficients for the relationship between each pair of indices and between each index and the quality of the group outcome (i.e., number of members giving the correct answer following the discussion). In general, the obtained correlations support the contention that input is a function of resources and that facilitative processing is a function of input. The greater the proportion of group members who can solve the problem, the greater is the frequency with which the correct solution is proposed. The more often the correct solution is mentioned, the more favorable are the reactions it evokes, and the greater is the probability it will be accepted by others. However, the connections between one step and the next are far from perfect, and the processes that transpire in a group may generate outcomes that are less good than the resources of the group are capable of producing.

All of the research cited in this section has concerned optimizing tasks. Empirical studies of maximizing disjunctive tasks have been extremely rare.

In summary, we may conclude that when a task is disjunctive a group's potential productivity is determined by the resources of its most competent member. If at least one person has the ability to perform the task perfectly, the group has the potential ability to perform it perfectly. However, the actual productivity of the group may fall below its potential productivity because the processes that transpire in the group deviate from the prescribed pattern. This will be the case if the most competent member does not employ his resources to perform the task or if the most competent member performs the task but other members do not accept his performance as the group's product. Evidence suggests that process is likely to be faulty when (a) a majority of the group members initially favor an outcome other than that generated by the most competent person; (b) the most competent person has low status in the group; (c) the most competent person is not very confident of his own ability to perform the task; or (d) the most competent person does not present his contribution very aggressively and does not evoke supportive reactions from others. If a task is of the eureka type, the probability that process will be effective appears to be greatly enhanced.

Conjunctive Tasks

When a task is unitary and conjunctive, each member of a group is required to perform essentially the same function, and everyone's success is determined by the effectiveness with which the least proficient member operates. Although the speed with which a team of mountain climbers can reach the top of a cliff is probably the best example of this arrangement, other illustrations can be cited. A column of marching soldiers can move no faster than its slowest member, and some discussion groups are no stronger than their least able participant, because the implicit rules governing the discussion decree that every member of the group must understand the complexities of any subtopic before the group can proceed to the next subtopic. Elementary teachers often complain that the amount of material that can be covered by a class is restricted by the inability or disinclination of a few stragglers to keep up with the crowd. Indeed, the conjunctive nature of classroom learning is a primary reason for the widespread practice of assigning students to homogeneous ability groupings.

Many conjunctive tasks are not unitary. Thus, for example, men who work on an assembly line perform specialized operations at a rate that cannot exceed a pace the least able man can maintain. Almost any division of labor introduces an element of conjunctivity into the work situation because all subtasks must ordinarily be performed adequately in order for the group to achieve a satisfactory outcome; consequently the progress of each worker depends on the ability and willingness of others to perform their functions properly. An entire building project is likely to be halted when the plumbers or masons go on strike, and failure of any member of a submarine crew to perform his role may endanger everyone on board. Complicated conjunctive arrangements of this kind will be examined later in this book; here we will concentrate on comparatively simple, unitary cases.

The demands imposed by a conjunctive unitary task are fairly evident. The least competent member must possess the resources required to meet the criterion of success. Prescribed process dictates that he apply his resources to the task, and that other members proceed toward the goal as expeditiously as conditions permit. The potential productivity of the group is established by the resources of the least competent member; if he does not function at the level permitted by his resources, or if other members function even less effectively than he does, actual productivity will fall below potential productivity.

Performance of a conjunctive unitary task was investigated by McCurdy and Lambert (1952). Six two-position electrical switches were located on small panels and clamped to the edge of a table. An individual seated before these panels was told that he could make a light go on by throwing one (and only one) of the six switches. The subject's task was to discover, through trial-and-error exploration, which switch needed to be thrown, while making as few wrong choices as possible. After the subject had succeeded in causing the light to appear, it was turned off by the experimenter, and the problem was repeated with a different switch serving as the key to success. On later trials, it was necessary to throw still other switches in order to make the light reappear. For the first eight trials, the switches that accomplished the task were, as numbered from the subject's left to his right, numbers 3, 1, 5, 3, 6, 1, 4, 1. After the eighth trial, this sequence was repeated, and it was continued throughout a 900-sec work period or until the subject had learned it well enough so he could go through it once without making any errors. The subject was not told that a repeating sequence of switch positions was being employed; he had to discover this for himself in order to master the task. His productivity score was the number of times he succeeded in turning on the light during the 900-sec work period.

Groups of three persons also worked on the experimental problem. Each subject sat at a different side of a table and had responsibility for two switches located in front of him. Aside from these changes, procedures were the same as those employed when only one subject managed all six of the switches. Members of groups were permitted to talk to one another, and, to varying degrees, they did so.

On first thought, this task may seem to have an additive character. Presumably, three persons can throw switches about three times as fast as can one person working alone, and thus a group might succeed in activating the light three times as often as does a single individual. However, the electrical circuitry was such that even the correct switch would not turn on the light if an incorrect one were thrown at the same time. Consequently, a person who operated an incorrect switch always nullified the vote of one who threw the correct one; when truth and untruth occurred together, untruth always triumphed over truth! Under these circumstances, the fact that three persons had the opportunity to operate switches can hardly be viewed as an advantage; any individual could impede the exploratory behaviors of the others, and could thus delay their discovery of the correct sequence of switch turnings. A group that contained at least one member who had not understood the instructions, who was not sufficiently motivated, or who was too unintelligent to sense the intricacies of the problem, should have done very poorly. Groups should have functioned at about the level their least productive member would have achieved had he worked alone. The findings reported by McCurdy and Lambert indicated that groups were, in fact, less successful than individuals who worked alone, but the data were not analyzed in a fashion that would test the contention that groups performed at the level of their least proficient members.

Steiner and Rajaratnam (1961) employed McCurdy and Lambert's data in an analysis that was expressly designed to compare the performance of groups with that of their least competent members. Individuals who had worked alone on the task were randomly assigned to three-person "nominal" groups, each of which was credited with the score earned by its least successful member when he worked individually. The mean score obtained by such nominal groups was found to be almost identical to the mean score earned by McCurdy and Lambert's actual groups, the difference being so small that it could readily be attributed to chance factors. However, only 11 persons had worked as individuals, so only three nominal groups could be created. This number was too small to provide a very sensitive or dependable test. Consequently, Steiner and Rajaratnam conducted a second analysis, based on sampling theory. Because the logic of this analysis is pertinent to several issues examined in this book, it will be described in some detail.

Consider a population in which the scores that individuals earn when working alone on a particular task are distributed in accordance with a normal, bell-shaped curve. If groups of size n are randomly assembled from this population, and the members of each group are rank-ordered with respect to their scores on the task, they will, on the average, divide the population into $n + 1$ equal parts. Thus, for example, the members of three-person groups will, on the average, fall at the 75th, 50th, and 25th percentiles of the population. The most competent member will tend to have a score that is higher than that of 75 percent of the population, the second most competent member will, on the average, have a score that surpasses that of 50 percent of the population, and the least competent member will have a score that exceeds that of only 25 percent of the population. If two-person groups are assembled, the more competent member will, on the average, fall at the 66.7th percentile, and the less competent will fall at the 33.3rd percentile. For four-person groups, the correct percentiles will be the 80th, 60th, 40th, and 20th.

McCurdy and Lambert's three-person groups appear to have been randomly assembled from a population in which individual performance scores were normally distributed. (Actually, the scores of the 11 subjects who worked alone were markedly skewed. On the assumption that this departure from normality was due to the manner in which performance was measured and did not truly reflect the character of individual productivity levels, McCurdy and Lambert transformed their scores in a way that generated a normal distribution.) Consequently, if the least competent members of McCurdy and Lambert's groups had functioned alone, they would presumably have performed at a level representing the 25th percentile of the population. If group productivity equaled that of the least competent member, the mean of the group scores should have surpassed the scores earned by 25 percent of the subjects who worked alone, and should have been lower than the scores obtained by 75 percent of the subjects who worked alone. Actually, the mean of the group scores exceeded the score obtained by only one individual (9 percent) and fell below the scores of 10 individuals (91 percent). Through the use of a complex statistical procedure, Steiner and Rajaratnam demonstrated that the difference between the obtained and predicted findings was small enough to be attributed to sampling errors. Although these results did not prove that group outcomes were determined by the behaviors of the least competent members, they were entirely consistent with that conclusion.

It should be noted that both nominal groups and the statistical logic employed by Steiner and Rajaratnam may be used to test a variety of hypotheses. One may determine whether it is reasonable to believe that a group's product equals that which its most competent member would have produced had he worked alone. The group's product may be compared with that which would have been obtained by the second most competent member, or the third, or the fourth. This is a very useful feature of the two research techniques because task demands sometimes make group success contingent upon the ability of some, but not all, of the members. If all but 10 of the soldiers who are to be moved to a new military site can be accommodated in available vehicles, the speed with which the convoy can move is established by the marching ability of the tenth most competent man. If only two oars are available for rowing a boat, the efficiency with which the craft can be propelled depends upon the strength and skill of the crew's second most competent oarsman. Because the number of persons who can or must participate in the performance of a conjunctive task is often limited by man-made rules, or by the scarcity of tools or work space, it is reasonable to expect that group productivity will often be determined by the behaviors of persons who are neither the most nor the least competent members of their groups.

Conjunctive tasks have not been very intensively studied, perhaps because the prescribed process is almost the only one a group can employ. Task demands dictate that the least effective member will receive total weight, and all that remains in doubt is who that person will be and how poorly he will function. Furthermore, when the group product cannot be better than that which its weakest member could have achieved working alone, there is not much room for uncertainty concerning how well the group will actually perform. When there is little uncertainty, there is usually little reason to do research. Another probable reason for the limited attention given to conjunctive group activity is the fact that tasks that are conjunctive with respect to one criterion of performance are generally nonconjunctive with respect to other criteria. Thus, for example, the task confronting a team of mountain climbers is conjunctive if the goal is to reach the summit as rapidly as possible. However, the task is probably additive if the important consideration is the amount of cargo that can be transported to the top. Tasks are most likely to be conjunctive when rapid performance is the critical goal (i.e., when they are maximizing tasks), and researchers have not usually found speed of performance to be as interesting as the quality or correctness of the product that is created. In our subsequent examination of the research literature, we will have occasion to identify experimental tasks that are disjunctive or additive because the investigator chose to emphasize one criterion of performance, but which would have been conjunctive if some other criterion (usually speed) had been emphasized.

Additive Tasks

When tasks are conjunctive or disjunctive, the group product reflects the contribution of a single member. In the case of conjunctive tasks, it is the least proficient member of the group (or the least proficient member who is involved in the conjunctive operations) who determines the quality of the group output. When tasks are disjunctive, the group may accept any member's outcome as its product. Additive tasks are strikingly different in that they permit the contributions of various members to be summed. Consequently, the group product is a combination of individual outcomes rather than the outcome generated by a single member.

During the 1920s, a German psychologist named Ringelmann (see Dashiell, 1935) compared the abilities of individuals and groups to perform a task involving the use of physical strength. His apparatus consisted of a rope attached to a weight-measuring scale. When an individual or group pulled on the rope, the strength of the pull was measured in kilograms. Some subjects worked alone whereas others worked in two-, three-, or eight-person groups. As might be expected, eight men pulling together exerted a greater force than did a single individual or a group of two or three members. However, eight men pulling together did not pull eight times as much as a single individual working alone; they pulled only about four times as much. Two-person groups pulled about 1.9 times as much as a single individual, and three-person groups pulled about 2.5

times as much. Although no restraints were imposed on the freedom of individuals to combine their efforts in a purely additive fashion, it is evident that they were not entirely successful in doing so. Apparently group process was not fully in accord with prescribed process, for groups obtained poorer outcomes than the resources of their members should have permitted them to obtain. Especially when groups were large (eight members) actual productivity fell far below potential productivity.

The process that is prescribed by Ringelmann's task can readily be specified. Each member should pull as hard as he can on the rope, and all should pull at exactly the same time and in the proper direction. If an individual does not pull at the same time as others do his contribution will not be added to those of his colleagues, and if he pulls in a different direction his efforts will be partially or entirely wasted. Failure of actual productivity to equal potential productivity indicates that (a) some or all of the individuals did not pull as hard in the group situation as they were capable of doing, or (b) not all members pulled at the same time and/or in the proper direction. Whatever the correct explanation may be, groups sustained a loss of productivity because their processes were not maximally efficient. When tasks are additive, the group product is the sum of the individual contributions, but there is no guarantee that members will contribute as much as they are capable of doing or that they will perform the summation process with utter precision.

In real life, many tasks are additive. Assuming an absence of social and physical restraints, the amount of snow that can be shoveled by a group equals the sum of the amounts the several members can shovel when working alone. Similar statements can be made about the ability of a group to mow lawns, carry supplies, or paint fences. Whenever all members of a group are capable of performing a task adequately and the criterion of productivity is the number of units performed, the task is at least potentially additive. However, even when these conditions are met, the task may not be completely additive because rules may permit only a few persons to participate, raw materials (e.g., snow to be shoveled) may be in short supply, or there may not be enough tools and space to enable everyone to function well. Ringelmann might have transformed his experimental task into one that was only partly additive for eight-man groups by providing a rope that could be grasped by only four men, or by announcing that it was unfair for more than four men to pull at once. Had this been done, the task would have included some disjunctive features. The group's product would have depended upon which four of the members were selected to do the work and upon the effectiveness with which the selected members combined their individual pulling powers. Outside the laboratory, complete additivity is probably rather rare.

Discretionary Tasks

Imagine that the members of a group are asked to agree upon a single best estimate of the temperature of the room in which they are sitting. The task is unitary because the intellectual operations by which estimates of room temperature are made cannot profitably be broken into subtasks and performed by two or more individuals. The group may arrive at its decision in many different ways. One member may do all of the work, the others acquiescing in his conclusion, or several members may produce individual estimates, the group selecting one of them as its official verdict. If several or all of the members express judgments, the group's estimate may also be generated by computing the average of the individual judgments. However, there are almost innumerable ways of computing an "average." The opinions of all members may be weighted equally, as is the case if all judgments are added and then divided by the number of judgments. However, the group may instead compute a weighted average, letting some members' estimates count more heavily than others'. Thus members who have often been right when controversial issues have been discussed in the past may be regarded as experts and accorded special consideration. Members who seem highly confident, or who occupy positions of high status in the community, may be more influential than those who do not. Whatever gives one member more influence than another favors the computation of a weighted average which deviates from the principle of "one man, one vote."

We are not suggesting that group members will self-consciously employ a complex mathematical formula when attempting to resolve their varied views of room temperature. Occasionally they may do so, but they are more likely to engage in a discussion process in which weights are unobtrusively assigned to one another's contributions, and in which members gradually converge upon a position that reflects the importance each person's judgment is accorded. Consequently, the process can be seen as one in which members' behaviors accomplish the operations that might be indicated by a mathematical formula.

The temperature-judging task permits a group to devise its own mathematical formula. Members are free to sum their several independent judgments if they wish, but it is unlikely that any group would ever devise its estimate in such an impracticable manner. Members are permitted to assign total weight to the contribution of a single person, or to the persons who produce the modal judgment. In the more typical case, each individual's contribution is likely to affect the decision that is reached, but the opinions of certain members will carry more weight than those of others. The group's estimate of the temperature of a room will probably be a weighted average of the members' estimates.

When viewed in this light, a disjunctive task may be said to require that total weight be given to the contribution of a single member (or to two or more members who have produced the same solution), but the group is free to decide which member will receive that weight. A conjunctive task not only requires that total weight be accorded a single member but also dictates that it is the least productive person who must receive that weight. When performing an additive task, individuals are weighted equally; thus a properly executed pull of one kilogram on Ringelmann's rope contributed one unit to the group's product regardless of who did the pulling. By contrast with each of these three types, the temperature-judging task permits the group to devise its own mathematical formula; members may be weighted in any fashion, and they are free to combine their weighted contributions in any manner they desire. To be sure, some of the techniques by which members are permitted to combine their individual products are unlikely to be employed because they cannot be expected to yield a high quality product. By comparison with the options that are open when tasks are disjunctive, conjunctive, or additive, this one offers members very great flexibility. Tasks that permit group members to select their own weighting and combinatorial rules will be called discretionary tasks. Within broad limits, members are free to employ whatever processes they prefer.

When an optimizing task is discretionary, the quality of the group product depends heavily upon the processes the group actually employs. Regardless of how inaccurately the individual members of a group judge the temperature of the room, there will almost invariably be one or more "prescribed processes" by which the individual estimates can be combined to produce the correct one. Consequently, the group's potential productivity (the level of success it can achieve if it makes the best possible use of its resources) will almost always entail perfect performance. This will be the case because prescribed process will compensate for poor individual outputs. Actual productivity will, of course, fall below potential productivity to the extent that group process is not in accord with prescribed process. The nature of the prescribed process will depend upon the distribution of individual contributions that are to be combined into a single product and upon the criterion value that is regarded as being correct. Thus, for example, if one member has correctly estimated the temperature of the room, prescribed process might involve assignment of total weight to that particular member. If no individual has been correct, the estimates of the members having scattered on both sides of the criterion value, prescribed process will involve some form of averaging of the individual contributions. Unfortunately, members will not ordinarily know which of many permitted processes is prescribed, and the group's success will depend upon the one they actually employ.

In many early studies, individuals were asked to make judgments of the kind under consideration here. They estimated the temperature of a room, the number of beans in a jar, or the numerosity of buckshot. The quality of their individual judgments was indexed by the accuracy with which they approximated the true values. In these investigations, however, individuals were not assembled into *ad hoc* groups and instructed to render a single decision. Instead, the experimenter himself created a "group product" by computing the unweighted mean of the judgments expressed by people whom he arbitrarily treated as members of "nominal" groups. Consequently, these studies did not examine group performance of discretionary tasks; they investigated the quality of the products groups would have generated had they employed a specific process. The reason for discussing such research at this point is that the process imposed upon the nominal groups was one that members might actually have used had they been assembled and permitted to interact freely.

In most of these studies, the unweighted average of the members' independent judgments was found to be rather accurate, and to be more nearly correct than the judgments of most of the members. Individual judgments tended to be scattered symmetrically around the true value, and when they were combined to produce an unweighted average, one person's excessively high estimate could compensate for another's excessively low one. If the judgments of individual members of a group are symmetrically distributed around the correct outcome, behaviors that abide by the rules for computing an unweighted average constitute a rather appropriate process. However, they do not necessarily represent the most appropriate (prescribed) process. In almost all of the relevant studies, it was found that the initial judgments of one or more members of a group were even more accurate than the average of all judgments; when this was the case, a more appropriate process would have been to assign total weight to the person who was most nearly correct. Needless to say, real-life groups would have been unlikely to know which member was most accurate and thus could not have employed this advantageous strategy.

A few of the studies using the paradigm described above have produced quite different findings. During World War II, Klugman (1947) asked soldiers to predict the dates when hostilities in the European and Pacific sectors would end. Of 109 subjects, 27 produced estimates of the former date that were more accurate than the average of all estimates, and 59 of the individual estimates concerning the Pacific sector were more nearly correct than the mean. Farnsworth and Williams (1936) required individuals to heft two boxes and then estimate the weight of a third that was lighter than either of the first two, but larger in bulk. In response to this size-weight illusion, subjects were inclined to overestimate the weight of the third box, and the average of all judgments was not very accurate. As might be expected, a large proportion of the individual estimates were more nearly correct than the unweighted average. In both of these studies, the process imposed on nominal groups was not very appropriate because the judgments of individuals were not symmetrically distributed around the true value. When this is the case, a process that assigns total weight to the most accurate person, or which weights accurate persons more heavily than inaccurate ones, will be more effective than one which abides by the rules for computing an unweighted average. It is reasonable to surmise that members of real-life groups, like the researchers who conducted these studies, might fail to employ prescribed combinatorial systems.

Studies of the kind reviewed above examine the quality of the product that will be created *if group action proceeds in a specified manner.* They do not indicate whether or not members of groups actually behave in the indicated fashion. With only a little change in the research paradigm, information can be obtained concerning the process that actually occurs. Imagine that after individuals have independently judged the temperature of a room they are assembled as an *ad hoc* group and asked to reach a single decision. The final judgment rendered by the group can be compared with the unweighted average of the individual judgments to determine whether it is reasonable to believe that group process followed the rules by which that statistic is computed. If the group output is not significantly different from the unweighted mean, it is plausible to conclude that members weighted one another equally and averaged their individual contributions. Of course, findings of this kind will not prove beyond all doubt that such combinatorial rules have guided the group process, for one will generally be able to concoct alternative "process models" that are also capable of "explaining" how the final decision was reached. However, many mathematical formulas will fail to generate the group's outcome and can be rejected as inaccurate statements of the process by which members have assembled their contributions.

These procedures for inferring group process have occasionally been used in studies involving divisible tasks, but they have almost never been employed when tasks have been unitary and discretionary. The findings yielded by such techniques can most conveniently be discussed in connection with our subsequent examination of divisible tasks.

As noted earlier, maximizing tasks seem never to be discretionary. When the goal is to produce as many units as possible, or to function at top speed, members of groups are not permitted to multiply their individual contributions by some factor in order to achieve an attractive outcome. Furthermore, an averaging process would be so blatantly inconsistent with task demands that it is, in effect, prohibited.

In summary, discretionary tasks permit group members to employ any of a wide variety of combinatorial rules. The nature of the prescribed process depends upon the distribution of individual contributions that are to be combined and upon the criterion of success. The quality of the group product reflects the degree to which the group process corresponds to that which is prescribed.

Summary

Unitary tasks cannot profitably be divided into subtasks and performed in piecemeal fashion by two or more individuals. Consequently, the group product must either be the outcome generated by a single member or some combination of the outcomes produced by several members. Task demands determine how the contributions of individual participants *can be* weighted and combined, and they prescribe the manner in which members *must* weight and combine their contributions if their actual productivity is to equal their potential productivity.

When a unitary task is disjunctive, members are permitted to assign total weight to the contribution of any member, but cannot distribute weights among members. The prescribed process entails assignment of total weight to the member who has performed most effectively.

Conjunctive tasks require that total weight be assigned to the least productive member. If each participant makes full use of his relevant resources, actual productivity will equal potential productivity because the contributions of individual participants are automatically combined in the only manner permitted by the task.

Additive tasks require that members' contributions be weighted equally and that they be summed. When these rules prevail, a group's product reflects the quality (or speed) of the work done by individuals, and the proficiency with which they accomplish the summation process (e.g., the precision with which all members succeed in pulling on a rope at exactly the same time and in the same direction).

Discretionary tasks permit members of a group to combine their individual outcomes in any of the ways described previously, or to employ processes that yield a weighted or unweighted average of the individual contributions. The process that is prescribed depends on the distribution of individual outcomes that are available to be combined and on the character of the criterion outcome that is assumed to represent ideal performance.

Maximizing tasks make success depend upon how many units of an outcome are produced, or how rapidly they are produced. Optimizing tasks make success a function of the degree to which the obtained outcome approximates a preferred or "best" value. Additive tasks usually involve maximization, and discretionary tasks seem invariably to require optimization. Conjunctive and disjunctive tasks may entail either maximization or optimization.

How well a group will perform a task depends upon the relevant resources of its members, on task demands that determine which processes are permitted and prescribed, and on the process that members of the group actually employ. When actual process corresponds to prescribed process, actual productivity will equal potential productivity (i.e., the group will make the best possible use of its available resources). Several factors may prevent this from happening. Among those identified in this chapter are (a) failure of status differences to parallel the quality of the contributions offered by participating members; (b) the low level of confidence proficient members sometimes have in their own ability to perform the task; (c) the social pressures that an incompetent majority may exert on a competent minority; and (d) the fact that the quality of individual contributions is often very difficult to evaluate.

Chapter 3

Group Performance
of Divisible Tasks

Jack Sprat could eat no fat; his wife could eat no lean.
And so you see, between the two, they licked the platter clean.

In simple form, this nursery rhyme suggests both the advantages and complexities of divisible tasks. When a work assignment can be broken into subtasks, a group may succeed even though none of its members can do the entire job alone. If each member is inclined (or can be induced) to work on that phase of the total task that he can do better than other members, the group product may be very good indeed. However, divisible tasks are not necessarily performed effectively. Members of a group may not know who is best qualified to eat fat or lean, or the rules under which the group operates may require that members take turns performing all subtasks, or even that members specialize on those subtasks for which they are least qualified. Depending upon who does

40

what, groups may perform far better than their most able member, or much worse than their poorest.

Divisible tasks come in many varieties. They differ from one another with respect to the ways they can be divided into subtasks, how people are "assigned" to subtasks, the manner in which two or more individuals may combine their efforts to perform a single subtask, how the outcomes of subtask performances can be assembled to form a group product, and many other ways. The number of variables that may reasonably be expected to affect group performance of divisible tasks is so large that no workable classificatory system is likely to be complete. In this chapter, attention will be focused upon a limited number of distinctly different kinds of divisible tasks. Some of the varieties that are not examined closely will be considered later in other contexts. The immediate aim is to note the major contingencies that exist when tasks are divisible.

Rules and the Performance of Divisible Tasks

Like other tasks, those that are divisible are performed according to rules that specify what may or must be done. Rules are sometimes imposed by the society or organization within which the group operates. Thus legislatures pass laws restricting the kinds of tools and raw materials that may be used, and organizations employ "job analysts" who decide how a task will be divided into subtasks and how the efforts of various workers will be coordinated and combined. Traditions specify what is proper and ethical behavior, and norms and role systems sometimes place severe restraints on an individual's or group's freedom to do whatever comes naturally. Employers and foremen usually specify how certain tasks shall be performed, and experimenters typically require their subjects to work in a predetermined fashion.

Other rules reflect the impact of equipment design, spatial restrictions, the logical necessities imposed by the character of the goal that is to be achieved, and other considerations. The structure of an assembly line determines how many men can work at once, what each must do, and how the several subtasks are combined to yield a group product. Many pieces of farm machinery are designed to be operated by a specific number of persons, and the behaviors that each must produce in order to achieve a favorable outcome are dictated by the nature and location of the instruments that are to be manipulated. Only three men can be accommodated in the Apollo spacecraft, a fact that severely limits the division of labor that can occur. If a task is composed of two unitary subtasks, there is only one way it can profitably be divided, and if it consists of only one unitary element, it cannot be divided at all. Sometimes the subtasks into which an assignment may be broken can only or most profitably be performed in a certain order. Thus, for example, Bales (1950) suggests that tasks requiring groups to reach decisions concerning very complex matters typically call for sequential answers to three questions:

(a) What are the relevant facts?
(b) How should the facts be organized and evaluated?
(c) What conclusion is justified by examination of the facts?

Needless to say, the second or third subtask cannot be very adequately performed until the first has been concluded.

Regardless of the manner in which rules are created, they affect the procedures by which tasks can or must be performed. Consequently, they influence the actual and potential productivity of groups. In the following sections, we will examine the implications of certain rules.

Self-Matching with Specified Subtasks

Sometimes the rules governing performance of a task clearly specify the subtasks into which the total endeavor must be divided, but permit members of a group to decide for themselves who will be matched with which subtask. For example, two or more persons may be instructed to respond to a true-false test by agreeing on a single answer for each question. Every item of the test may constitute a subtask which is disjunctive and unitary. Consequently, a member of the group may receive total weight on a specific item (his answer is selected as the group's answer) or no weight at all; he is either matched with a specific subtask or he is not. The group's score on the task is additively determined by counting the number of subtasks performed correctly. In an instance of this kind, the group's potential productivity equals the number of items at least one member can answer correctly. Actual productivity will approximate potential productivity to the degree that members are always matched with items they can answer correctly.

Imagine that individuals and groups are confronted by a large board on which a number of bolt heads are visible. The bolts are clustered in pairs, and each pair is said to represent a decision point. When a stylus is applied to the "correct" bolt head, a light flashes and the individual or group proceeds to the next decision point. The goal is to learn through repeated trials which of the two options is the correct one at each point, and eventually to move through the entire maze without making any errors. Gurnee (1937) employed a task of this kind in a study that compared individual and collective learning. College students worked alone or in groups of about ten persons. At each decision point, members of groups voted by acclamation on the path to be followed, but if neither bolt head received strong support, a show of hands was demanded. The acclamation procedure permitted individual members to express their judgments vociferously when they believed they had learned the correct response to a particular pair of bolt heads, and to remain silent when other choice points were encountered. Thus members were free to match themselves with specific subtasks. By contrast, individuals who worked alone were compelled to assign total weight to themselves at every step in the maze.

Gurnee's findings reveal that, after proceeding through the maze once, groups made many fewer errors than did individual subjects. However, when members of groups were asked to work as individuals after their sixth trial, they made almost as many errors as did subjects who had worked alone throughout the experiment. Therefore, it appears that people did not actually learn any faster in groups than alone, and that the superiority of groups reflected the advantageous pooling of what members had learned. Gurnee noted that members who were correct tended to announce their answers more rapidly than those who were not. The task was clearly a divisible one because each choice point was treated as a separate subtask. Although members were not explicitly assigned responsibility for specific subtasks, they seem to have made such assignments for themselves. Presumably, groups functioned effectively because individual members chose to perform those phases of the task they could do most effectively and to leave other subtasks to their associates. Together the members of groups accomplished more than any one of them might have achieved working alone. In this respect, they were like Jack Sprat and his wife who were able to lick the platter clean because each chose to eat the only kind of meat he could consume.

It should be noted that the goal imposed by Gurnee made his task additive; success was defined by counting the number of subtasks that were correctly performed. The subtasks themselves, though, were disjunctive because they required an "either-or" weighting of group members. Whether a particular subtask was adequately performed depended on the correctness of the outcomes generated by individual members and on which member was accorded total weight. It is characteristic of divisible tasks that they do not fit cleanly within any one of the classes discussed in the previous chapter. Specific subtasks may prescribe one type of process, but the method by which subtasks performances can (or must) be combined to generate a group product is often quite different.

Other researchers have also employed divisible tasks composed of disjunctive subtasks that must be combined additively. Faust (1959) asked individuals and four-person groups to solve four "spatial problems." One of them required that nine dots be connected by four straight lines drawn without removing the pencil from the paper. Another involved 16 matches that were laid out in a way that produced five squares; subjects were required to produce four squares by moving three matches to different locations. Problems of this kind are probably unitary in that they cannot profitably be subdivided into smaller parts, each of which is performed by a different person. Furthermore, they are disjunctive because various hypothetical solutions cannot meaningfully be added or averaged. The group must accept somebody's outcome as its official solution, and must apply a weight of zero to all others.

When confronted by a divisible task of this kind, the process that is prescribed for a group is fairly evident. If any individual member possesses the resources needed to solve a problem, he should employ them for that purpose and should present his correct solution to the group. His associates should, in turn, accept his proposal and proceed to the next problem. The process should then be repeated with the group again adopting the outcome that is offered by its most proficient member. Needless to say, the member who is most proficient on the second problem may not be the one who was most effective on the first. If the prescribed process is followed, the group will solve every subtask for which at least one of its members possesses the needed resources. Unless a single member is the one who is most competent on all subtasks, the group's score (number of subtasks performed correctly) will exceed that which any of its members might have earned working alone.

Faust's findings suggest that groups did, in fact, employ the prescribed process. On the average, groups solved significantly more of the four problems than did individuals who worked alone. Furthermore, group scores were approximately equal to the scores of "nominal" groups assembled to test the proposition that "truth triumphs over untruth" on every subtask. To accomplish this test, Faust randomly assigned individuals who had worked alone to purely hypothetical groups that were credited with solving a problem if any member had solved it while working individually. On this basis, nominal groups solved an average of 2.03 problems whereas real groups solved 2.31. The difference is not statistically significant. The ability of real groups to make such advantageous use of their members' resources probably reflected the fact that the subtasks had a strong "eureka" flavor; the correctness of the proper solution to a problem was highly evident once it was discovered.

Barnlund (1959) examined group performance of a task that was structurally similar to those employed in the Faust study, but which lacked the eureka quality. College students worked individually on a test that contained 30 items, each of which presented the premises of a syllogism and required the respondent to select the conclusion that most logically followed from those premises. The following is a sample item.

> Some Communists are advocates of heavy taxes;
> All advocates of heavy taxes are conservative Republicans;
> Therefore:
>
> a.   Some advocates of heavy taxes are not Communists.
> b.   Some Communists are conservative Republicans.
> c.   Some conservative Republicans are Communists.
> d.   Some Communists are advocates of heavy taxes.
> e.   None of these conclusions follows.

Every item of the test presented a conclusion that was logically correct along with four others that were not. However, the correct conclusion was often one that might be expected to contradict the beliefs or prejudices of individual subjects.

Eight or nine weeks after they had responded to the test instrument, subjects were assembled in groups of four to six members. Efforts were made to compose homogeneous groups consisting of persons who had earned identical or very nearly identical scores during the previous, individual sessions. Of course, different members of the same group had obtained their scores by solving different items correctly, but this kind of heterogeneity tends not to be very pronounced on tests of syllogistic reasoning. Consequently, although Barnlund does not report data concerning responses to specific test items, it is reasonable to believe that groups were not only very homogeneous with respect to ability to perform the total task, but also rather homogeneous with respect to their ability to perform particular subtasks. The latter aspect of the composition of groups is especially pertinent because it tends to restrict the degree to which one member's ability can complement another inability. If Jack Sprat and his wife had both been able to eat lean but not fat, their capacity to lick the platter clean would have been severely restricted.

Groups assembled in the manner described above were given a "parallel form" of the 30-item syllogistic-reasoning test and asked to reach a group decision on each item. (A parallel form is one that is designed to measure the same variable as another test and contains items of the same kind. The two forms of the instrument employed by Barnlund had been found in earlier research to yield highly correlated scores. In order to compensate for any possible difference in the difficulty of the two forms, Barnlund gave half of his subjects form A and half form B during the first session; the parallel form received by groups during the second session was the one to which members had not responded earlier.) After all groups had completed the task, their scores on the parallel form were compared with the scores individual members had made when working alone on the original form. Groups were found to score significantly higher than the average member had scored during the earlier session (21.9 items correct versus 17.5 for individuals) and also higher than the most successful member had scored when working alone (18.8 items correct). Barnlund did not assemble nominal groups of the kind used by Faust to estimate the scores groups would have obtained if truth had triumphed over untruth *on every item* of the test. Consequently, we cannot assert that groups followed prescribed process with great precision. However, the fact that they scored markedly higher than their best single member had done when working alone strongly suggests that (a) different members were correct on different items and (b) groups were rather successful in assigning total weight to whichever member was correct. Thus despite the relative homogeneity of members' resources and the fact that subtasks lacked a strong "eureka" flavor, groups seem to have been able to function in a complementary manner. If any member was able to perform a subtask, it appears to have been performed.

Barnlund offered a somewhat different interpretation of his groups' successes. Perhaps individual members worked harder when functioning in a group than when operating as separate individuals. If this were the case, the outcomes from which a group could select its official verdict may have been better than the outcomes the same persons would have produced working alone. Group success may therefore have been more strongly indicative of members' willingness to use their resources to generate good outcomes than of their ability to select among outcomes once they were generated. The available data do not permit us to decide which aspect of the total process was more directly responsible for group superiority. However, research that is examined later in this book (see Chapter 6) indicates that reasoning problems are generally performed more accurately by individuals who work alone than by people who work in social situations. Consequently, Barnlund's alternative interpretation is unlikely to be correct.

Ryack (1965) also examined group performance of a task that permitted individuals to match themselves with clearly delineated subtasks. Subjects were exposed to a series of nonsense syllables each of which was projected on a screen for a 4-sec interval. After all syllables in the series had been exposed, individuals or groups of two subjects were allowed 5 min in which to recall as many of them as possible. Members of groups were permitted to talk freely during the recall period, but were required to prepare a single list of syllables. After the 5-min response period, the syllables were again exposed to the subjects who were allowed another 5 min in which to recall what they had seen. The process was repeated until the individual or group had correctly listed all syllables on two successive trials. Success was measured by counting the number of errors (omitted or incorrectly remembered syllables) committed before the two completely correct trials occurred.

Two-person groups were found to obtain significantly better scores than the average individual who worked alone. Furthermore, group scores proved to be better than the scores the more competent members of the groups would have made had they worked alone. (The scores that better members of dyads would have made working alone were deduced in accordance with the technique recommended by Taylor and by Lorge and Solomon; see page 20 of this book.) In order to determine whether it was reasonable to presume that truth triumphed on every subtask, a second formula proposed by Lorge and Solomon (1955) was used to deduce the scores groups would have made if they had successfully recalled every syllable that either member could remember. These estimated values were quite comparable to the scores groups actually obtained, suggesting that members were highly effective in matching themselves with subtasks. If either individual could correctly recall a syllable, he presumably was permitted to perform that phase of the total task.

The studies by Gurnee, Faust, Barnlund, and Ryack are similar both with respect to procedures and findings. All of them examined group performance of a divisible task consisting of subtasks that were unitary and disjunctive. In each study, subtasks were clearly prescribed, but members were free to decide who would perform which subtask. In every case, the group's success depended upon the number of subtasks performed correctly. Under these circumstances, groups were more productive than individuals working alone and they seemed to be remarkably successful in matching members with subtasks (i.e., in assigning total weight to the particular person who could best perform a specific subtask). However, it cannot be assumed that group process will always correspond so closely to that which is prescribed by the task. As has already been noted, disjunctive tasks (or subtasks) *permit* a group to assign total weight to members who are not most competent, and a variety of circumstances may lead it to do so. An extreme case that probably does not often occur in real life involves a complete mismatch of members and subtasks, each phase of the work being allocated to the person who is least competent to perform it. This arrangement would prevail if Jack Sprat chose (or was assigned) to eat the fat, which he could not consume, and his wife were assigned responsibility for the lean, which was anathema to her. Under these circumstances, group productivity would necessarily be lower than that which even the poorer member might have achieved by working alone.

All of the preceding studies deal with situations in which any member of a group can be matched with any number of subtasks. This will be the case whenever the several subtasks need not be performed simultaneously and when there are no rules dictating that everyone should do his "fair share" of the work. If the goal is to proceed as rapidly as possible through a series of subtasks, the demands of the task may require that different persons work simultaneously on different phases of the total endeavor.

It should also be noted that in real life, members of groups are often required to perform the matching process *before* they know what outcome each participant can or will produce. In the studies examined above, all members of a group were permitted or required to perform each subtask and the actual matching occurred after their individual outcomes were available for inspection. These circumstances undoubtedly maximized the effectiveness with which matching was accomplished. Imagine, for sake of example, that two golfers are instructed to function as a team and that each is permitted to take a first shot. After observing one another's success on this shot, the members are permitted to decide whose performance will be accepted as the team's effort. If this procedure is then repeated for each succeeding shot, the team will undoubtedly obtain a very good score. Because golfers can readily recognize a good shot when they see it (golf is a eureka task), the better of the two performances will be accepted at every stage of the game and the matching will be perfect. However, if the two players are required to use only one ball and to decide who will take each shot before it is made, the situation is quite different. Assuming that one man is known to be very effective off the tee and the other is thought to excel on the green, a realistic basis for matching exists. Unless the participants are strikingly unequal in their abilities to perform specific subtasks (and their abilities are correctly perceived), matching that occurs prior to performance will be less than perfectly executed. The actual productivity of the team is likely to fall below its potential productivity. It is regrettable that laboratory studies that deal unequivocally with such matching processes are not available.

Self-Matching with Unspecified Subtasks

In each of the studies cited in the previous section, subtasks were clearly specified by the experimenter or by the situation he created for his subjects. Certain problems were to be solved, or specific materials were to be learned. Success depended upon how many of these unmistakably prescribed subtasks were performed adequately. However, tasks can sometimes be divided into almost countless parts, and the individual or group is required to discover what those subtasks are, and to perform as many as possible of them. When this is the case, success depends upon the number and character of the subtasks that are discovered as well as upon the facility with which they are performed.

Experimental tasks employed by Taylor, Berry, and Block (1958) emphasized the discovery of subtasks. In a study designed to evaluate the effectiveness of "brainstorming" techniques, groups of four Yale students were asked to suggest as many ways of attempting to solve a problem as they could. Each suggestion was announced orally and members of groups were instructed to avoid any criticism of one another's contributions. Instead, they were urged to emphasize quantity of suggestions and to express any idea no matter how "wild" it might seem. Comparable instructions were given to individual subjects who worked alone on the same tasks.

One problem entailed developing a program to induce Europeans to visit America. Another called for suggestions concerning ways of meeting the teacher shortage, and a third required an enumeration of the advantages and disadvantages that would ensue if humans were suddenly endowed with an extra thumb on each hand. Many different acceptable suggestions could be made in response to each of these three problems, and the experimenters noted that more than 475 different solutions were actually proposed for each of them. Consequently, the task that confronted a group or individual was not to produce "the correct" solution, but rather to propose as many different "partial" solutions as possible.

The total task posed by a single problem was to discover and perform the maximum number of subtasks (i.e., to discover and announce the maximum number of suggestions). Any member of a group might match himself with any subtask he could discover, provided it had not already been performed by someone else.

The number of subtasks performed by groups far exceeded that for individuals who worked alone. However, when nominal groups were concocted and credited with making every suggestion any member had offered when working individually, the scores of these hypothetical groups were found to be almost twice as large as those of real groups. Thus it appears that interacting individuals were not highly successful in discovering a wide range of subtasks. Groups did better than solitary individuals, but not as well as the combined abilities of their members should have permitted. The experimenters concluded that members of groups probably felt somewhat reluctant to express seemingly deviant ideas, and that working in a group may have led people to pursue a single, shared train of thought. Either of these two kinds of social constraints might explain why actual group productivity fell far below potential productivity. It is also possible that members of groups could not remember what suggestions their associates had made and were loath to offer solutions that might duplicate those others had already mentioned. Whatever the correct explanation may be, it seems apparent that individuals failed to discover as many subtasks when serving as members of a group, and/or failed to "perform" all of those they did, in fact, discover.

In real life, it is sometimes important to identify a large number of possible ways of coping with a problem, but success ordinarily requires that additional steps be taken. The individual or group is usually compelled to evaluate available alternatives, select one or a few for implementation, and employ available resources to execute the option(s) that have been chosen. Brainstorming is therefore a highly atypical task because it involves only one phase of a larger sequence of actions, and because the aim is to identify and perform as many subtasks as possible rather than to discover and implement the best possible combination of subtasks. Tasks that emphasize the latter aims have been employed in a number of studies.

In 1948, Bavelas suggested a procedure by which the complex communication structures found in large and rather formal organizations might be reduced to manageable size and examined in the laboratory. Each of five persons could be given one-fifth of the information needed to solve a problem, and the freedom of these individuals to communicate with one another could be restricted by rules permitting messages to flow along only certain specified channels. Figure 3.1 shows several possible communication "structures" each providing a different combination of open channels. Thus in the case of the chain, adjacent persons can communicate directly with one another, but persons

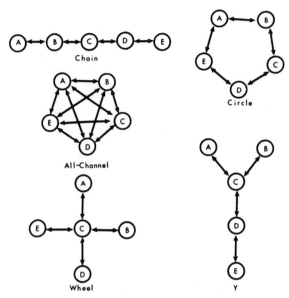

Fig. 3.1. Five-person communication networks.

who are not adjacent can establish contact only by having their messages relayed by one or more intermediaries. The wheel allows direct, two-way communication between person C and each of the other members of the group, but persons A, B, D, and E can reach one another only be sending their messages to C. Experimentally contrived arrangements of this kind were said to parallel real-life organizational structures. in that they permitted people to pool their highly specialized resources (information) only by employing a predetermined set of communication channels. Much of the research stimulated by Bavelas' suggestions was designed to determine how effectively (accurately, rapidly) groups could solve problems when their communicative activities were guided by one versus another pattern of available linkages.

In an early study, Leavitt (1951) required subjects to solve the "common symbol" problem. Each of five persons was given a card on which was printed all but one of six symbols ○, △, ◇, □, +, *, the cards being designed in such a fashion that a different symbol was omitted from each, and only one of the six symbols was included on *all* cards. Members of groups were instructed to communicate with one another with the aim of discovering the symbol that was present on every card. However, communication could occur only in the form of written notes that were sent along the channels provided by a circle, chain, Y, or wheel, Whenever any individual had received the necessary information from others in his group he could, of course, reach a decision and inform his colleagues of his conclusion by sending more notes along whatever channels the communication structure provided. When all members had indicated to the experimenter that they had obtained a solution, the task was said to be completed. Success was measured (inversely) by the number of seconds required to finish the task, the number of messages transmitted, and the number of erroneous conclusions reported to the experimenter. In order to accumulate reliable data, each group worked on the task 15 times, the "correct" symbol being changed from one trial to the next. However, all 15 trials were performed on a single communication network (circle, chain, Y, or wheel).

Leavitt's major findings have been corroborated a number of times by other investigators. Groups working with a circle pattern tended to require more messages and to take more time to solve the problem than did groups working with a wheel pattern. The chain and Y networks produced intermediate results. Relatively few errors were made regardless of the network employed, though there was some indication that circle groups were especially error prone but, at the same time, rather capable of correcting errors.

It is pertinent to inquire whether groups worked at about their maximum level of efficiency on tasks of the kind employed by Leavitt. Did actual productivity approximate potential productivity? Did groups obtain better scores on the wheel than on the circle because potential productivity was higher when working on the former? To answer these questions, we must examine the constraints that various networks imposed on group behavior and infer the level of productivity they permitted groups to attain.

Consider first the level of accuracy a group should manifest if its members make full use of their resources. Regardless of the network that is employed, members of a group collectively possess all the information that is needed to solve the problem. Furthermore, the problem itself is so simple that a college student can hardly fail to solve it correctly once he is given all the necessary facts. Surely any group of five students will contain at least one member who can identify the common symbol after receiving messages telling him which symbols are on each person's card. All networks not only permit such messages to be sent to any of the five members, but also allow any member, once he has deduced the correct answer, to send return messages telling his associates which symbol is the common one. To be sure, in some cases messages must be relayed several times, but in every network all individuals can communicate (directly or indirectly) with all others. Consequently, it seems fair to conclude that every network permits completely accurate performance. If a member announces the wrong answer, it is because someone did not do what his own abilities and the rules of the task permitted him to do. Someone failed to transmit a message that he could have transmitted, failed to deduce the common symbol when he had resources to do so, or failed to inform others of the correct answer once it was discovered. The processes that are *permitted* by every network always include at least one that will eventuate in everyone's having the correct answer, but other processes are also permitted and there is no guarantee that the prescribed process will actually occur.

How many messages must members send in order that everyone obtain the correct answer? Inspection of the networks shown in Fig. 3.1 indicates that the job can always be accomplished with eight messages. For example, in the case of the chain, persons A and E can send their information to B and D respectively (two messages), who may, in turn, report what they know to person C (two more messages). Having received all the necessary information, person C can deduce the common symbol and transmit the solution to B and D (two more messages) who can relay the correct answer to persons A and E (two more messages). Similar sequences can be employed in other networks; it is possible to transmit all necessary information to any member of any structure using only four messages, and only four additional messages are required to inform everyone of the correct solution. Whenever a network permits everyone to communicate directly *or* indirectly with everyone else, it is possible for groups of size n to solve the common symbol problem using $2(n - 1)$ messages. If productivity is measured by the number of messages groups employ in reaching the correct solution, all of Leavitt's networks have the same *potential* productivity. Discrepancies between the actual productivity scores obtained by groups working within different networks cannot be attributed to discrepancies in potential productivity.

When productivity is measured by the amount of time required to solve the problem, the task is somewhat more difficult to analyze. However, if we assume "standard" individuals, all of whom require the same amount of time to write and send a message, the total communication time required by the four networks can be deduced. Because no individual can prepare and send more than one note at a time, the eight messages by which chain-groups can solve the problem will require five units of time. (During the first interval, persons A and E send their information to B and D. During the second interval, B and D transmit their knowledge to C. Person C then deduces the correct solution and, during the third communication period, informs either B or D of the answer. During the next interval, C informs his other adjacent neighbor of the correct answer, and during the fifth time interval the solution is relayed to persons A and E.) The reader may determine for himself that the wheel and Y networks also require a minimum of five units of time. The circle and all-channel networks permit the correct solution to be obtained in three units, but the communication pattern that allows this to happen is so complex that groups cannot reasonably be expected to discover it. Consequently, it seems appropriate to assume that the minimum amount of time required to perform the total task is the same for all networks. The fact that groups actually completed the job more rapidly in some networks than others reflected the manner in which networks were used rather than any difference in the effectiveness with which they could have been used.

The foregoing analysis has been concerned with prescribed process—process that *must* occur if a group is to obtain the best score the rules permit it to obtain. The fact that actual scores varied across networks while potential scores did not indicates that groups sometimes failed to employ the prescribed process. Leavitt's data do not provide a detailed picture of who actually did what, but other research has yielded information concerning the subtasks into which groups tend to divide the total endeavor, and about the manner in which members are matched with subtasks.

Guetzkow (1960) employed the common symbol problem in a study that compared the performances of groups that were required to function in circle, wheel, or all-channel networks. During the first few trials, little specialization of function was observed to occur. Members usually sent all the information they possessed to anyone else with whom they were directly connected. Thus far more messages than necessary were sent, and information flowed helter-skelter along available channels until everyone had obtained all the facts necessary to draw his own conclusion. Although this procedure enabled groups to obtain correct answers, it was highly inefficient with respect to time and number of messages written. By about the fifth trial, many groups began to develop a hierarchical structure in which members played one or another of two or three distinct roles. One such role was that of "keyman"; it involved receiving information from others, deducing the correct solution, and transmitting the answer to others. A second role entailed sending one's own information to one or more associates and waiting to receive the solution that was discovered and transmitted by the keyman. Guetzkow refers to this role as that of an "endman." A third role often emerged in the circle network, but rarely occurred in wheel or all-channel groups. Some members received information from endmen and relayed it, along with information concerning their own symbols, to the keyman. When the latter supplied the solution to these "relayers," they forwarded it to the endmen.

It is to be noted that performance of these roles resulted in a process that was fully in accord with prescribed process. To be sure, the circle and all-channel networks did not require members always to play the same roles, but continuity from trial to trial guaranteed that all aspects of the prescribed process would occur. In the case of the wheel, only the member located at the center of the network could act as keyman without loss of efficiency, and when he performed that role, no relayers were needed. (The all-channel network can be used as a wheel, and in most instances groups with that option avoided the relayer role.)

The dependability with which groups developed an efficient hierarchical structure was contingent upon the network that was imposed. Wheel groups almost always organized themselves effectively, and all-channel groups had a high rate of success. Only 14 of 40 circle groups evolved an organization that assured good performance. The relatively low ability of circle groups to employ prescribed process is especially noteworthy because Guetzkow, unlike Leavitt and most other experimenters, permitted his subjects to send one another notes concerning organizational matters after each trial on the common symbol task. Apparently there is something about a circle network that makes effective organization difficult. In part, this is probably due to the fact that three, rather than two, roles are required in order to operate efficiently within a circle network. However, Guetzkow found that his circle groups sometimes succeeded in dividing the task into the three essential subtasks, but failed to function well because members were not appropriately matched with subtasks. Two or more participants sometimes attempted to function as keymen, and on many trials there was a dearth of relayers or endmen. Whatever the explanation for inadequate organization may be, groups functioned well when the prescribed subtasks were created and "assigned" to appropriately located members; groups functioned poorly when this did not occur.

Guetzkow's research identifies two factors that undoubtedly affected the organizational effectiveness, and hence the productivity, of Leavitt's groups. Of the four networks employed by Leavitt, only the wheel prescribed a process involving just two roles. The circle, chain, and Y required a three-part division of labor, and were therefore more difficult to organize properly. Furthermore, of these three complex structures, the circle required the group to make more organizational decisions than did either the chain or Y. In effect, the chain almost automatically matched two persons with the endman role, and the Y matched three members with it. By contrast, the circle permitted any person to be matched with any of the three roles, but the prescribed process required that there always be two endmen, two relayers, and one keyman. It seems apparent that important aspects of the matching process were solved in an advantageous fashion by the rules under which chain, wheel, and Y groups operated, but were left to the discretion and caprice of circle groups. With these considerations in mind, we may suggest that Leavitt's wheel groups functioned best because the prescribed organization of the wheel network was simpler than that of the other structures and because the wheel strongly encouraged an appropriate matching of individuals and subtasks. Chain and Y groups were next most effective because, although the prescribed division of labor was complex, the nature of the imposed structure strongly favored an advantageous matching of members and subtasks. Circle networks offered neither of these advantages. Consequently, although potential productivity was the same for all networks, the prescribed process was more dependably achieved in some cases than others because it was a simpler process and/or because the network permitted fewer nonprescribed processes to occur.

Studies such as those by Leavitt and Guetzkow deal with only a few of the contingencies that may exist when both division and matching are left to the discretion of the group. Research of this kind examines situations in which almost every member is competent to perform any subtask, and the prescribed pattern of specialization is arbitrarily dictated by the experimenter. In real life, division of labor may be prompted by the inability of specific individuals to perform certain activities adequately, or by the incapacity of any single person to do everything that is required. When, as in the case of Jack Sprat and his wife, specialization is necessitated by the idiosyncratic resources of individuals, matching and division of labor reflect a single decision; subtasks are tailored to "fit" the resources of specific members of the group. Under these circumstances, a group may be *able* to employ only one or a few of the many different processes that task demands permit it to employ. Chapter 5 examines some effects of group composition on process.

In network studies, each individual is virtually compelled to produce certain minimum behaviors. If a single members fails to contribute the unique information he has been given, the group cannot solve the problem. In this respect the task is conjunctive, as are many real-life tasks that permit or require a division of labor. However, outside the laboratory, it is sometimes possible to circumvent a participant who performs his phase of the job poorly, or to have several persons work collaboratively on critical parts of the task. Furthermore, in many situations it is unimportant whether every member of a group receives and accepts the correct solution to a problem; acceptance by the majority, or even by a minority, is sometimes sufficient.

In spite of the fact that network studies examine the impact of a special set of circumstances, they provide substantial insight concerning the productivity of groups. When both division into subtasks and the matching of individuals with subtasks are left to the discretion of the group, productivity depends not only upon the adequacy of members' resources, but also upon which of the permitted patterns of division and matching is employed. In cases of this kind, group process includes the actions by which the task is subdivided and those by which members are assigned to particular facets of the total endeavor. The greater the number of patterns from which the group may choose, the lower is the probability that the best possible pattern will be chosen (or the greater is the amount of effort that must be expended to identify the most effective one). Rules that impose a single, advantageous division of labor upon a group may therefore result in higher productivity than do rules that permit a high degree of choice.

Specified Matching with Specified Subtasks

Task demands sometimes specify how the total task must be divided and who must perform each subtask. Situations of this kind are prevalent in industrial settings, but are also found in more informally organized environments. Thus anthropologists have reported that even the seemingly spontaneous behaviors of close acquaintances may be determined by conventions that dictate who must do what.

When both division and matching are specified, productivity will be strongly affected by the character of the particular role system that is imposed upon the group. Are people matched with the subtasks they can perform most comfortably and well? Does the specified pattern of subtasks represent a functionally appropriate division of labor? These are questions which personnel specialists and efficiency experts ask concerning the operation of formal organizations. They are important questions whenever individuals are required to work on designated subtasks.

Specified matching. The quality of a group's performance may be low because the wrong persons are required to do the right things. Division into subtasks may be completely adequate, but if Jack Sprat and his wife are required to do what they dislike doing, or are totally unable to do, productivity will undoubtedly be low.

Smelser (1961) conducted a study in which pairs of male college students operated toy trains on a circular track. A freight and a passenger train were oriented in opposite direction making it imperative that one of them be moved to a siding in order that the other might pass. The announced criterion of group productivity was the number of mutually completed trips during 3-min trials. Thus, if one train circled the track eight times and the other only four, the group's score equaled four rather than eight. There were six trials.

The movement of the trains could be controlled by electrical switches that were located in front of each of the two subjects. Although it was physically possible for either member of a dyad to control both trains, Smelser assigned specific roles to the members of his experimental groups. One person was told to manage the passenger train and to give orders to the other individual whose duty it was to operate the freight train in accordance with instructions he received from his more powerful partner. In half of the experimental groups, the member who was assigned the dominant role was the one who had scored higher on a paper-and-pencil measure of dominance administered during an earlier session. In the other half of the groups, the person who had received a score indicating less dominance was matched with the dominant role.

Control groups operated the trains without having been assigned roles. For subjects in the control condition, the task involved self-matching with unspecified subtasks whereas for experimental subjects both division and matching were predetermined by the experimenter.

Dyads in which the dominant role was assigned to the more dominant member completed an average of 160.4 mutual trips during six trials, while dyads in which members were matched in reverse fashion completed only 116.4. Control groups obtained an average score of 141.2. Therefore, when individuals were advantageously matched with subtasks, groups performed better than when members were permitted to evolve their own division of labor. However, when individuals were inappropriately matched with specified subtasks, performance was notably worse than that of groups on which neither a division nor matching was imposed. Unfortunately, Smelser did not examine the impact of experimental conditions that permitted members to match themselves with *specified* subtasks.

The effect of appropriate matching is also suggested by studies in which particular kinds of persons are assigned to function as the "central" person in a wheel network. As noted earlier, the wheel does not dictate that the central man must operate as a "keyman," but the group cannot function very effectively unless he does. Moreover, the central man's position strongly encourages him to assume that role. Consequently, it seems reasonable to anticipate that wheel networks will function most effectively when the individual assigned to the central position is "naturally" inclined to accept responsibility for making decisions and is willing to exercise authority. Findings consistent with this expectation have been reported by Shaw (1959) who examined the effectiveness of four-man wheel networks when the central man was one who had scored high versus low on a measure of willingness to exercise authority.

It might also be predicted that the productivity of centralized networks will be low if the person who is most advantageously located to perform the "keyman" role is disliked by his associates. Under these circumstances, the individual who is "selected" by the network to function as the dominant member of the group may be reluctant to make decisions for others, and his colleagues may refuse to accept his decisions even if he is willing to make them. Mohanna and Argyle (1960) found that wheel networks with unpopular central members were, in fact, less productive than those in which a popular person was assigned to the central position.

Laboratory research has not often dealt with the case in which people are deliberately matched with subtasks they are *least able* to perform, perhaps because such arrangements seem not to occur very frequently in real life. In general, social psychologists have shown little enthusiasm for research that investigates the impact of externally imposed matching systems. Self-matching has received moderate attention, but studies in which subjects are assigned specialized roles have been rare and have usually involved random assignment procedures.

Division into subtasks. Divisible tasks can usually be divided in several different ways, some of which are likely to permit greater productivity than others. Consequently, the success with which a group performs a task may be strongly influenced by the particular division of labor it is compelled to employ.

Lanzetta and Roby (1956) compared the productivity of groups on which "horizontal" versus "vertical" divisions had been imposed. In the former case, each individual was required to perform all aspects of the task whereas in the latter each performed only a specialized portion of the work assignment. Three-person teams of Air Force cadets were instructed to perform a task that simulated work they might later be required to do as military officers. Three target-areas were to be defended against attack—a goal that could be achieved by monitoring incoming messages about the movement of hypothetical enemy aircraft, by computing the future locations of attacking forces, and by dispatching "friendly" planes to intercept enemy craft. In half of the groups, each person was made responsible for one target area, while in the other half each member performed one of the three critical subtasks. In order to manipulate task difficulty, some groups were required to cope with a total of 15 planes, whereas others worked with only 10. Horizontal division proved to be slightly more effective than vertical when the task was easy (10 planes), but when the burden placed on groups was heavy (15 planes), vertical division was somewhat superior. The investigators suggest that certain aspects of the total task (e.g., computing future locations) were probably more difficult than others and that when a single individual was required to perform all three aspects (horizontal division), high task load induced him to neglect the easier ones. According to this interpretation, specialized assignments were more likely to result in all aspects of the task being performed adequately.

A similar study was conducted by Thomas (1957). Groups of five women were seated around a table and asked to construct miniature cardboard houses. The job entailed tracing the pattern of a house, cutting the design out of cardboard, scoring selected parts with a surgeon's knife, gluing the house together, and painting it. Groups were urged to construct as many houses as possible during a limited time. In half of the groups, each member was required to perform all five functions, whereas in the remaining groups each person was assigned two of the five subtasks, the pattern of assignments being such that each member's progress was contingent on the rate at which she received materials from other members. The latter arrangement led to a significantly higher level of productivity (more houses completed) than did the former. Thus, like Lanzetta and Roby, Thomas found vertical division to be more productive than horizontal when groups functioned under heavy work loads. According to Thomas, the superiority of vertical division may reflect the fact that specialization of function makes each person responsible for the efficiency of others; so in this study each woman undoubtedly realized that she would impede the performance of her associates if she did not complete her subtasks as rapidly as they. Consequently, vertical division may have stimulated very intense motivation.

However, it is easy to imagine conditions under which vertical division will not be more productive than horizontal. If one or more members of a group lack the resources to perform their assigned subtasks, the entire group may be immobilized and produce nothing. To the extent that each person's progress is contingent upon the performance of everyone else, vertical division makes the task conjunctive. Even though individuals may be highly motivated to avoid becoming a "dead weight" or "bottleneck," their personal resources may be so inadequate that they cannot perform effectively. Moreover, there is no assurance that a conjunctive task will always prompt high motivation; an individual may wish to sabotage the groups effort rather than to promote it, or he may be so unconcerned about the success of others or the goal they seek that he is not inclined to work hard. When individuals are required to perform specialized but interlocking functions the "chain is no stronger than its weakest link," and a single incompetent or uncooperative person may prevent any progress whatever. Such dire consequences were not observed in the Thomas (1957) study because all of the subtasks were very easy to perform, the task was described as a measure of "general work intelligence," and participants undoubtedly wished to demonstrate their own individual competence. In real-life situations, these favorable circumstances may not prevail.

Dashiell (1935) reports a study by Lorenz in which the performance of employees in a shoe factory was examined. Six-member groups made gymnasium shoes, each of the workers performing one of the six operations by which the product was created, and each receiving one-sixth of the pay for doing the job. It was known that individual employees who completed all six operations produced an average of 43 pairs of shoes per day whereas specialization of function raised efficiency to an average of 60 pairs. When Lorenz had individuals work alone on a different phase of the task each day until all phases had been performed, they produced an average of 56 pairs per day. Thus horizontal division was almost as effective as vertical if individuals functioned according to a plan involving *temporal* specialization. The slight superiority of vertical division over the temporally but horizontally organized work arrangement may reflect the kinds of motivational considerations mentioned above, or it may be a consequence of favorable matching that can occur when different members of a group are most competent to perform different phases of the task. The very great advantage of temporal "division" over ordinary horizontal division is probably due to the fact that the former minimizes losses in time and energy that are almost inevitable when an individual must repeatedly shift from one subtask to another.

Tasks that are divided vertically may generally be broken into any of several different patterns of specialization. If some patterns are more effective than others, a group's productivity will be determined in part by the particular pattern it is required to employ. Roby and Lanzetta (1956) compared two different vertical patterns and contrasted each with horizontal division. Three-man groups were responsible for manipulating six four-position electrical switches in response to information that was received on visual displays. Each member manned two of the switches and, when division was horizontal, received all the information he needed from his own display. In the case of vertically organized groups, some of the necessary information was not revealed by the individual's own display but could be obtained by telephonic communication with other members. Thus each person's role included gathering and transmitting information to associates as well as receiving and using the information that was pertinent to the operation of the two switches he personally controlled. A comparatively simple vertical division made each member dependent on one other member for information, whereas a more complex pattern made each person dependent upon both of his colleagues. Both vertical divisions made the task conjunctive because no member could perform his own subtask effectively unless he received accurate information from others. As might be expected, horizontal division proved to be more productive than the more complex vertical division which, in turn, was less effective than the simpler pattern. The study illustrates the conjunctive character of many tasks that are organized vertically, and suggests circumstances under which vertical division is unlikely to be superior to horizontal. If people are matched with specialized subtasks calling for resources (e.g., information) they do not possess, they will be unable to function very well. Vertical division may be very effective when it involves a pattern of specialization that "fits" the specialized resources of the group members, and quite ineffective when it does not. Whether a particular way of dividing a task into subtasks will permit high productivity depends not only on the pattern of subtasks that is created, but also on the manner in which resources are distributed among the individuals who are required to perform the subtasks.

As has been noted previously, vertical division usually means that persons who work on different subtasks are conjunctively interdependent. This is the case whenever all subtasks must be completed in order to generate a single unit of the group product. Conjunctivity also exists if some members cannot perform their specialized functions until others have performed theirs, or if the several subtasks must be performed simultaneously, each being synchronized with the other. Temporal aspects of group performance are discussed in the paragraphs that follow.

Temporal programming. When tasks are divided into subtasks, productivity generally depends not only upon who does what, but upon who does what *when.* Sometimes subtasks must be performed sequentially, as for example when completion of one subtask presupposes completion of another (e.g., a house cannot be painted until it has been constructed; a book cannot be printed until it has been written), or when rules require that an individual or group solve one problem before proceeding to the next. In other cases, several subtasks must be performed simultaneously; in the game of baseball the pitcher and catcher must act jointly, and when time pressures require rapid completion of several subtasks, it is generally essential that many specialized functions be performed at the same time. Divisible tasks are not unique in this respect, for many unitary tasks also require that activities be performed sequentially or simultaneously. Mathematical problems typically require that several operations be completed in a specified order, and many puzzles can best be solved by a series of simultaneous or alternating mental and motor behaviors. Because all aspects of a unitary task are performed by a single individual, the critical coordination is *intra*personal rather than *inter*personal.

There are exceptions to this generalization. A team of mountain climbers has the potential ability to move as fast as its slowest member can climb, but this level of productivity will be achieved only if the behaviors of members are temporally coordinated. The strength of the force a group can exert on a rope depends in part upon the success with which members synchronize their efforts. When unitary tasks are additive or conjunctive, combinatorial rules sometimes make productivity contingent on the simultaneity with which individual members act. There are also instances in which a group cannot be successful unless members perform their unitary task at *different* times. Mintz (1951) instructed groups of 15 to 21 persons to remove aluminum cones from a glass jug which would soon be filled with water from an aperture in its side. There were as many cones as people, and each cone could be removed by pulling on a string that extended upward through the mouth of the jug. Each member of a group was told to grasp one of the strings and be responsible for extracting the attached cone when the experimenter gave the signal to begin. In some groups, the announced goal was to remove all cones before any were moistened by the incoming water, and in other groups each subject was instructed to get his own cone out while it was still dry. The task was unitary in that all members were required to perform the same behaviors. However, because the mouth of the jug was large enough to accommodate only one cone at a time, it was imperative that no two persons respond simultaneously. Any single member could impede the progress of others merely by contesting their right to act first; if two cones entered the mouth of the jug at the same time, a serious and time-consuming "traffic jam" was created.

Because the water did not enter the jug very rapidly, ample time was available to remove all cones. Groups that had not evolved a plan of action specifying when each person should act typically succeeded in withdrawing only a few of them. Given the conjunctive character of the task, inappropriate behavior by one or more members was sufficient to guarantee that the group would fail. Groups in which all members were instructed to get *their own* cones out were less proficient than those in which success could be achieved only by removing all cones. Apparently the individualistic orientation that prevailed in the former groups inhibited temporal coordination. Later in this book, we shall have occasion to view the Mintz study from other perspectives.

When tasks are unitary, all participants perform the same act (or none at all). Consequently, when the task is to remove cones from a jug, it does not really matter who acts first; the important consideration is that no two persons act simultaneously. When several persons are instructed to cooperate in pulling as hard as possible on a rope, the critical concern is that *everyone* pulls at exactly the same time. Thus unitary tasks may require temporal coordination, but success depends on *what* is done *when,* rather than upon *who* acts *when.* If everyone is matched with the same "subtask," whether John Doe or Jim Smith acts first is unimportant, and it does not matter very much which particular member of a group fails to pull on a rope at the appropriate time. "Whoness" is essentially irrelevant. When tasks are divided into specialized subtasks, success is likely to depend not only upon which subtask is performed when but also upon who performs which subtasks. Temporal programming and matching are joint requirements either of which can interfere with the other.

If several different subtasks must be performed simultaneously, a single individual cannot ordinarily be matched with more than one of them. However, if subtasks are sequentially ordered, a single person may sometimes be successively matched with all of them, or with as many as his resources permit him to perform more effectively than anyone else in the group. Consequently, successively ordered subtasks permit greater flexibility of matching than do those that must be performed simultaneously. The latter arrangement may require that certain phases of the endeavor be handled by persons who are not most competent to perform them. When this is the case, the best possible matching will be less productive than that which would be permitted by successive ordering. Therefore an optimally effective matching of persons with subtasks may prevent simultaneous programming, and simultaneous programming may prohibit use of the best conceivable matching system. Whenever success depends upon who does what when, the way any two of these factors are linked tends to determine how the third must be handled. If person A is to act before person B, then A cannot be matched with a subtask that presupposes the prior performance of B's subtask (who-when must be consistent with what-when). If person A is to perform subtask 1, and person B is to perform subtask 2, sequential programming will dictate the order in which the two individuals must act (who-when must be consistent with what-when).

It should be noted that although successive programming permits a single member of a group to be matched with any number of subtasks, this freedom may be negated by other restrictions. Formal or informal rules may require that everyone do his fair share of the work, or specify that nobody is permitted to perform more than one subtask. Furthermore, the time and energy that are expended when a single person shifts from one subtask to another may be so great that it outweighs the advantage of always matching persons with subtasks on which they excel.

Role assignment and productivity. When both division and matching are specified, group productivity depends upon the appropriateness of the role system that is imposed upon the members of the group, and upon the adequacy with which members perform their assigned roles. If, as is generally the case, the role system specifies when each function must be performed as well as who must perform it, actual productivity will equal potential productivity provided each participant performs his role to the best of his ability. (Potential productivity equals the best performance a group can achieve given its fund of resources and the rules under which it must operate.) However, potential productivity will depend upon the resources of the members, the degree to which members are matched with subtasks they can perform better than anyone else in the group, and the extent to which the specified division and temporal programming meet the demands imposed by other aspects of the task. Potential productivity will be low if the wrong person is required to do the right thing, or if the right thing is programmed for the wrong time. Even if the imposed role system specifies an optimally advantageous arrangement of whoness, whatness, and whenness, a group may function poorly because members are not motivated to employ their resources in the prescribed manner. The adverse effect that complete specification sometimes has on the motivation of workers is widely recognized by industrial psychologists, and will receive attention in later chapters of this book. Here it is sufficient to note that a role system may establish a high level of *potential* productivity, but actual productivity may be low because members of the groups are not inclined to enact the roles that are imposed upon them.

Organizational Decisions

Process includes all those intrapersonal and interpersonal actions by which people transform their resources into a product, and all those nonproductive actions that are prompted by frustration, competing motivations, or inadequate understanding. Included among these actions are the intellective and communicative behaviors by which members of a group decide who shall do what when. In its full scope, process involves those activities by which a group organizes (or reorganizes) itself for action, as well as the behaviors that occur once organization has been achieved.

The organizational aspects of process entail asking and answering the following questions.

How are we permitted to divide the task into subtasks? If more than one pattern of subtasks is permitted, which shall we employ?

Who is permitted to perform which subtask? Which pattern of matching shall we choose?

Must the subtasks be performed in a specific sequence? If more than one sequence is permitted, which shall we employ?

Although groups may not ask or answer these questions in a deliberate or self-conscious manner, they usually cannot avoid the issues that are involved in them. If several persons are to work collectively on a task, it must somehow be divided into parts (even though all parts may be exactly alike). Individuals must be assigned (or assign themselves) to subtasks which they perform in some temporal order. To be sure, organizational decisions may be made in a trial-and-error fashion, and the members of a group may not even realize they are being made, but in one way or another organizational problems must be resolved.

When division and/or matching are specified by the environment or by outside agencies, a group is spared some of the responsibility for deciding how its activities will be organized. Part of its process has already been performed and it has no option but to accept the decisions that have been made for it. Consequently, members can proceed directly to the production of behaviors that are specified by the predetermined organizational arrangement. Under these circumstances, we might say that group process is truncated or abbreviated because it does not include critical aspects of the complete sequence. However, even when groups do not make their own organizational decisions (i.e., even when their only decision is to accept that which is unavoidable), it is important to remember that decisions are made and that they influence the outcome of collective action.

A group on which neither division nor matching is imposed must, of course, devise its own organizational system. If the same product is needed on many occasions, the group may be required to solve its organizational problems only once. Having discovered a tolerably effective way of performing the task, the group may "decide" to employ the same strategy each time it encounters the situation, and thus may spare itself the effort and turmoil that would be entailed in starting afresh each time. This energy-saving ploy is, of course, responsible for the emergence of enduring role systems and for a good deal of the inflexibility that so often characterizes group activity. It also accounts for some of the maladaptive behaviors that occur when groups confront tasks that are slightly different from those they have already performed. Instead of devising a new and wholly appropriate organization, groups are likely to employ the less appropriate one they have used successfully in other settings.

It is pertinent to note that studies comparing the productivity of individuals and groups have sometimes examined the outcomes generated by groups that have not yet solved their organizational problems. When *ad hoc* groups of strangers are instructed to perform a novel task, the members must ordinarily discover how they can work together before their resources can be effectively employed to create the required product. Unless unlimited time is allowed, group performance is likely to be rather poor and may be inferior to that of individuals who work alone. This aspect of group research has been highlighted by Anderson (1961) who repeated a study conducted by Watson (1928). The latter investigator had found that small groups did not perform as well on an anagrams task as did nominal groups which were credited with every success their members had achieved while working individually. Theorizing that Watson's *ad hoc* groups had been allowed insufficient time to organize themselves, Anderson permitted his groups (and individuals) 50 percent more working time than Watson had allowed. Anderson's groups not only functioned much better than their most competent members might have been expected to do working alone, but earned scores that were about as high as those obtained by nominal groups. It seems evident that the findings of studies that have failed to reveal group superiority over individuals should be accepted with caution, and that they may be quite atypical of results that would be obtained from a comparison of individuals with *organized* groups. Inappropriately organized groups, and those which are not yet organized, may indeed function less well than individuals, but appropriately organized groups should be expected to perform many tasks more effectively than individuals who work alone.

As we have noted throughout this chapter, some imposed patterns of division and/or matching are likely to promote a higher level of productivity than others. The same statement should be made about organizational arrangements that are devised by the group itself. Organizational decisions restrict subsequent phases of group process and thus tend to determine the quality of the product that will be obtained.

Summary

When tasks are divisible, they can profitably be broken into specialized subtasks each of which may be performed by a different person. Although it is generally possible to divide such tasks in any of several different ways, social and environmental constraints sometimes dictate that only one of the possible patterns is acceptable. Regardless of whether a particular division is *specified* or the group is permitted to select its own pattern, individuals must somehow be *matched* with subtasks. Matching may also be specified or left to the discretion of the group. Thus, in theory, a division of labor may be established in any of four different ways: specified matching with specified subtasks; unspecified matching with specified subtasks, unspecified matching with unspecified subtasks; or specified matching with unspecified subtasks. However, the last of these four arrangements is purely hypothetical; matching involves the assignment of particular individuals to particular subtasks, and it cannot be specified unless the subtasks themselves are also specified.

When two or more persons are matched (or match themselves) with the same subtask, their performance may be disjunctive, conjunctive, additive, or discretionary. In theory, the process by which several subtask outcomes are combined to form a single group product may also involve any of these four types of activities. However, in the majority of cases this phase of the group's task is likely to be disjunctive; if any member can combine the available subtask outcomes into a good product, the group has the ability to do so. It should be noted that some tasks do not require the group to perform the integrative function. Thus, in several of the studies described in this chapter group productivity was evaluated by counting the number of subtasks performed satisfactorily, and it is possible to imagine situations in which a group's success is assured if it correctly performs a single subtask. In real life, however, most divisible tasks probably require that a set of outcomes be assembled in a way that generates a complex product.

When division and matching are specified, a group's potential productivity is determined by the appropriateness of the imposed role structure and by the resources of the members who are required to perform specific roles. Certain ways of dividing a task into parts are likely to permit a higher level of productivity than others, and potential productivity will be higher when people are matched with the subtasks they are most suited to perform than when they are not. A group's actual productivity will fall below its potential productivity if members do not function as effectively within their assigned roles as their resources permit them to function.

When division or matching is unspecified, a group is required to make organizational decisions concerning who shall do what when. Potential productivity equals the level of performance that can be achieved if the best possible organizational decisions are made and if everyone performs his role to the best of his ability. Actual productivity will fall below this level if the group employs a system of division and matching that is not most advantageous, or if members do not perform as well as they are able. In cases of this kind, group process includes both the behaviors by which organizational decisions are made and the actions by which those decisions are implemented.

Chapter 4

Effects of Group Size

Will a large group perform a task more effectively than a small group? Like the question concerning the comparative outputs of individuals and groups, this one has no simple answer. Research indicates that large groups are often more successful than small groups, but there is also evidence that they sometimes do not perform as well as their smaller counterparts.

Whether an increase in group size will be responsible for an improvement in productivity depends upon the same factors that determine whether a group will be more successful than a single individual. If an increase in group size augments the group's potential productivity without creating serious "process losses," it will be responsible for improved performance. However, if the increment of potential productivity occasioned by the addition of new members is very small, and the increment of process loss is big, enlargement of the group will bring a decrease in actual productivity. Depending upon the nature of the task, the initial size of the group, and the resources of the persons involved, group enlargement may have either of these consequences.

Size and Potential Productivity

Potential productivity is the maximum level of productivity that can occur when an individual or group employs its resources to meet the task demands of a work situation. It is the level of productivity that will be attained if the individual or group uses its resources in the most advantageous way permitted by the rules under which it must operate. Because large groups often command a bigger fund of relevant resources than small groups, it may be anticipated that the former will often have a higher level of potential productivity than the latter.

Disjunctive Tasks

When task demands permit any single member of a group to supply the group's product, the potential productivity of the group depends upon the resources of its most competent member. If one or more members can perform the task adequately, the group has the potential to perform it adequately. The size of the group is an important consideration because it affects the likelihood that at least one member will be able to do the work satisfactorily.

As noted in Chapter 2, Taylor (1954) and Lorge and Solomon (1955) reported a formula by which it is possible to calculate the percentage of randomly assembled groups of size n that will include at least one person who is competent to perform a given task. If P equals the proportion of individuals in the population who can perform the task, and Q equals the proportion who cannot, $100(1 - Q^n)$ percent of all groups should contain at least one member with the needed ability. Inspection of this formula reveals that the percentage of potentially successful groups will ordinarily increase as group size increases. The rate at which it will increase depends upon the proportion of competent persons in the population (task difficulty) and upon whether the increase in group size involves adding members to a small group or to one that is already rather large. If the task is so easy that everyone in the population can perform it, Q will equal zero and the potential productivity of a single individual will be as high as that of any group regardless of its size. If the task is so difficult, however, that it can be handled by only a small fraction of the available individuals, the average group will have a higher potential productivity level than the average individual, and large groups will have a higher potential for success than small ones. The more difficult the task (i.e., the larger the Q,) the more rapidly will the group's potential productivity increase as its size is enlarged.

The effect of increasing the size of groups also depends upon whether they are already fairly large. If a group contains only two members, adding a third increases the probability of its containing a competent individual by a margin that equals $(Q^2 - Q^3)$. This increment will be larger than that contributed by adding a fourth member, $(Q^3 - Q^4)$. Indeed, each additional person will add a

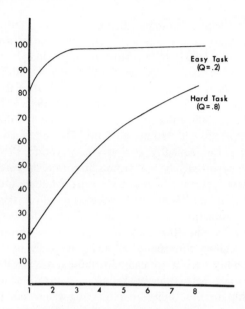

Fig. 4.1. Relationship between group size (abscissa) and the percentage of groups containing at least one person who can perform a disjunctive task (ordinate).

smaller increment to the group's potential than the last previous member. Therefore, the relationship between group size and potential productivity is curvilinear. A curve depicting successive increases in potential productivity as group size is enlarged will rise more rapidly as the first few members are added than when the tenth or twentieth is added. Eventually, a size will be reached beyond which additional members will contribute almost nothing to potential productivity. This point will be reached sooner if the task is easy rather than difficult. Fig. 4.1 shows these effects for an easy ($Q = .2$) and a difficult ($Q = .8$) task.

The previous discussion has dealt with cases in which success is defined dichotomously by an unambiguous pass-fail criterion. In many instances, productivity is evaluated in a continuous fashion; the individual or group receives a score that may vary from extremely low to extremely high, and success is defined as a positive function of the score that is obtained. In situations of this kind, a group's potential productivity equals the score its most competent member is able to earn, and the size of the group tends to determine how high that particular score will be. When success is treated as a continuous, rather than a dichotomous variable, the procedures described by Steiner and Rajaratnam (1961) may be used to infer relationships between group size and potential productivity.

As noted in Chapter 2, samples that are randomly drawn from a population in which an ability is normally distributed will, on the average, divide that population into $n + 1$ equal parts. Thus if single individuals are randomly selected, the average of their ability levels will fall at the 50th percentile of the population (i.e., they will be more competent than half of the population and less competent than the other half). If two-person samples are drawn, the more competent members of the pairs will, on the average, fall at the 67th percentile, and the less competent will fall at the 33rd. The logic may be extended to samples of any size. Consequently, it is very easy to infer the percentile scores that the most competent members of groups of various sizes are likely to obtain.

Unfortunately, percentile scores have a troublesome quality. The difference between the ability levels of persons who fall at the 20th and 30th percentiles is not ordinarily the same as the difference between the abilities of people who score at the 30th and 40th percentiles. Equal intervals on a percentile scale seldom correspond to equal intervals on the ability scale. However, if the ability itself is normally distributed, it is possible to remedy this fault by transforming percentile scores into "standard" scores that have the desired relationship to the ability that is being examined. (The reader may consult a textbook on psychological statistics for a discussion of standard scores and their relationship to percentile scores.) Table 4.1 reports the average percentile scores that most and least competent members of various sized groups should be expected to earn. Standard score equivalents of these percentiles are also reported. It should be noted that the standard score corresponding to the 50th percentile (the median) equals zero, and that the standard scores for percentiles below the 50th carry negative signs.

Table 4.1 indicates that as groups increase in size, the ability of their most competent members also tends to increase, and that this relationship is curvilinear. The increment contributed by adding the third person is smaller than that contributed by adding the second, etc. Thus when the task is disjunctive and success is treated as a continuous variable, a curve depicting the relationship between group size and potential productivity will resemble those shown in Fig. 4.1. However, the amount of increase in actual *ability* (as contrasted to the increase in standard score) occasioned by adding a new member to the group will depend upon the heterogeneity of the population from which the members are drawn. If the task is one for which only small differences in ability exist, a given increment in standard score will reflect only a small increase in actual competence, and a curve representing *changes in ability* will not be very steep. However, if individuals differ widely in their competence to perform the task, a curve representing changes in ability will rise very rapidly. The difficulty of the task will affect the slope of the "ability" curve only if it affects the heterogeneity of the population or causes the distribution of individual abilities to deviate from normality.

TABLE 4.1

Average Percentile and Standard Scores of Most and Least Competent Members of Groups[a]

Group size	Most competent member		Least competent member	
	Percentile score	Standard score	Percentile score	Standard score
1	50	0	50	0
2	67	.43	33	−.43
3	75	.68	25	−.68
4	80	.84	20	−.84
5	83	.97	17	−.97
6	86	1.08	14	−1.08
7	88	1.17	12	−1.17
8	89	1.22	11	−1.22

[a]The values in this table are based on the assumption that groups are randomly assembled from a population in which competence is normally distributed.

In deriving the above conclusions about relationships between group size and potential productivity, we have assumed that groups are randomly assembled from a population. In many real-life situations an attempt is made to select only individuals who are believed to possess the ability to perform the task at hand (e.g., to select only persons who have received certain specialized training, are physically strong, or have scored high on a test that is thought to be related to task performance). When this is the case, members of groups are drawn from a preselected population that is likely to be rather homogeneous and to represent a high average level of ability. However unless extremely accurate techniques are available for identifying competent people, and unless the agent that makes the final choices has dictatorial control over those he would like to select, the members of groups may represent approximately random subsets of the preselected population. When this is true, the logic of the preceding discussion will still be applicable. Unless preselection procedures identify populations that are not normal, the most competent members of the resulting groups will have ability levels that are distributed as shown in Table 4.1. The curve describing the relationship between group size and potential productivity will, however, be somewhat flattened due to the homogeneity of the population from which members are drawn. If group success is measured dichotomously, the curve will be comparatively flat due to the high P value in the preselected population. However, regardless of whether success is treated as a continuous or dichotomous variable, the relationship between size and potential productivity should be curvilinear. As group size increases, potential productivity should increase at a decelerating rate.

Conjunctive Tasks

When a task is conjunctive, a group's potential productivity is determined by the resources of its least competent member. The effect of group size on potential productivity can be inferred using the models described previously.

When success is measured dichotomously, a group has the potential to succeed on a conjunctive task if its least competent member has the ability to perform it adequately. If groups of size n are randomly assembled from a population in which P is the proportion of the people who have the ability to perform the task, the least competent members of $100P^n$ percent of these groups should be able to perform the task, and the least competent members of $100(1 - P^n)$ percent of these groups should be unable to perform it. The larger the n, the lower will be the percentage of potentially successful groups; as the size of groups increases, potential productivity will decrease. This relationship is shown in Fig. 4.2 for an easy task ($P = .8$, $Q = .2$) and for a hard task ($P = .2$, $Q = .8$). When the task is difficult, potential productivity is low even for two-person groups, and it decreases at a decelerating rate as additional members are added. In the case of an easy task the potential productivity of very small groups is relatively high, but decreases rapidly as size is increased. For both difficult and easy tasks, the decrement in potential productivity caused by the addition of a new member is always smaller than that caused by the addition of the last previous member. Thus potential productivity is a negative, curvilinear function of group size. Of course, if the task is so difficult that nobody in the population can perform it, or so easy that everyone can, potential productivity will be unrelated to group size. These are extreme conditions, however, that are unlikely to prevail when groups are required to perform tasks.

If group success on a conjunctive task is treated as a continuous variable, the potential productivity of a group will depend upon the ability of its least competent member. The right-hand column of Table 4.1 reports standard scores representing the comparative ability levels of least competent members of various sized groups. It can be seen that potential productivity decreases as group size increases, and that the relationship is curvilinear. As noted earlier, whether a difference between two specific standard scores represents a large or small difference in potential productivity depends upon the heterogeneity of the population from which the group is assembled. If the task is one with respect to which abilities vary widely, potential productivity will decrease rapidly as group size increases. However, if the task is one that everyone can perform almost equally well, a difference between two standard scores will represent only a small difference in competence, and enlarging the size of the group will have little effect on potential productivity.

Task demands sometimes require that some, but not all, of the members of a group perform the same unitary task, and success is contingent upon the

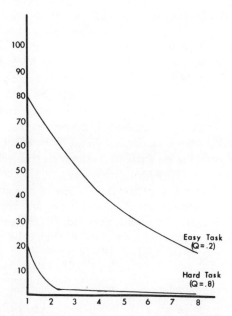

Fig. 4.2. Relationships between group size (abscissa) and the percentage of groups in which the least competent member can perform a conjunctive task (ordinate).

ability of the least competent of the individuals in that subset. For example, if all but ten of the soldiers to be moved to a new military site can be accommodated in available vehicles, the speed with which the convoy can move is established by the marching ability of the tenth most competent man. If only two oars are available for rowing a boat, the efficiency with which the craft can be propelled depends upon the strength and skill of the crew's second most able oarsman. Because the number of persons who can or must participate at the same time in task-oriented activities is often limited by man-made rules or by the availability of tools or work space, it is reasonable to expect that potential productivity will frequently be determined by the abilities of persons who are neither the most or least competent members of their groups. When the requirements imposed by the situation make the group's potential productivity depend upon the resources of the ith most competent member, the task may be regarded as quasi-conjunctive. The competence of the ith most competent members of groups can be inferred using techniques analogous to those described above.

For example, consider a situation in which at least two members of a group must be able to perform a task in order for the group to succeed (e.g., at least two members must be able to speak German in order for the group to produce a conversation in that language). In cases of this kind, the potential productivity of the group depends upon the ability of its second most competent member. If the proportion of persons in the population who have the necessary ability is known, the percentage of randomly assembled groups of size n that will contain at least two competent persons can be calculated from the appropriate terms of the binomial expansion. When this is done for groups of varying sizes it is found that the percentage increases as a negatively accelerated function of group size. Thus, the larger the group, the greater is the likelihood that it will contain at least two (or some other specified number) competent persons. Although potential productivity is positively related to group size in such quasi-conjunctive situations, the curvilinear shape of the function indicates that increments of potential productivity become progressively smaller as more and more "extra" members are added.

If success on a quasi-conjunctive task is treated as a continuous variable, the logic described by Steiner and Rajaratnam may be employed to infer the ability of groups' ith most competent members. On the average, the ith most competent members of groups will have a level of ability that corresponds to the

$$\frac{100(n + 1 - i)}{n + 1} \text{ th}$$

percentile score for the population. In order to compare the ability levels of the ith ranked members of groups of different sizes, the appropriate population percentiles can be computed, and the standard score equivalents of these population percentiles determined. Therefore, it can be shown that the second most competent members of randomly assembled four-person groups will, on the average, have a standard score of +.25. The second most competent members of groups with five, six, and seven members will, on the average, have standard scores of +.43, +.57, and +.67 respectively. It is apparent that potential productivity is again found to increase as a negatively accelerated function of group size.

In summary, when tasks are truly conjunctive (i.e., when success depends on the poorest member of the group), potential productivity decreases as the group is enlarged, the rate of the decrease being dependent upon how many members are already in the group and on task difficulty (if the criterion of success is dichotomous), or on the heterogeneity of ability levels in the population from which members are assembled (if the criterion of success is continuous). When tasks are quasi-conjunctive (i.e., when success depends on the ability of the ith most competent member), potential productivity will increase as a negatively accelerated function of group size.

Additive Tasks

When tasks are additive, one person's accomplishment is (or may be) added to that of another. The amount of snow shoveled by a group equals the sum of the amounts shoveled by the individual workers, and the total force exerted on a rope equals the sum of the forces exerted by the separate members—provided they all pull at the same time and in the same direction.

Given that a task is additive, we may expect potential productivity to increase as a linear function of group size. If groups are randomly assembled, the second member will on the average, be as competent as the first, and the third will be as competent as the second. Therefore, if the size of a group is doubled, its ability to perform the task is also doubled. However, there are severe limits on the validity of this generalization. Additive tasks generally permit additivity to occur only when the group's size and outcome fall within a restricted range. Unless an unlimited supply of snow is available to be moved, there will be a ceiling on the number of persons whose shoveling processes can be summed, and unless the rope on which members are to pull is endless, repeated enlargements of the group will eventually provide more members than can possibly be used on the pulling task. Because there always seems to be an upper limit or ceiling on the amount or quality of work to be done, tasks that are additive for groups of certain sizes will lose their additivity if group size is drastically increased. For some such tasks the "ceiling effect" will occur when groups are still fairly small, whereas for others it may be delayed until very many members have been accumulated. However, sooner or later, a curve depicting the relationship between size and potential productivity must level off. If the job assignment is to exert a force of at least 5 pounds on a rope, one person is enough and the potential productivity of a dyad is no greater than that of a solitary worker. If the task is to exert a maximum force on a rope that is 50 feet long, perhaps as many as 25 persons can maintain an additive relationship to one another. In every case however, there will be a maximum group size beyond which extra members can add little or nothing to potential productivity.

There may also be "threshold effects." If the job is to pull a one-ton boulder as far as possible in 10 min, a single individual can accomplish nothing at all. Two or three persons may be no more effective than one, for their collective efforts may be inadequate to overcome the inertia and friction that is involved. However, if the rope on which individuals must pull is long enough, 6 or 8 people may be able to move the boulder several yards, and 20 or 30 may be capable of pulling it half a mile. Of course, if the group is enlarged to 100 or so, the boulder can probably be pulled as fast as the slowest member can run; when this size is reached, additional members will be of value only to the degree that they can be substituted for others who are slow runners (i.e., the task ceases to be additive and becomes quasi-conjunctive).

Although the relationship between group size and potential productivity is positive and linear when a task is additive, threshold and ceiling effects usually permit additivity to prevail for only a limited range of group sizes and outcome values.

Discretionary Tasks

When tasks are discretionary, members of a group are free to combine their individual outcomes in any way they desire. Such freedom is unlikely to exist except when the goal is to reach the best possible conclusions concerning an issue for which a multitude of continuously distributed conclusions are available. When these unusual conditions exist, any group has the potential to obtain the most preferred conclusion, for there are always ways in which the judgments of individual members can be combined to produce it. Consequently, when tasks are discretionary, group size is unrelated to potential productivity.

Divisible Tasks

Divisible tasks may be conceived to involve two or more "stages." At one stage, subsets of group members work together on specialized subtasks, and at another stage the outcomes generated by the various subtask performances are combined to yield a group product. Sometimes, of course, several subtasks are performed sequentially rather than simultaneously, and when the job that is to be completed is extremely complex there may be several "layers" of subtasks. Thus if an automobile is to be constructed, the work by which each of thousands of parts is manufactured may constitute a separate subtask. At a higher "layer," assembling the parts that make up the carburetor, the transmission, or the fuel pump may also be distinct subtasks. Finally, the products created by the performance of each of many nested series of subtasks are combined in a specified fashion to yield the finished automobile. Although many divisible tasks are broken into such multistage problems, we will concern ourselves with only relatively simple cases in which the group product is obtained by combining the outcomes generated by a single layer or sequence of subtasks outcomes.

The bigger the group that is available to work on a divisible task, the larger is the number of subtasks into which the total can be broken and/or the greater is the number of persons who can be matched with each subtask. If all phases of a divisible task must be performed simultaneously, it is generally advantageous to break the total endeavor into as many subtasks as possible. The larger the group, the greater is the number of subtasks that can be identified and assigned to different individuals—provided the number of available individuals does not exceed the number of unitary functions involved in the total work assignment. Even when the number of persons is larger than the number of subtasks into which the job can profitably be broken, large groups are likely to enjoy an advantage over small ones. If subtasks are additive or disjunctive, assignment of several persons to the same function will tend to establish a higher level of potential productivity than will assignment of only one or a few. Furthermore, if a large number of persons are available to be assigned to a small number of subtasks, individuals may be more effectively matched with subtasks than would be the case if only a few persons were available. If subtasks can or must be performed sequentially, the same arguments are applicable. The larger the group, the greater its ability to perform disjunctive or additive subtasks should be.

On first thought, it might seem that large groups have less ability to perform conjunctive subtasks than do small groups. However, this is the case only when rules require that *every* member be assigned to such subtasks. If, as is usually the case, groups are free to match only one or a few members with each conjunctive subtask, large groups should enjoy an advantage. On the average, the larger the group from which the critical individual or subset of individuals is chosen, the more competent the selected person(s) *can* be. Consequently, in the majority of situations, large groups should have greater *potential* to perform conjunctive subtasks than should small groups.

It is reasonable to conclude that the ability of groups to perform disjunctive, additive, or conjunctive subtasks is a positive function of group size. However, curves depicting these relationships should be negatively accelerated; as more and more persons are added to the group, the increment contributed by each new member should tend to be smaller than that added by the last previous member. As noted earlier, group size should not affect potential to perform discretionary subtasks.

The previous discussion has dealt only with potential to perform subtasks; it has not been explicitly concerned with the ability of groups to combine their subtask outcomes into a total product. However, the processes involved in the final stage of a multistage task are not likely to be very different from those that have occurred at earlier stages. The final stage (i.e., combining subtask outcomes) may conceivably be disjunctive, conjunctive, additive, or discretionary. However, unless unusual rules have been imposed, it will generally be disjunctive or quasi-conjunctive—if any individual or subset of individuals can assemble the available subtask outcomes properly, the group has the ability to do so. The larger the group, the greater, on the average, will be the likelihood that it will contain one or more members with the necessary competence.

There is one complexity that may favor small groups over large ones during the final stage of task performance. If large groups have achieved higher efficiency at earlier stages by dividing the task into a greater number of specialized subtasks, the outcomes that must be combined will be more numerous. Consequently, the job of assembling outcomes into a finished product will sometimes be more difficult to perform when groups are large, and this consideration may cancel the advantage that large groups enjoy by virtue of their greater probability of containing members who are especially competent to combine subtask outcomes. However, because the quality of the subtask outcomes that are available to be combined can be higher when groups are large, potential productivity should tend to increase as a positive (but negatively accelerated) function of group size. Most divisible tasks cannot be performed very well unless *all* subtasks are handled effectively. Large groups are more likely than small ones to have the ability to handle all subtasks effectively.

Summary

If a task is unitary and disjunctive, potential productivity will tend to be a positive, decelerating function of group size. If a unitary task is conjunctive, and if all members are required to work on it, potential productivity will tend to decrease at a decelerating rate as group size is increased. If the task is additive, the relationship between size and potential productivity will be positive and linear. However, tasks that are additive for groups of intermediate sizes may not be additive for groups that are extremely small or extremely large. Threshold and ceiling effects may cause a curve depicting the relationship between size and potential productivity to assume the shape of the letter S. When tasks are discretionary, potential productivity should be unrelated to group size.

Divisible tasks may take many different forms, and the relationship between group size and potential productivity will depend upon which kind of divisible task is being examined. However, in the majority of instances, potential productivity may be expected to be a positive but decelerating function of group size.

Size and Actual Productivity

An increase in group size may augment potential productivity without creating a corresponding increase in actual productivity. Too many cooks may spoil the broth because they get in one another's way, or because each insists on adding his own favorite seasoning. This can happen even if, collectively, many cooks know more about brewing broth than do few cooks. Although superior resources often permit large groups to have a higher level of potential productivity than smaller groups, size also tends to complicate the procedures by which resources must be used if maximum efficiency is to be attained. The larger the group, the more people there are to be assigned differential weights, to be matched with specific subtasks, and to be assimilated within a delicately balanced pattern of ongoing activity. If organizational problems (who will do what when?) are less appropriately solved when groups are large, the addition of new members to a group may contribute less to its actual productivity than to its potential productivity, and may even be responsible for a decrease in actual productivity.

It is to be recalled that potential productivity represents the highest level of success a group can achieve; it equals the outcome that will be obtained if members use their available resources in the most advantageous manner permitted by the rules under which they are obliged to work. Failure to employ prescribed process will result in "process losses," and will cause actual productivity to fall below potential productivity.

Actual productivity = potential productivity
−losses due to faulty process

Consequently, the impact of group size on actual productivity is a function of its effects on potential productivity and on the efficacy of the procedures by which resources are transformed into a group outcome.

Size and the Complexity of Organizational Problems

If only one person is available to perform a task, organizational problems are likely to be comparatively simple. The individual must decide what he should do when, but questions concerning who should do what, or who should act when, have already been answered. Actual productivity may fall below potential productivity because the individual does not perform the necessary steps to the best of his ability, or because he performs them in the wrong order. But there can be no process losses due to inappropriate matching of individuals with subtasks, or poor interpersonal coordination. The recipe for maximum success is relatively easy to discover, for it does not require that a series of complex interpersonal relationships be established.

When two persons work collectively on a task, all of the decisions required of a single person remain pertinent, and others are added. If the task is unitary, a productive way of combining individual outcomes must be discovered and adopted, and in some cases patterns of temporal and spatial coordination must also be established. If the task is divisible, prescribed process entails allocating particular subtasks to members who are most qualified to perform them, and the selection of the most appropriate procedure for assembling subtask outcomes into a group product. When a monad becomes a dyad, the number of different ways a task can conceivably be attacked increases dramatically, and unless the rules taboo the use of most of these alternatives, the dyad may be required to make a very difficult discovery—only one or a very few of the permitted organizational patterns will yield the highest possible level of success, and the comparative merits of the available options are not ordinarily apparent. Even if the dyad succeeds in selecting the best possible organizational pattern, it may experience grave difficulties in establishing and maintaining the kinds of interpersonal coordination that are required. Two persons often possess more resources than one, but a dyad is more vulnerable to process losses than a monad.

When a third member is added to a group, organizational problems are likely to be complicated still further. If a task is unitary and does not require close temporal or spatial coordination of behaviors (e.g., the horse-trading problem), the additional complexity may be rather inconsequential. Three-person groups may be compelled to choose among three individual outcomes rather than two, and the possibility that two members will coalesce in opposition to the third introduces a new element of uncertainty. However, in cases of this kind, complexity probably increases no faster than group size, and it may increase less rapidly. However, if a task is unitary and requires a high level of interpersonal coordination, the picture is very different. Thus, if two men are asked to pull as hard as possible on a rope, maximum productivity can be achieved only if they pull at the same time and in the same direction. The situation is one in which coordination is needed along one "link"—person A should coordinate his behavior with that of person B, and *vice versa*. If three persons are confronted by the rope-pulling task, coordination is needed along three links: persons A and B, persons A and C, and persons B and C. If a fourth member is added to the group, coordination may be required along six links, and a fifth member will raise the number of potentially critical coordination links to 10. Table 4.2 reports the number of such connections for groups as large as size eight. It is apparent that the number of linkages along which coordination may be essential increases much more rapidly than group size.

The Ringelmann study (see Dashiell, 1935) which was described earlier, suggests that process losses may be very substantial when large groups perform tasks requiring interpersonal coordination. It is to be recalled that individuals and groups of two, three, or eight members pulled on a rope, the strength of their pull being measured in kilograms. The young male subjects appeared to be highly motivated and it is probably safe to assume that they pulled about as hard as they could. Consequently, it is reasonable to believe that *when individuals worked alone* actual productivity was very nearly equal to potential productivity. The average force exerted by individuals was 63 kilograms and we may regard that figure as a rough indication of the average potential productivity of individual subjects. The potential productivity of dyads should therefore have been 126 kilograms, and that of three- and eight-person groups should have been 189 and 504 respectively. But, as Table 4.3 indicates, the actual productivities of two-, three-, and eight-person groups were only 118, 160, and 248 kilograms. The discrepancies between the potential and actual productivities of these

TABLE 4.2

Number of Person-to-Person Linkages along Which Coordination May Be Needed

Group size	Number of linkages	Group size	Number of linkages
2	1	6	15
3	3	7	21
4	6	8	28
5	10		

TABLE 4.3

Potential and Actual Productivity of Ringelmann's Groups

Group size	Number of coordination links	Potential productivity	Actual productivity	Process losses	Relative process losses[a]
1	–	63	63	–	–
2	1	126	118	8	.87
3	3	189	160	29	3.17
8	28	504	248	256	28.00

[a]Entries in this column reflect the relative magnitudes of the process losses shown in the adjacent column, and the number of coordination links in the groups of various sizes. If 28 links are responsible for a loss of 256, 3.17 links should be responsible for a loss of 29, etc.

groups form an interesting progression; they are very nearly proportional to the number of links along which coordination was needed—one, three and 28. That the obtained discrepancies deviated slightly from this pattern (they can be expressed by the progression .87, 3.17, and 28.00) may have been due to sampling errors; Ringelmann observed only a few groups of each size. Process losses appear to have been a linear function of the number of links along which coordination was needed. As groups became larger, actual productivity lagged behind potential productivity by increasingly large margins.

As has already been noted, some unitary tasks do not require continuous interpersonal coordination, and others undoubtedly call for coordination along only a few of the links connecting pairs of workers. Thus when several persons cooperate in removing the snow from a pathway, coordination is unlikely to be a very serious problem; all that may be necessary is that each participant adjust his own behaviors to harmonize with those of persons who are working immediately adjacent to him. In instances of this kind, certain links are far more critical than others, and process losses need not increase very markedly as the group becomes larger. Indeed, even the rope-pulling task employed by Ringelmann might conceivably have been performed by eight-person groups without large losses due to improper coordination. A single member might have functioned as a "coordination specialist" who assembled his associates into a straight line and gave the signal to pull. Had this occurred, the number of links along which coordination was needed would have been $n - 1$ rather than $n(n-1)/2$. Later in this chapter we will consider other procedures by which large groups can sometimes avoid heavy process losses. At this point, it is sufficient to note that unless effective integrative techniques are discovered and employed, the addition of new members to a group may generate process losses that cancel any advantage that accrues in the form of increased potential productivity. Furthermore, if a group is already large enough to possess all the relevant resources needed to perform a task well, the addition of new members may cause process losses without adding anything whatever to potential productivity.

When tasks are divisible, groups can ordinarily achieve their full potential only if they are successful in establishing rather complex patterns of interpersonal coordination. Prescribed process generally involves a division of labor, different individuals performing different functions. The quality of the collective effort depends heavily upon who does what when, and upon how various subtask performances are synchronized and combined. Moreover, there is a strong element of conjunctivity because poor performance of any subtask may jeopardize group success. If the tuba player behaves erratically, the fate of the entire band is affected adversely; if the navigator is incompetent or unmotivated, the ship may run aground. The potential productivity of the group represents the level of success that will be achieved if people are ideally matched with subtasks, if each performs his duties to the best of his ability, and if the actions of all members are coordinated in the most advantageous manner. Needless to say, members of the group may not know how they should resolve their organizational problems (who should do what when), or may be unwilling to adopt the prescribed pattern of action even if they realize what should be done in order to maximize productivity. Because prescribed processes are likely to be especially complex when tasks are divisible, and because any deviation from prescribed processes is likely to be rather costly, it may be expected that actual productivity will often fall below potential productivity.

When many persons are available to work on a divisible task, both potential productivity and process losses may be high. Large groups ordinarily possess more resources than small ones, can break the total task into a larger number of subtasks (which is sometimes a distinct advantage), and enjoy greater flexibility in matching individuals with subtasks. Consequently, large groups often have higher potential productivity than do small ones. However, as groups become larger, organizational problems are likely to increase at a very rapid rate. This is the case because the number of subtasks into which the total task must be broken in order to achieve maximum success is likely to increase as more members are added. The number of ways in which available persons can be matched with a given number of subtasks necessarily increases very dramatically. If two persons are available to be matched with two subtasks, only two different patterns of specialization are possible. By chance alone, the group has a .5 probability of selecting the better of the two, and the simplicity of the situation is likely to permit members to make a better-than-chance decision. If three persons are available, there are six different ways of assigning at least one individual to each of two subtasks, and if the group contains four members there are 20 different ways of doing it. Small increases in group size produce very large increases in the number of organizational opportunities from which the group must choose, and they greatly reduce the probability that the best of all possible organizational decisions will be made by chance alone. Moreover, as the number of alternative arrangements increases the ease with which members of a group can discern the relative merits of available options undoubtedly decreases. Consequently, organizational decisions are probably less likely to surpass chance levels when groups are large. For both of these reasons, process losses are likely to increase much more rapidly than group size.

Summary. As a group increases in size, its organizational problems become more difficult to solve in the best possible manner. If the task is unitary, large groups must discover and establish a procedure for coordinating and combining the efforts of many persons, whereas for small groups the required integrative processes are generally less complex. If the task is divisible, the number of subtasks into which it must be divided in order that a large group can make full use of its available resources is likely to be great, but even if the number of subtasks is constant, an increase in group size will compound the complexity of the problem of matching individuals with subtasks. Consequently, as new members are added to a group, process losses are likely to increase, sometimes at an accelerating rate. In certain cases, the increment of process loss entailed by enlarging a group will exceed the increment of potential productivity that is contributed by new members. When this happens, large groups will, of course, manifest lower actual productivity than small groups.

Size and Motivation

The previous discussion has dealt entirely with process losses that occur due to less than maximally effective organization of collective efforts, and has concluded that losses of this kind are likely to increase rather rapidly as groups become large. However, process includes not only the events by which the outcomes generated by individual members are combined to form a group product, but also the actions by which individual members utilize their resources to create individual outcomes. Process losses may therefore occur because members are unwilling to make full use of their resources, and thus contribute poor individual outcomes to the group. When this happens, the actual productivity of the group will fall below its potential productivity even though appropriate answers have been found to organizational questions. Even if interpersonal coordination, matching, and temporal programming are ideal, the product created by combining individual contributions is likely to be inferior if the individual contributions themselves are of low quality. There is evidence suggesting that individuals are less willing to do their best when the group of which they are members is large than when it is small.

Shaw (1960) compared the willingness of members of large and small groups to work in behalf of their associates. College students were assembled into *ad hoc* groups of two to five members (small groups) or six to eight members (large groups) and told they were about to participate in an investigation of "cooperative studying." Subjects were informed that each person would be given an article describing a different stellar constellation, and that each would be asked to abstract certain information from the article he received. The group would subsequently study all the abstracts members had prepared and take a test over the material contained in the articles. Subjects were permitted to choose the article they would abstract from a list that named several esoteric constellations and indicated that both long and short articles were available on each topic. Although the short (one-page) articles were reported to include all the information needed to produce an adequate abstract, longer (up to 10 pages in length) ones were said to provide more complete coverage and to permit a more thorough report. The length of the article chosen by the individual was employed as a measure of his motivation to contribute to the group. Members of small groups chose significantly longer articles than did members of larger groups.

Shaw interpreted his results as indicating that people who are responsible for performing a large share of the total task are more strongly motivated to perform well than are individuals who are responsible for a small share. The greater the individual's weight in determining the quality of the group outcome, the greater is his incentive to function effectively. Because a single member generally exercises greater weight when the group is small, individuals tend to work harder in small groups than in large ones.

However, the member's belief that he exercises greater control over the collective outcome is not the only reason why he may work hard when the group is small. As Thelen (1949) has pointed out, nonparticipation and poor individual performance are especially visible in small groups. When only a few persons are involved in an activity, each can more readily be monitored by the others, and negative feedback from outside sources will reflect more directly upon the willingness and competence of every participant. Consequently, fear of social reprisal is likely to prevent the individual from standing by while others do the work. According to behavior setting theory (Barker, 1960, 1968), the degree of responsibility felt by members of organizations varies inversely with the number of people available to carry out the organization's activities. When people are sparse, members sense that the fate of the group depends upon them; consequently they impose high standards of conduct upon themselves and upon their associates. When people are plentiful, demands on individuals are less stringent; other persons are available to carry on the desired activities, so felt responsibility and actual effort are lower. Thus Wicker (1969) found that members of large churches spent less time and energy on their organization's programs than did members of smaller churches. The former were also inclined to be less critical of associates who participated in minimal fashion.

The evidence cited previously concerns participation in large organizations, but there is reason to believe that similar relationships prevail in group settings. Latané and his associates (Darley and Latané, 1968a, b; Latané and Rodin, 1969) found that the likelihood that a person would come to the aid of an associate in distress varied inversely with the number of persons present. Apparently it was easier to avoid feelings of individual responsibility and to assume that someone else would perform necessary functions when groups were large.

Another line of research suggests that people are likely to obtain fewer personal satisfactions from participation in large groups than from small ones. Many investigators (see the reviews by Golembiewski, 1962, and by Thomas and Fink, 1963) have found that members of large groups report less opportunity to contribute freely and to influence the course of events. Moreover, members of large groups are more inclined to complain that activities are poorly organized and that their group does not function very well. These criticisms probably reflect the coordination problems discussed earlier, but they may also have serious motivational implications. If people believe that large groups are unduly restrictive of individual freedom and initiative, and that they do not operate very effectively, motivation to work in such groups may be adversely affected. Unless other incentives increase as a direct function of group size, members of large groups should, on the average, be rather unwilling to incur heavy costs in behalf of their groups.

However, people may also fail to contribute their resources when groups are extremely small. If only a few members are available to work on a task, the group may appear to lack sufficient resources to accomplish its purpose. Gross undermanning may make any effort seem futile, and may lead to apathy or resignation instead of task-oriented behavior. Three men are unlikely to work very hard to extinguish a forest fire, and a two-man basketball team will not struggle very persistently to defeat a five-man team. Some tasks cannot be performed at all unless a certain number of individuals are available, and many others can be handled successfully only when the group reaches or approaches a critical size. Gross undermanning is likely to have detrimental effects on motivations. Consequently, the relationship between group size and task motivation should sometimes be curvilinear. Depending upon the nature of the task, the addition of a third or fourth member to a group may raise the probability of success to a level that justifies a maximum effort, but the addition of a sixth or seventh member may lead to overmanning, decreased feelings of personal responsibility, frustration due to coordination problems, and to a consequent slackening of effort.

A study by Slater (1958) suggests that both undermanning and overmanning have adverse effects on motivation. *Ad hoc* groups of two to seven college students discussed a human relations problem for 40 min and prepared a written report regarding ways in which it might be solved. At the conclusion of the discussion period, subjects responded to a 60-item checklist calling for evaluations of their group and its activities. One item provided an opportunity for members to indicate that their group was too small to achieve maximum success, and another offered individuals the chance to say their group was too large. The percentage of persons checking the former item declined steadily as group size increased from two through four, and the percentage of persons checking the latter item increased as group size rose above five.

Members of five-man groups were most satisfied with the size of their group. As might be expected, reasons expressed for dissatisfaction in larger groups centered on lack of coordination, insufficient opportunity to speak one's mind, poor use of time, and mediocre accomplishment. Members of small groups (sizes two through four) did not explicitly identify the deficiencies that led them to say more members were needed. Consequently, we cannot be sure that they felt their available fund of resources was too meager. (Apparently the checklist did not offer options that clearly expressed this sentiment, but subjects might have been reluctant to endorse such self-incriminating alternatives even if they had been included in the list.) Slater offers indirect and somewhat speculative evidence that members of very small groups (particularly those containing only two persons) felt compelled to treat one another with so much kindness and restraint that they were unable to function as well as they wished on a task that called for frank and open advocacy of personal views. In fact, this may have been the case, but it is reasonable to guess that subjects also believed that a discussion group ought to contain about five members in order to represent a variety of viewpoints and to possess a full range of useful resources. As James (1951) has indicated, real-life groups that are charged with the responsibility for making decisions generally contain at least five members. If Slater's groups had been required to play basketball rather than discuss a human relations problem, members of very small groups would undoubtedly have communicated their thoughts about undermanning regardless of what the checklist encouraged them to say.

Of course there is nothing magic about the number five. For some tasks, (e.g., reading a book) a single person is likely to be enough, and the addition of a second individual will constitute overmanning. For other tasks (e.g., winning a tug-of-war), the critical group size may be determined by the number of people on the opposing team, and a group with ten members may feel that is hopelessly undermanned. The important conclusion to be derived from research of the kind reviewed here is that although motivation may increase as new members are added to a group, a size will eventually be reached beyond which the addition of new members will almost certainly be detrimental to motivation. Whether the detrimental effect will commence with the addition of the second or the thirtieth member will depend in part upon the group's apparent need for additional resources in order to accomplish its task.

Summary. There are several reasons for expecting a negative relationship between group size and task motivation. The larger the group, the less influence any single member is likely to exercise over the group outcome. Consequently, as groups increase in size, the rewards that accrue to the individual as a consequence of group success are less completely contingent upon his own behaviors. Moreover, in large groups, individuals are not easily monitored by their associates, and feedback from external sources is unlikely to reflect very directly upon the performance of any single participant. As group size increases, members tend to enjoy their roles less and to complain that neither they nor their group is able to function very well. Coordination problems are often solved less satisfactorily by large groups, and members experience fewer opportunities to make major contributions. Thus several kinds of reinforcement that encourage good performance by members of small groups probably have less effect when groups are large. In addition, if a large group is successful, the payoff will normally be divided among more people than is the case when a small group is successful.

There is little reason to expect task motivation to increase with group size. To be sure, the addition of new members to a group that is grossly undermanned may have a salutary impact on motivation, but once the apparent shortage of personnel has been remedied, further increases in group size should have a detrimental effect on incentives to work hard. (Due to a process called "social facilitation," individuals who function as members of groups may sometimes be more intensely motivated than those who work alone. However, this phenomenon, which is discussed in Chapter 6, is unlikely to be responsible for large differences in the motivation of individuals who are members of different sized groups.)

In conclusion, it is reasonable to anticipate that motivation will ordinarily be lower in large groups than in small ones. If other conditions remain constant, task motivation will tend to fall as new members are added to a group. Although it is possible to imagine circumstances under which this generalization may not be valid, there is probably a maximum size beyond which it becomes a true statement about any group working on any task.

Actual Productivity

The effect that a change in group size will have on actual productivity depends upon the impact of the change on (a) potential productivity, and (b) process losses.

$$\text{Actual productivity} = \text{potential productivity} - \text{process losses}$$

As has already been noted, an increase in group size will ordinarily lead to an increase in potential productivity. The major exceptions to this trend occur when a task is so easy that a single individual possesses all the resources that are needed, when all members of the group are required to work on a conjunctive task, or when the task is discretionary. However, even when the task calls for more resources than the typical person can muster, and when it is disjunctive or divisible, the increment of potential productivity contributed by a new member will tend, on the average, to be inversely related to the number of persons already included in the group. (In the case of additive tasks, each new member should contribute as much as the one who preceded him, but as group size increases, a point will eventually be reached beyond which the task is no longer additive. Ceiling effects will activate the "law of diminishing returns.") In the majority of real-life and experimental situations, potential productivity may be expected to increase at a decelerating rate. Sooner or later a size will be reached beyond which new members will add almost nothing to the group's potential productivity.

Process losses occur when (a) organizational problems are not solved in the best possible manner, and/or (b) members of the group are not optimally motivated to employ their resources to create a group outcome. The effect of group size on process losses will depend, therefore, upon the manner in which size influences the solution of organizational problems and affects the task motivation of group members. In most instances, an increase in group size will complicate the organizational problems that must be solved if the group is to make full use of its members' resources. The likelihood that this most appropriate pattern of organization will be discovered, and the probability that it will be adopted and maintained, will tend to decrease as groups become larger. To be sure, process losses associated with malcoordination are sometimes not very serious; certain tasks do not require that a group maintain a high level of interpersonal coordination or that an intricate system of weighting or matching be established. However, whenever the prescribed process entails a complex division of labor or continuous temporal programming of members' activities, the process losses created by an increase in group size may be very heavy. Observation of groups that were performing tasks of this kind led the noted time-study man, F. W. Taylor (1911), to conclude that industry should rarely assign more than three or four persons to work in close concert with one another.

Because an increase in group size will typically cause potential productivity to increase at a decelerating rate, and process losses to increase at an accelerating rate, we should be prepared to find that actual productivity often tends to be curvilinearly related to group size. Unless the task is conjunctive or the first member of the group possesses all the resources that are needed, the addition of a second member is likely to augment the quality or quantity of the product. A third member will bring still another increment in actual productivity unless he contributes less to the group's potential than he subtracts in the form of process losses. A fourth, fifth, or tenth person will also improve the group's outcome provided the positive effect of his resources is greater than his negative impact on coordination and/or motivation. Sooner or later the negative effect of adding new members will outweigh their positive contributions, and actual productivity will begin to decrease. Depending on the nature of the task and the characteristics of the population from which members are drawn, this size may be reached when only a single individual is available to do the work, or it may not occur until the group has become very large.

Empirical evidence concerning the effect of group size on actual productivity is highly fragmented and incomplete. In a review of the pertinent literature, Thomas and Fink (1963) found only ten experimental studies that examined the impact of size on the quality of group decisions or collective judgments. Carefully controlled research into the effect of size on the performance of motor tasks has been even more rare. Furthermore, investigators have almost invariably compared only two or three different group sizes within a single study, and evidence concerning groups with more than eight or ten members is extremely sparse. Consequently, unambiguous data concerning the shape of the actual productivity curve are not available for any single task, and comparison of such curves for different kinds of tasks (or different kinds of populations) is, at best, a highly speculative process. Fragments of evidence can be assembled in a manner that suggests empirical regularities, but firm conclusions must await additional research.

Positively accelerated increases in productivity. Apparently nobody has reported evidence indicating that actual productivity increases more rapidly than group size. However, it is not difficult to specify circumstances under which such findings might be obtained. As noted earlier, a single individual can not pull hard enough to move a one ton rock even an inch. Probably a two- or three-person group will do no better, but a six-man group may be able to pull the rock several feet during a given interval of time, and a ten-man group may have the capacity to move it 100 yards. Whenever a certain minimum fund of resources is needed in order to perform a task, threshold effects may permit productivity to increase at an accelerating rate. It takes two men to operate an old fashioned cross-cut saw effectively, and at least three or four to manage a moderate sized sailing ship. If a task is additive, a certain minimum output may be required in order to achieve any success whatever, and if n subtasks must be performed simultaneously, a group with fewer than n members will fail. Needless to say, the positively accelerated increases in productivity that occur when the critical size is reached are unlikely to persist when many more members are added. Increments of process loss should tend eventually to cancel the contribution that extra members can make to the group's potential productivity.

The absence of research reporting accelerated increases in productivity is easy to explain. Situations that are likely to yield such outcomes go unexamined because the experimental evidence they might yield seems trivial. Everyone knows that a five-man basketball team will overwhelm a comparably constituted four-man team, and that one person cannot pull hard enough to move a huge boulder. Because empirical research documenting such obvious conclusions would generate little enthusiasm among editors of technical journals, it is not conducted. Instead, investigators understandably elect to explore situations with uncertain outcomes. Tasks that cannot be performed by a single individual are avoided, as are those for which large groups would clearly be inappropriate. This selective process tends, of course, to introduce a serious bias into the experimental literature; the situations that are examined in the laboratory are not broadly representative of those that occur outside it, and the bulk of our empirical findings concern tasks that differ substantially from many of the real-life work assignments that are our major interest.

Negatively accelerated increases in productivity. The findings of several studies reveal a tendency for productivity to increase less rapidly than group size. Taylor and Faust (1952) instructed individuals and two- and four-person groups to play a game of "twenty questions." To start the game, participants were told only whether an object was animal, vegetable, or mineral. Task rules required subjects to ask the experimenter questions that could be answered "Yes," "No," "Partly," "Sometimes," or "Not in the usual sense of the word." Productivity was measured (inversely) by the number of questions required to identify the object, failure to make the correct identification after asking the full allotment of questions, and number of minutes to obtain the correct solution. On all three criteria, dyads were significantly more successful than individuals, but four-person groups were superior to dyads only when productivity was measured by avoidance of failure. Thus it appears that the second member of a group added a larger increment of actual productivity than did the third and fourth members combined. Had Taylor and Faust examined the performance of much larger groups they might have found that the tenth or twentieth member was responsible for a diminution of productivity.

Gibb (1951) performed a study that was unusual in that it examined the impact of a wide range of group sizes. Individuals and groups containing 2, 4, 6, 12, 24, 48, and 96 members were asked to suggest ways of improving the public relations policy of a university. Productivity was indexed by the number of acceptable suggestions offered during a 30-min interval. The relationship between group size and actual productivity proved to be curvilinear; doubling the size of small groups led to dramatic improvements in the number of acceptable suggestions, but doubling the size of large groups had much smaller effects. Indeed, groups containing 96 members were only slightly superior to those that contained 48 members. Apparently groups of 48 persons commanded about all the relevant resources that could effectively be used on the task, and a further increase in group size added little to the potential productivity of the unit. That actual productivity did not decline when groups became very large probably reflects the fact that the task required very little interpersonal coordination. The rules under which participants operated resembled those imposed in the "brainstorming" study cited earlier (Taylor *et al.*, 1958) and permitted each member to function in a highly individualistic manner. Had members of Gibb's groups been required to reach consensus on each suggestion, groups of 96 persons might have proven to be hopelessly cumbersome and ineffective. When tasks are essentially additive and require little interpersonal coordination, a very large number of people can contribute to the group outcome.

As has already been noted, the Ringelmann study (see Dashiell, 1935) also revealed a curvilinear relationship between group size and actual productivity. However, increments of productivity declined much more rapidly than was the case for Gibb's groups. Ringelmann's rope-pulling task required a very high level of interpersonal coordination, and eight-man groups pulled only about twice as much as two-man groups. Although both tasks had an additive character, process losses undoubtedly increased much more rapidly as new members were added to the rope-pulling groups than when they were added to Gibb's brainstorming groups. It should also be noted that Gibb's task probably lost some of its additivity when groups became very large. Only a limited number of brainstorming suggestions can be expressed concerning any one problem, or during a 30-min period, and ceiling effects may have restricted the increment that the 80th or 90th member could contribute to the group's potential productivity. Gibb's study of "diminishing returns" undoubtedly reflected decreasing increments of potential productivity, whereas in the Ringelmann investigation they were almost certainly due to rapidly increasing process losses.

Ziller (1957) asked individuals and groups of two to six persons to perform two different tasks: estimate the number of dots on a card that was displayed for 5 sec (the correct number was 3159) and select the four facts (from a list of 15) that were most critical in determining the correct answer to a complex problem. On both tasks, there was a significant positive relationship between group size and quality of performance, and in both cases there was a tendency for this positive relationship to become weaker as more and more members were added to the group. Thus, on the dot-judging task three-person groups were 74 percent more accurate than individuals who worked alone, but six-person groups were only 9 percent more accurate than three-person groups. On the other task, three-person groups scored 51 percent higher than individuals, and six-person groups earned scores that were only 18 percent higher than those of groups containing three members. Although the overall tendency for improvement to decrease as size increased was not statistically significant (Ziller observed only a few groups at each size), the data suggest that size and productivity are curvilinearly related for both tasks.

The dot-judging exercise yielded data that are difficult to assimilate to our model. The task was clearly discretionary because subjects were free to combine their individual estimates in any manner they chose. There was always a way of "averaging" such estimates to produce an errorless group product; consequently, potential productivity should have been a constant for groups of all sizes. Under these circumstances, the fact that large groups performed better than small ones suggests that process losses *decreased* as groups became larger. How could this happen?

When everyone feels quite unsure of his ability to make a judgment, and when nobody has an intense personal commitment to any specific alternative, disagreements are likely to be resolved by "computing" the unweighted average of individuals' judgments. Such a procedure is comparatively easy to follow and it avoids dissension-producing discussion that may be required in order to weight members unequally. Furthermore, one can readily demonstrate (Steiner, 1966) that the unweighted average tends to be a rather accurate resolution of individual differences provided the judgments that are to be combined are symmetrically distributed around the correct estimate. When this is the case, the accuracy of the unweighted average tends to increase (at a decelerating rate) as groups become larger. Thus it may be suggested that Ziller's large groups performed better than his small ones because the particular system of interpersonal coordination employed by groups of all sizes was one that was more appropriate for large groups. Of course, this pattern of outcomes is likely to occur only when the situation encourages groups to favor the unweighted mean over other joint products, and when errors in individual judgments tend to be symmetrically distributed around the correct estimates. It is unlikely to be generated under other circumstances.

Ziller's second task required groups to choose among the several alternatives favored by individual members, and to perform the selection process four times. Consequently, the task may be seen as one that was divisible and for which each subtask was disjunctive. As group size increased, potential productivity should have risen at a decelerating rate, and process losses should have increased at an accelerating rate. Data on actual productivity are consistent with these assumptions.

Decreases in productivity. There is little available evidence indicating that repeated enlargement of a group leads eventually to a decrease in productivity. In a review of the literature, Thomas and Fink (1963) noted several studies in which large groups outperformed small ones, a few in which size appeared to have no effect on outcomes, but none in which small groups were significantly more productive than large groups. However, most of these investigations examined groups that contained no more than six persons, and only one employed groups with as many as thirteen members. Failure to obtain evidence of negative effects may only indicate that sufficiently large groups were not observed. Had experimenters extended the size of their samples to include groups of 15 or 20 members, process losses might have outweighed increments of potential productivity and led to a downward trend in actual performance. Moreover, studies of group size have rarely employed tasks of the kind that are most likely to reveal a negative relationship between size and productivity. Researchers have seldom chosen to investigate group effectiveness on tasks a single individual can perform with great skill and on which groups are likely to sustain heavy process losses. The probable findings of such research are too obvious to be very interesting.

It is possible to specify conditions that should permit a single individual to be more proficient than a group of any size. The task should be easy enough so it can be readily performed by a single person, but complex enough so that two or more people are likely to get in one another's way, or to create mutual interference by attempting to pursue incompatible but equally acceptable courses of action. Thorndike (1938) asked individuals and groups to design a crossword puzzle, and found that groups performed very poorly. The task was one for which any college student undoubtedly possessed adequate resources; consequently, the potential productivity of groups was probably no greater than that of individual subjects. However, there were a multitude of different ways in which an acceptable product could be created, and members were apt to pursue different strategies. As Thorndike noted, "there is no predetermined right answer ... and the interrelations of many parts must be kept continuously in mind. Individual suggestions follow diverging lines ... Groups found it very difficult to work together on this complex fluctuating pattern ... [pp. 412–413]." It seems clear that process losses seriously impaired the performances of groups, and caused them to function less effectively than individuals who worked alone.

Under somewhat parallel circumstances, Kelley *et al.* (1965) obtained a negative relationship between group size and productivity. Members of groups containing from four to seven persons were told they could avoid an impending electrical shock by pressing a switch. However, it was explained that escape could be accomplished by only one person at a time. If one, and only one, member activated his switch for a 3-sec interval, he escaped; but if two or more members operated their switches simultaneously, none escaped. Thus the task required that individuals perform an exceedingly simple operation, but necessitated a very high degree of interpersonal coordination. A single impetuous member could block the progress of everyone. Groups were allowed work periods equaling 6 sec per member, and were informed that the electrical shock would be delivered to anyone who did not escape during the allotted time. In order to heighten subjects' awareness of the passage of time, an apparatus consisting of two interconnected bottles was placed where it could be seen by all. When the starting signal was given, colored water began flowing from one bottle to the other; the amount of water in the former bottle was such that is was completely transferred to the second by the time the group's work period ended.

A single individual, unimpeded by anyone else, should have been able to escape in slightly more than 3 sec (the 3-sec interval during which his switch had to be depressed plus a fraction of a second to allow for "reaction time"), and two persons should have been able to escape in slightly more than 6 sec. Potential productivity (the number of persons who could escape per second of elapsed time if no process losses occured) should have been a constant for all groups. The number actually escaping per second was .13 for four-person groups, while for five-, six-, and seven-person groups the numbers were .09, .05, and .08, respectively. Except in the case of the seven-person groups, the findings reveal the expected decreases in actual productivity.

Kelley *et al.* surmised that the unexpectedly high rate of success for seven-person groups may have been due to subjects' awareness that the allotted time was far longer than actually needed. Because the time allowed per person was very generous (6 sec instead of slightly more than 3), and because the flow of colored water informed subjects of the time remaining to them, members of large groups may have felt less urgency than those in small groups for whom the total surplus time was smaller. (Four-person groups had about 12 extra seconds whereas seven-person groups had about 21.) A lower level of experienced urgency may have permitted large groups to avoid some of the coordination difficulties their size would otherwise have created. To explore this possibility, Kelley *et al.* did a second study which, although it employed the same time schedules as the first, did not keep subjects informed concerning the amount of time remaining before electrical shock would be delivered. For four-member groups, the number of persons escaping per second was .16, and for five-, six-, and seven-member groups the numbers were .08, .04, and .04. Seven-person groups again performed slightly better than might be anticipated, but their outcomes were not grossly inconsistent with the general trend. As groups became larger, productivity decreased, but apparently at a decelerating rate.

In studies of this kind, the shape of the productivity curve is, of course, influenced by the criterion of success. Had Kelley *et al.* required that *all* members escape in order for a group to be regarded as successful, the conjunctive nature of the task would have placed large groups at a serious disadvantage. If, for example, every group had been allowed 18 sec, it would have been impossible for those containing six or seven members to succeed. Potential productivity would have entailed "perfect" performance for all groups of size four or five, and "complete failure" for all groups of six or seven. Under these circumstances, the process losses created by adding a fifth member to a group would undoubtedly have been responsible for a moderate decrease in the proportion of group successes; the addition of a sixth member would have brought a precipitous drop in productivity, while the addition of a seventh would have had no effect whatever.

Summary. The effect that an increase in group size will have on actual productivity depends upon the impact of the increase on potential productivity and process losses. If the task is additive, disjunctive, or divisible, group enlargement generally leads to decelerating increases in potential productivity. Increasing the size of groups ordinarily results in accelerating increases in process losses. Consequently, in many situations the net effect of group size on actual productivity can be represented by a curve that rises at a decelerating rate as groups become larger, but which eventually reaches a maximum level and begins to descend. Depending upon the nature of the task and the characteristics of the population from which members are drawn, the point of maximum productivity may occur when only a single individual is available to do the work, or it may not be reached until the group has become very large. Under special circumstances, (i.e., when a small group lacks the resources to perform the task) productivity may increase at an accelerating rate when certain critical sizes are attained. However, if the group is enlarged beyond this critical range, diminishing returns will be noted and a size will eventually be reached beyond which group productivity will decrease.

Empirical evidence concerning the effect of size on actual productivity is far from complete because researchers have usually elected to examine only comparatively small groups and have not systematically sampled the full range of tasks. Although the fragmentary nature of available data makes an *ex post facto* analysis especially difficult and speculative, laboratory findings appear to support the above contentions.

Size and Other Variables

It is apparent that large size can be both a blessing and a curse. On the one hand, the resources of many persons may be needed in order to perform a task adequately, or at all. However, the organizational difficulties encountered by large groups may prevent members from making maximum use of their resources, and motivation may fall to a level that endangers productivity. Recognizing these contradictory implications of group size, Thelen (1949) proposed that groups achieve maximum productivity when they contain only as many members as are needed to supply the necessary task and interaction skills. Although this proposal neglects nonskill resources, it suggests that a group needs to be large enough to command a sufficient fund of relevant task resources, and small enough to avoid the organizational and motivational problems that are responsible for heavy process losses. Stated in the language of this book, a group is most successful when it contains the number of members that maximizes the positive discrepancy between potential productivity and process losses.

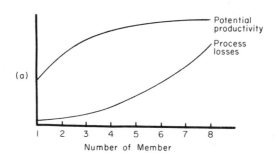

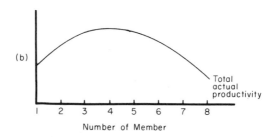

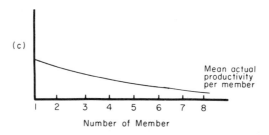

Fig. 4.3. Illustrative curves depicting relationships between group size and potential productivity, process losses, total actual productivity, and mean actual productivity per member.

Figure 4.3a is a schematic diagram of the way group size might affect the determinants of actual productivity. The curves are, of course, illustrative and hypothetical; in a general way they probably approximate the truth concerning certain tasks and populations, but they undoubtedly misrepresent the facts about many others (e.g., situations in which the task is conjunctive or in which college students are designing a crossword puzzle). Although the curves are not intended to depict universal trends, they indicate relationships that are postulated to prevail in many situations: As group size increases, potential productivity rises at a decelerating rate, whereas process losses increase at an accelerating rate. Given the relationships described by Fig. 4.3a, the effect of size on actual productivity is as shown in Fig. 4.3b. Actual productivity equals potential productivity minus process losses, and in the present example it reaches its maximum when the group contains four or five members. The average productivity per member is greater when a single individual works alone on the task, and it declines steadily as more persons are added (see Fig. 4.3c). The most desirable group size depends upon whether one wishes to maximize total productivity or productivity per man.

However, the problem confronting anyone who wishes to maximize total or average productivity is not simply that of determining the most advantageous group size. One can sometimes alter both of the curves shown in Fig. 4.3a. Depending somewhat upon the nature of the task, the slope and elevation of the potential productivity curve can be manipulated by changing the composition of the groups that are assembled. Selection procedures that recruit individuals with abundant resources, or training programs that endow participants with needed task skills, may cause the potential productivity curve to start at a high level, and, in the absence of ceiling effects, may permit it to rise very rapidly. The following chapter examines some consequences of group composition.

Process losses may also be affected by group composition, and they are often susceptible to other influences as well. Thus it is sometimes possible to intensify the motivation of participants by manipulating the extent to which their behaviors are monitored, or by altering the scheme by which rewards are distributed. Organizational problems are likely to become less serious after a group has had time to evolve a pattern of matching and a system of temporal programming. Intervention by external agents, emergent or designated leadership, and the development or imposition of group structure can affect the elevation and slope of the curve representing process losses. Each of these factors is examined in later sections of this book.

Because both of the curves shown in Fig. 4.3a can be altered, the size of a group is only one determinant of the effectiveness with which it will perform a given task. People who wish to maximize the productivity of a work unit should attempt to raise the potential productivity curve and to accentuate its upward slope. They should also endeavor to prevent process losses from increasing at a very rapid rate as new members are added to the group. The success with which these aims are accomplished will tend to determine whether a group must be large or small in order to achieve maximum productivity.

Critical Sizes

As group membership is enlarged, the addition of the nth person may bring a noticeable change in the trends established by earlier increases in group size. Thus, for example, the addition of the seventh member may cause actual productivity to decrease whereas each previous person has contributed an increment of productivity. Or, when groups are grossly undermanned for the tasks they are to perform, the addition of the tenth person may induce members to believe that their probability of success is high enough to justify an all-out effort. As noted earlier, Slater found that the tendency of members to complain that their group was too small decreased steadily until five persons were included; above size five there was an increasing propensity to say the group was too large.

In the illustrations cited above, the number of members constituting a critical size undoubtedly depends upon the nature of the task and the resources of the participants. The size beyond which productivity begins to decline clearly reflects the demands of the task, and three-person groups with insufficient resources may welcome a new member whereas those with adequate resources may not (Ziller and Behringer, 1960). However, there is reason to believe that certain group sizes may be critical in a fairly wide variety of situations.

The Dyad

A single individual, working alone on a task, must decide what to do when. But a dyad confronts a new kind of organizational question: Who shall do what when? Both intrapersonal and interpersonal coordination are needed, and a system of weighting or matching must be developed. Opportunities for process losses are therefore more numerous in the dyad.

As Simmel (1950) has noted, the dyad is a unit in which members are likely to feel intense responsibility to one another. Each participant can, should he choose to do so, terminate the group's existence. Moreover, the dyad, being the smallest possible group, offers each member maximum control over the group's success. Consequently, each is likely to feel a strong obligation to adjust to the other's preference and style of behavior. Fear of alienating the associate may induce members of a dyad to employ what Slater (1958) has called "a kind of 'pussy-footing' or 'kid gloves' approach to problem solving [p. 137]." The more competent member may be loath to assign himself the weight he deserves, and both participants may be reluctant to match themselves with the subtasks for which they are more suited. If this is the case, the dyad is a unit in which the most productive solutions to organizational problems are unlikely to be adopted.

Bales and Borgatta (1955) have reported evidence supporting this view of dyads. Groups of two to seven persons discussed a human relations problem and formulated recommendations for its solution. By comparison with larger groups, dyads manifested strong tendencies to avoid the expression of disagreement or antagonism, and to accentuate activities that are affectively supportive or neutral. Thus members of dyads adopted a gentle, kindly approach to one another.

Bales and Borgatta did not report productivity data, but other investigators have obtained evidence suggesting that the unwillingness of dyads to adopt an appropriate system of weighting or matching sometimes has adverse effects on group outcomes. When two-man groups work on tasks that require a division of labor and very close interpersonal coordination, productivity is found to be more highly correlated with the ability of the less competent member than with that of the more competent (Comrey, 1953; Comrey and Deskin, 1954a, b). However, when the task does not require specialized role performances or intense interpersonal coordination, the ability of the more competent member is the better predictor of group success (Comrey and Staats, 1955; Wiest, Porter and Ghiselli, 1961). In the former case, the propensity of dyads to maintain equality of influence apparently has the effect of reducing the more able member to the level of his associate. When the task requires little coordination, or even encourages individuals to operate "on their own," the contribution of the superior member can be decisive. Whether or not the task has a strong eureka flavor may also be critical; even in a dyad members are likely to receive unequal weights if it is clear that one is markedly more successful than the other.

A study conducted by Wegner and Zeaman (1956) suggests that larger groups are more likely than dyads to establish an advantageous weighting system. Groups containing two or four members worked on a pursuit rotor task. Productivity was measured by the proportion of time a stylus was kept in contact with a small spot on a rotating disk. In order to enable several persons to work simultaneously, the stylus was equipped with a handle for each member of the group. Although the task could be performed fairly well by a single individual, a group could contain a higher score, *provided the efforts of the members were advantageously weighted and coordinated.* A single, incompetent member would, of course, seriously restrict productivity if his behaviors were permitted to dominate the group's activities (or even if his efforts were accorded a weight equal to that assigned other members). On the other hand, a highly competent member could cause the group to be successful if his associates adjusted their own behaviors to his. The outcomes achieved by dyads were found to be proportional to the scores their poorer members had obtained on individual practice trials, whereas the productivity of four-person groups was more strongly correlated with the scores their most competent members had earned while working alone. It appears that larger groups were more successful in assigning heavy weights to their most able participants.

The dyad is a group in which feelings of interpersonal responsibility are likely to inhibit members from adopting nonequalitarian solutions to organizational problems. Whether or not this characteristic of the dyad results in large process losses presumably depends upon the extent of the needed coordination, the heterogeneity of the members, the degree to which the task calls for unequal weighting, and upon whether the task has strong eureka qualities.

The Triad

The triad is the smallest group in which certain phenomena can occur. When a group gains its third member, a coalition can form, one individual may provoke or mediate disagreements between others, and the continuance of the group no longer depends upon the willingness of every member to participate. More important, perhaps, is the fact that any member can be outvoted by his associates. Consequently, the "will of the group" need not reflect the preferences of all its members, and a triad may become a "super-individual entity" to which members conform or acquiesce without being personally convinced of the wisdom of their actions. Simmel has argued that this feature of the triad tends to absolve the individual of responsibility for his own behaviors and for the consequences of the group's decisions. Furthermore, members need not feel very directly responsible for the unhappiness of their associates; the actions that cause displeasure are approved by a majority which includes one other person.

By comparison with the dyad, the triad should be a unit in which the ideology of equality, and other extra-task considerations, have little influence on the way organizational problems are resolved. Groups containing more than three members should, of course, reveal the same absence of "pussy-footing" behavior as the triad. The justification for regarding the latter as a critical size is that it presumably represents a rather sharp break with the dyad.

Although the propensity of triads to generate coalitions has been widely studied (Gamson, 1964), there is little empirical evidence bearing on other alleged consequences of adding a third man to the group. Bales and Borgatta (1955) have reported striking discontinuities in interaction patterns, and Simmel (1950) has interpreted a variety of historical events to indicate that triads operate very differently from dyads. However, carefully controlled laboratory studies dealing with both process and productivity seem not to have been performed.

Other Critical Sizes

If a group is repeatedly enlarged, a size will eventually be reached beyond which direct, face-to-face interaction among all members is prohibitively cumbersome. In order to maintain such a pattern of interaction, each participant in a group containing n members must monitor $n - 1$ communication channels, and transmit messages along many of them. Unless messages are exceedingly simple and deal with matters that are familiar to all, coping with more than a few channels will constitute an intolerable burden. If n rises above a certain level, members may be expected to discontinue their use of some of the channels and to concentrate their attention on only a few. When this occurs, full scale face-to-face interaction is replaced by a structured arrangement in which some pairs of participants maintain only indirect contact with one another.

We do not know how large a group may become before this transformation is necessary. The critical size probably varies somewhat, being smaller when the task requires rapid, continuous, and complex communication than when it does not. However, there is evidence suggesting that no more than about eight or ten persons can be directly responsive to one another in a group discussion setting, and that mutual responsivity becomes difficult even before that size is reached. Castore (1962) observed psychotherapeutic groups ranging in size from five to twenty members, and counted the number of persons to whom each individual directed at least one remark during an hour's session. The percentage of available communication channels actually employed fell sharply when size nine was reached, and continued to decline as groups became larger. Even though Castore employed a very lenient criterion of responsiveness, groups with five or six members failed to make full use of the channels available to them, and groups with ten or more members manifested a high degree of selectivity.

Evidence that available channels receive unequal usage has also been provided by Bales (1950) and by Stephan and Mishler (1952). Even in very small groups composed of three or four persons, some pairs of members communicate less frequently to one another than do other pairs. As the size of the group increases, such inequalities are accentuated; they become very noticeable by the time six or eight members are included. Bales has also reported that people who are infrequently the originators or targets of communicative acts tend to direct their comments to high participators who, in turn, address a large proportion of their messages to the group as a whole rather than to specific individuals. The emerging picture is therefore one in which communication patterns become increasingly polarized as group size is enlarged. However, neither Bales nor Stephan and Mishler reported evidence of sharp discontinuities such as might be expected to occur if groups steadfastly maintained an each-to-each interaction pattern until a critical size had been attained and members were compelled to accept a more polarized arrangement. Probably the burden of manning an increasingly large number of communication channels induces participants to accept some degree of polarization before they are actually required to do so.

Other research also suggests that unrestricted face-to-face interaction becomes extremely difficult when groups contain more than about eight or ten members. Hare (1952) noted that groups of 12 Boy Scouts tended to divide into two or three small subgroups when they were instructed to evaluate the merits of various items of camping equipment. Similarly, Theodorson (1953) reported that discussion groups containing 15 to 22 members formed subgroups of less than 7 persons in order to facilitate communication and to avoid problems of organization and status differentiation. Hollingshead (1949) found that cliques in a public school varied in size from 2 to 9 for boys and from 2 to 12 for girls. The modal size was 5 for both sexes. James (1951) observed that free-forming groups encountered outside the laboratory rarely included more than 7 persons, and suggested that this phenomenon is a consequence of the difficulty with which face-to-face relationships can be maintained in groups of larger sizes.

Although communication problems are not the only factor that may limit the size of face-to-face groups, it appears likely that the costs and complications entailed in each-to-each communication become unacceptable when more than 8 or 10 persons are involved. Above that size, groups either divide into subgroups or adopt a polarized pattern of interaction. Depending upon the nature of the task, one or another of these changes may occur before size 8 is attained.

Homans (1950) has suggested that another critical size may be reached when a group accumulates about a dozen members. Within a highly polarized group structure, a leader or supervisor is said to be unable to interact in a reciprocal fashion with more than about 12 other people. Thus the "span of control" that can be exercised by a single individual is seriously limited. In support of this argument, Homans cites the familiar pyramidal structure found in armies, factories, and other organizations. First-line supervisors (squad leaders, foremen) are often required to manage the activities of about a dozen subordinates, and a single official at the next higher level in the structure may have responsibility for overseeing the activities of about a dozen first-line supervisors.

However, data on the size of industrial work groups indicates that they sometimes contain many more than 12 persons. Although Handyside (1952) found that the modal size of such groups in British Industry fell between 10 and 15, the range was from less than 5 to 150. It seems apparent that a single supervisor can coordinate the work of many more than a dozen men if their activities are highly routine and/or are regulated by an appropriate role system. Under these circumstances, only minimal control need be exercised by the coordinating agent. A single conductor can "integrate" the behaviors of a hundred-man symphony orchestra because each musician has been trained to do what the musical score requires him to do (Steiner, 1955). The critical size that marks the upper limit on polarized groups appears to be a function of the extent and nature of the interaction that must occur between the central individual and each of his associates.

Possible Consequences

Some of the critical sizes mentioned above are direct consequences of the shapes and elevations of the curves representing potential productivity and process losses. Thus the size beyond which actual productivity per man will decrease is determined by factors that are summarized by those two curves. So also is the size beyond which total productivity will decrease. Other critical sizes may affect the curves themselves rather than being determined by them. Thus the dyad should, under certain circumstances, have heavier process losses than an inspection of the curve depicting such losses for larger groups would lead one to expect, and the triad should sustain smaller losses than those one might project from a comparison of data on individuals and dyads. On some tasks, the actual productivity of groups containing seven or eight persons should probably show an unexpected improvement over that of groups with five or six members; this should be the case when a shift to a more polarized structure reduces process losses. (The perplexing success of the seven-person groups studied by Kelley *et al.* may reflect such an effect.)

Data are far too limited to provide an adequate test of these suppositions. Whether the critical sizes noted above have appreciable effects on the curves that determine actual productivity is a question that cannot be answered until much more detailed research has been conducted.

Summary

The effect of group size on potential productivity can often be inferred with considerable precision if one knows how the relevant resources are distributed in the population from which group members are drawn. Assuming random selection and a disjunctive task, potential productivity will tend to increase at a decelerating rate as group size is enlarged. When tasks are conjunctive, increases in group size will cause potential productivity to decrease at a decelerating rate, and when they are additive the relationship between size and potential productivity will be positive and linear. Size should not affect the potential productivity of groups that are performing discretionary tasks. Relationships between size and potential productivity are more difficult to infer for tasks that are divisible. However, such relationships should typically be positive and curvilinear, increases in group size being responsible for decelerating increases in potential productivity.

As groups become larger, process losses will ordinarily increase at an accelerating rate. The complexity of the coordination problems that must be solved in order for a group to realize its full potential tends to increase more rapidly than group size, and optimal motivation is very difficult to maintain as more and more members are added. Although the development of role systems and the emergence of specialists who perform integrative and motivational functions may minimize the process losses for a time, repeated enlargement of the group will eventually produce a size beyond which such losses will increase at a rapid and accelerating rate.

Actual productivity equals the positive discrepancy between potential productivity and process losses. Depending upon the shapes and elevations of the curves depicting relationships between size and these two factors, and upon the number of persons already included in the group, an additional member may contribute either an increment or decrement to actual productivity. However, repeated enlargement of the group will eventually lead to a decline in the quality or quantity of the group's outcome. Whether this size will be reached when a group is very small, or delayed until it is extremely large, depends on a variety of considerations that affect the two curves. It appears that certain sizes may be critical in that they permit the determining factors to produce irregularities in the shape of one or the other of the curves.

Chapter 5

Consequences
of Group Composition

The productivity of a group is inevitably conditioned by the resources, attitudes, and dispositional properties of its members. The resources that individuals bring with them into the work situation determine how well the group can meet existing task demands, and the personological qualities of members may be expected to influence the success with which available resources are combined and utilized. Although we do not yet know a great deal about the effects of dispositional variables on group process, or even about the impact of resources on actual productivity, it is clear that much of what transpires in a group is a consequence of the properties of the members. A conclave of kindergarten children is unlikely to solve a calculus problem, and a group of schizophrenics will probably make poor use of the insights of its members.

Two aspects of group composition are critical. On the one hand, a group may do well or poorly because, on the average, its members have many or few relevant resources, or possess certain dispositional qualities to a high or low degree. In other cases, the average endowment of the members may be less important than the dispersion of individuals around the group average. Thus, for example, when task demands require that participants perform highly specialized roles it is probably advantageous to have a diverse assortment of group members, and when everyone must do exactly the same thing the ideal arrangement may be one in which all persons are very much alike. Whether, and how much, heterogeneity is desirable should therefore depend upon the nature of the task. It should also depend upon which particular dispositional or ability variable is under consideration. Even when the task favors a group whose members each possess a unique type of resource (heterogeneous abilities), uniformity of motivation, sex, or social status may be advantageous. We cannot expect to discover a single, all-purpose answer to the question: Is heterogeneity more desirable than homogeneity?

Although a completely satisfactory description of the composition of groups must deal with members' average scores on attributes as well as with their dispersion around these averages, this chapter is primarily concerned with the latter aspect of composition. The probable importance of group averages has been widely recognized, and researchers have generally employed experimental or statistical techniques that prevent differences in average scores from confounding the conclusions they reach. However, the critical impact that homogeneity-heterogeneity can have on group processes and productivity has been far less universally noted, and is often neglected by theoreticians and experimenters alike. Furthermore, the consequences of homogeneity-heterogeneity are likely to be mediated in a more subtle manner by task demands than are the effects of average membership qualities. Thus they are especially deserving of careful attention.

Experimental investigations into the effects of homogeneity-heterogeneity have typically involved the deliberate creation of *ad hoc* groups that vary in composition. Subjects with similar (or different) characteristics are assembled into groups and asked to perform a task or carry on some other activity. Differences among the outcomes generated by differently constituted groups are called "assembly effects" and are viewed as consequences of group composition. Outside the laboratory, it is often difficult to compose groups with varying membership characteristics, but careful examination of real-life groups sometimes permits investigators to derive conclusions concerning the effects of composition.

Homogeneity-Heterogeneity

Any single individual may be regarded as a composite of many attributes. He possesses certain skills to a high degree and others in meager measure; he is well informed about some topics and ignorant of others; his personality involves a concatenation of interrelated propensities that may be patterned in myriad ways. Humans are multi-faceted beings any two of whom may resemble one another with respect to one property but may be very dissimilar with respect to another. For this reason, research dealing with group composition always requires a simplification of unmanageable complexities.

If groups are assembled to be heterogeneous with respect to ability X, they may also be heterogeneous with respect to ability Y, or with regard to a wide assortment of dispositional characteristics. Similarly, homogeneous groups may be homogeneous on many variables in addition to the ones that have provided the basis for member selection. We know that a group whose members vary in height is likely to be one that is also heterogeneous with respect to members' weights, and that a group of college graduates will ordinarily represent a narrower range of IQ scores than a group of first-grade children. However, we do not know whether a group consisting of persons with highly varied abilities to perform a particular task will be one whose members are also heterogeneous with respect to personality variables, attitudes, or cultural perspectives; if such a group behaves differently from one whose members have more uniform abilities to perform the task in question, we cannot be sure whether the observed differences are due to the distribution of abilities or to the distribution of unmeasured dispositional qualities associated with those abilities. Because we know relatively little about the way attributes cluster with one another, and cannot possibly measure or manipulate all potentially relevant variables, studies of group composition usually leave the experimenter with an uncomfortable margin of uncertainty. He can rarely be sure that the variables on which he has matched (or deliberately mismatched) his subjects are the ones that are responsible for the assembly effects he obtains.

There is another problem that complicates research and theory dealing with composition effects. Heterogeneity with respect to a given attribute may augment potential productivity but greatly increase the complexity of the processes that must occur in order for the group to realize its full potential. Thus, for example, a group whose members each possess unique information concerning a topic may have the potential to produce a high quality judgment because their total available information is very great. Such a group is likely to experience greater difficulty in evaluating and pooling information than a group with more homogeneous members. Probably heterogeneity is also more likely than homogeneity to promote antagonisms among members. Consequently, it may be anticipated that heterogeneity sometimes establishes a high level of potential productivity which, however, is not fully attained because process losses are also high.

The foregoing discussion suggests that a theory of composition effects should deal with two important issues. It should be concerned with the identification of variables on which homogeneity-heterogeneity really matters, and it should relate homogeneity-heterogeneity on these variables to the consequences they are likely to promote (e.g., effects on potential productivity, process losses, or actual productivity). At the present time, no very satisfactory body of theory exists, and a good deal of additional research will be required before we can move far beyond the realm of hunch and speculation. However, on the pages that follow, a tentative and incomplete formulation will be proposed. The probable effects of certain kinds of homogeneity-heterogeneity will be examined, and an attempt will be made to incorporate these notions into the theoretical framework developed in earlier chapters. Attention will first be focused on questions relating to heterogeneity of resources; heterogeneity with respect to dispositional qualities will be examined later.

Heterogeneity of Resources

Disjunctive tasks. When tasks are disjunctive, the potential productivity of a group is determined by the ability of its most competent member. Thus if the aim is to exert a maximum force on a rope that is long enough to be grasped by only one person, it is the pulling power of the group's most able member, rather than the average pulling power of all members, that determines how well the group can possibly perform. If two groups have equal averages, the more heterogeneous of the two will have the higher potential productivity. The same may be said about the performance of other disjunctive tasks provided success is measured in a continuous (rather than dichotomous) fashion and is not restricted by a ceiling or upper limit above which recorded performance cannot rise.

When success is measured dichotomously (e.g., right-wrong), the situation is somewhat different. If the task is extremely easy, or the average ability of individuals is very high, even a rather homogeneous group is likely to contain at least one person who has the resources to succeed. Thus, for example, if the goal is to solve a simple multiplication problem, almost any group of eighth-grade children, regardless of its homogeneity, will contain one or more persons with the necessary skills. However, if the goal is to spell an obscure, technical word, a group whose members are heterogeneous with respect to the requisite resources is more likely than a homogeneous group with the same average ability level to include a member who can do the job. When tasks are disjunctive, heterogeneity never depresses potential productivity; unless there are ceiling effects due to the ease of the task, or to the manner in which performance is measured, heterogeneity augments potential productivity.

Heterogeneity may also complicate the processes that must be followed in order for a group to realize its full potential, and may therefore be responsible for large process losses. If a group is comparatively homogeneous, it does not matter very much which particular member is chosen (or permitted) to act in behalf of all; everyone has the ability to function almost equally well. In a heterogeneous group, matching is a more critical matter. Success depends upon the facility with which the most competent person can be identified, upon that individual's readiness to assume responsibility for the group's fate, and upon the willingness of his associates to allow him to do so. To be sure, if the task has a strong eureka flavor and everyone is free to demonstrate his competence, these contingencies may not be serious. If the quality of individual contributions is not clearly apparent, or if members must choose their functionary without having had an opportunity to observe his performance (as would be the case, for example, if only one person were allowed to pull on a rope and no practice trials were permitted), there is a strong possibility that the matching process will not be performed very advantageously. As we have noted earlier (see Chapter 2), under these circumstances social status, members' self-confidence and general ascendance, and informal social alliances may be expected to influence the choice of agent, and may lead to the selection of a person who is very poorly qualified to perform the particular task that confronts the group. Thus Torrance (1954) found that pilots were much more likely than gunners to provide the group's solution to the horse-trading problem even when the latter were able to solve it correctly and the former were not. The high potential productivity of heterogeneous groups will be transformed into high actual productivity only if members do a better-than-chance job of selecting their most competent associate to serve as their agent. Of course, the same may also be said about more homogeneous groups, but since their range of talent is smaller, the consequences of the selection process are less critical.

The effect of homogeneity-heterogeneity on process losses is sometimes mediated by the average ability of group members (or by its functional counterpart, task difficulty). In the Thomas and Fink (1961) study cited earlier, it was found that groups tended to select as their solution to the horse-trading problem whatever answer had been obtained by the majority of members when they worked alone. This propensity to converge on the modal response resulted in high quality group products if the majority of members had solved the problem correctly (i.e., if the average ability level was high), but led to an inferior product if the majority had independently reached the same wrong conclusion. Thus homogeneity appeared to have salutory effects on process when the average ability was high, but adverse effects when it was quite low. If anyone in a group can perform a disjunctive task, the group has the potential to perform it. Group potential is most likely to be realized however, when a large proportion of the members possess the needed resources.

These notions are illustrated by a study conducted by Goldman, McGlynn, and Toledo, (1967). College students responded to an intelligence test consisting of 50 problem-solving items. Seven weeks later they were assembled into

TABLE 5.1

Percentage of Correct Decisions by Three-Person Groups on Items for Which
Initial Responses of Members Were Distributed in Four Different Ways [a]

Initial responses of members	Percentage of correct decisions
All members correct	100
Two members correct and one wrong	93
One member correct and two giving different wrong answers	86
One member correct and two giving the same wrong answer	57

[a]Adapted from M. Goldman, A. McGlynn, and A. Toledo, Comparison
of individual and group performance of size three and five with various initially
right and wrong tendencies. *Journal of Personality and Social Psychology,*
1967, 7, 222–226.

three-person groups and asked to reach a consensus concerning the correct
response to each item. Table 5.1 reports the results that are most pertinent to
the present discussion. If all three members of a triad had given the correct
answer to an item when working alone, groups always reached the correct
solution; if only two members had been correct, group achievement was still
very high (93 percent of all such group solutions were correct). However, if only
one person had succeeded when working alone, group achievement was lower,
and especially so if the two inaccurate members had reached the same wrong
answer. Under the latter circumstances, the tendency of participants to select
the response with greatest popular support was probably so strong that the single
individual with the ability to solve the problem could not prevail against it. In
each of the four conditions, potential productivity was as high as it could
possibly be because every group contained at least one member who had
demonstrated his competence to perform the task. Process losses apparently
increased as a function of heterogeneity, and were responsible for variations in
actual productivity.

It is necessary to append a rider to the previous conclusion. Groups in
which two persons had reached the same wrong conclusion did not do as well as
those in which the two incorrect members had given different answers. We do
not know that the former were more heterogeneous than the latter with respect
to ability level, and it seems unlikely that they were. A cautious interpretation
would be that the two kinds of groups were equally heterogeneous with respect
to ability, and that the superior performance of groups in which there were two

different wrong answers reflected a different kind of heterogeneity. Many disjunctive tasks, like those employed by Goldman *et al.,* permit individuals or groups to be wrong in several different ways, but offer only one way of being right. When this is the case, it is often unclear whether one wrong response indicates more competence than another; different wrong answers may merely reflect different prejudices concerning the problem at hand. Evidence to be reviewed later in this chapter suggests that when members of a group hold diverse prejudices they are more likely to settle upon the correct answer to a problem than when their prejudices coincide.

A variety of dispositional characteristics may lead an individual to prefer one wrong response over another, or to choose a wrong response rather than the correct one. Because such dispositional variables may be associated with ability level, they complicate the conclusions we can draw from studies that compare the performances of groups that are homogeneous versus heterogeneous with respect to task-relevant abilities.

In summary, when tasks are disjunctive, heterogeneity of members' abilities tends to promote high potential productivity, but this effect is most likely to be manifested when tasks are difficult (when average ability is comparatively low). On the other hand, heterogeneity is often responsible for large process losses, especially when tasks lack the eureka quality, and when members differ substantially from one another with respect to social status, proclivity to dominate group actions, or other dispositional qualities that affect the weighting process. If the task is exceedingly difficult (average ability is low), diversity of prejudices concerning the proper group outcome may prevent precipitous action and thus encourage an advantageous weighting of members' contributions.

Conjunctive tasks. When tasks are conjunctive, potential productivity depends upon the resources of the group's least competent member. A team of mountain climbers can move no faster than its slowest man, and the verdict of a jury can be no better than that to which its least perceptive member will subscribe. In cases of this kind, homogeneity is likely to be an advantage, for it means that the least resourceful member is not much less competent than anyone else. For any given level of average competence, homogeneous groups will have higher potential productivity than heterogeneous groups.

Process losses should not be greatly affected by homogeneity-heterogeneity. The least capable member necessarily establishes the maximum productivity of the group, and his associates can do nothing to alter that fact. They can implore him to do his best, but they cannot supplement his efforts. Perhaps a heterogeneous group should be expected to exert greater pressure on the poorest member, for he is a more serious impediment to the progress of others than is the case when groups are homogeneous. Social pressures may either stimulate or inhibit individual performance, and there seems little basis for predicting that they will have any very uniform effect on process losses.

However, homogeneity-heterogeneity should have a dependable impact on the permanence of groups that perform conjunctive tasks. When groups are heterogeneous, the most able members far exceed the level of competence represented by the poorest individual, and the former may be expected to become discouraged or disgruntled by the latter's ineffective performance. Although such a group may endure for a short period of time, we may anticipate that the most competent members will attempt to form a more productive work team. Thus the group will not be very cohesive, and will probably splinter into smaller aggregations if external conditions permit it to do so. Birds that fly at very different speeds are unlikely to flock together for very long.

However, it should be remembered that the tasks performed by real-life groups are seldom totally conjunctive. Mountain climbers accept a conjunctive relationship with respect to *speed* of locomotion in order that the *safety* of each can be increased. When safety is seen as the goal that defines task demands, the resources of members are almost additive, and the slowest member may contribute as much as anyone else to the security of his colleagues. Needless to say, the ideal arrangement in cases of this kind is one that involves as much homogeneity as possible with respect to the resources that combine conjunctively, and a high average (or total) level of the resources that combine additively.

When tasks are conjunctive, homogeneity is advantageous because it permits a high level of potential productivity and is less likely than heterogeneity to generate dissatisfactions among superior members of the group.

Additive tasks. When a task is additive, potential productivity is unaffected by the heterogeneity of group members. If the goal is to pull as hard as possible on a rope, the group's maximum possible performance is established by the total pulling power of the members; how pulling ability is distributed among the members is irrelevant. The same is true if the task is to stuff as many envelopes as possible, or to shovel snow from a pathway. When task demands permit resources to be used in an additive fashion, heterogeneity of members should have no effect on potential productivity.

Heterogeneity may, however, have an adverse effect on motivation, and be responsible for large process losses. If highly competent individuals are teamed with others who are noticeably less able, the former may feel that they should receive a share of the payoff that is commensurate with their greater contribution to the group's success. Unless rewards are allocated in a manner that reflects the unequal resources of the members, the more competent may be loath to work to their full capacity. They may also be inclined to disassociate themselves from the group when the opportunity arises.

Research bearing on these matters has been reviewed by Gamson (1964). In a series of studies, triads have been confronted by a situation from which no individual can expect a positive outcome unless he works in concert with one of his associates and in opposition to the other. Although this kind of research setting involves the trappings of a competitive game (the two persons who coalesce win points whereas the third wins none), it has yielded insights into the considerations that motivate individuals to combine their efforts, and has provided evidence concerning subjects' conceptions of a fair and reasonable distribution of payoffs. Many of the findings support a "minimum resources" theory which maintains that (a) people prefer large payoffs over small ones, but want the payoff system to be equitable, and (b) an equitable payoff system is one in which rewards are distributed among the members of a coalition in proportion to the resources they have contributed. Given these assumptions, and the fact that only a specific quantity of resources is needed in order to "win," it follows that individuals will prefer to align themselves with whichever of their coparticipants possesses barely enough resources to permit the resulting coalition to succeed. By choosing to unite with a person whose contribution is minimal but adequate, the individual maximizes the importance of his own role in the partnership, and thus stakes his claim to a large but equitable share of the booty. According to this theory, of course, people will expect payoffs to be distributed roughly in proportion to the resources of the participants.

Although empirical results have often tended to support this formulation, they have rarely been very strong, and have sometimes been inconsistent with the theory. Perhaps a desire to obtain the greatest possible payoff occasionally overrides equity considerations; personal friendships, and other extra-task factors may influence decision; or subjects may not understand the rather complicated situation well enough to permit the equity principle to function very systematically. (Gamson has labeled the latter explanation the "utter confusion" theory.) However, it is also possible that subjects understand the situation perfectly, but do not regard a proportional distribution of rewards to be equitable. They may, instead, reason that since neither member of the coalition can win alone, each is indispensable and exercises "pivotal power." Under these circumstances, individuals may expect to share equally in the proceeds of the group action even though one contributes far more resources than the other.

It is noteworthy that bargaining sessions dealing with the distribution of payoffs have tended to produce decisions that represent a compromise between the "minimum resources" and "pivotal power" predictions. The less resourceful member of the coalition typically obtains a share of the payoff that is larger than his resources would suggest he should receive, but a smaller share than is allocated to the member with the greater resources. Such a compromise may reflect an awareness of the role of pivotal power, or the impact of an equity norm that maintains everyone should share alike because individuals' needs are likely to be approximately equal. Of course, pivotal power is a notion that has maximum applicability only when the fund of resources needed to assure a successful outcome is clearly defined, and when it is obvious that resources in excess of that minimum will be of no practical use. These conditions have almost invariably prevailed in the settings created by students of coalition formation, but they are unlikely to exist in many real-life situations. Outside the laboratory it is frequently the case that the total amount of payoff available for distribution is a direct function of the total fund of invested resources. Moreover, even when the amount of payoff is inflexibly prescribed, people are unlikely to know just how large the total investment of resources needs to be in order to assure success. Consequently, the circumstances that enable a small contributor to expect and demand a disproportionately large share of his group's outcomes probably do not occur very often in everyday life.

The reason for this prolonged excursion into the intricacies of coalition research is that the findings tend, on balance, to assert that when resources are unequally distributed, people expect payoffs to be somewhat proportional to investments. This contention has been advanced by Homans (1958) who has argued that people both expect and prefer that rewards be distributed in proportion to the costs individuals incur. A group in which such a pattern of distribution is not employed will seem unattractive to its members, and especially so if members' abilities are highly heterogeneous. We may surmise that those who are most competent will be inclined to malinger (reduce their costs) or to leave the group when the opportunity arises.

The pertinence of the foregoing discussion is not limited to situations in which groups perform additive tasks. It is relevant to any occasion when the expectation of proportional payoffs is thwarted. However, when tasks are additive, everyone does the same thing, and the superior ability of certain members is likely to be especially apparent. Furthermore, many additive tasks require comparatively little interpersonal coordination. (Rope pulling is an exception to the general rule; most additive tasks more closely resemble stuffing envelopes or shoveling snow, and thus permit each person to function as a relatively independent agent.) Miller and Hamblin (1963) reviewed a large number of studies concerned with the impact of equal versus proportional distribution of rewards, and concluded that the effect of the reward system depends on the nature of the task. When the experimental task involved the discussion of issues, or the performance of puzzle-problems, proportional rewards were found to produce lower levels of productivity, presumably because they discouraged interpersonal coordination which was essential for success. However, when tasks were additive and required little real coordination of members' actions (e.g., solving a large number of routine arithmetic problems, moving objects from one place to another), no such effect was evident. Although proportional distribution of rewards did not always lead to greater productivity on such tasks, the modal outcome was clearly in that direction. Because additive relationships typically entail low levels of interpersonal coordination, proportional distribution of rewards can be employed to motivate individuals without seriously interfering with necessary teamwork. Consequently, heterogeneity, if it is not accompanied by a system of proportional rewards, is especially likely to create large process losses when tasks are additive.

In conclusion, we may say that homogeneity-heterogeneity does not affect potential productivity when tasks are additive. However, under certain circumstances heterogeneity may undermine motivation and thus be responsible for large process losses. These effects are most likely to occur when the total amount of payoff is thought to be a direct function of total resources, when no provision is made for proportional distribution of payoffs, when the inequality of members' abilities is highly apparent, and when the task requires relatively little interpersonal coordination.

Discretionary tasks. When members of a group are free to combine their individual outputs in any manner they choose, the task is said to be discretionary. Such freedom is likely to exist only when the goal is to render the best possible judgment concerning the position an object or event occupies on a specified dimension (e.g., judgments concerning weight, length, numerosity, temperature, etc.). As has been noted earlier, in cases of this kind it is always possible to devise a combinatorial system that will translate the judgments of two or more individuals into the correct judgment; consequently, potential productivity is always "perfect," regardless of the homogeneity-heterogeneity of the group. However, the particular combinatorial procedures that must be employed in order to achieve maximum productivity are not independent of the group's composition, and the group's chosen manner of pooling its individual outcomes is likely to reflect the homogeneity-heterogeneity of its members.

If members are perfectly homogeneous with respect to relevant resources, there is no *a priori* basis for weighting one person's contribution more heavily than another's. A simple, unweighted average of the individual judgments permits "errors" that are symmetrically distributed around the correct value to compensate for one another; consequently, the mean or mode tends to be a good group solution. However, if members are heterogeneous with respect to relevant information or abilities, superior performance will be achieved when a more complex, weighted average is "computed"—members with greater ability being accorded more weight than their less competent associates.

Whether groups will actually employ the best possible combinatorial system undoubtedly depends upon a variety of factors, one of which is the accuracy with which members perceive their own homogeneity-heterogeneity. A homogeneous group that inaccurately perceives certain members to be more competent that others is likely to assign unequal weights to its participants, and thus restrict the extent to which opposing errors can compensate for one another. Conversely, a heterogeneous group that believes itself to be homogeneous will probably employ a system of equal weights, and lose a margin of accuracy that might have been achieved by according greater potency to the most competent members.

These issues have not yet received careful attention from empirically minded investigators. Jenness (1932) reported a study suggesting that groups whose members express diverse views before discussing an issue tend to reach more accurate group decisions than do those whose members are in closer accord before the discussion begins. However, it is not at all clear that heterogeneity of views signified heterogeneity of abilities to express accurate judgments. Perhaps, as some authors have suggested, the salutory effect of heterogeneity noted by Jenness reflected a propensity on the part of disagreeing individuals to reexamine their initial assumptions which, in turn, led to an improvement in the quality of the individual judgments that were contributed for group consideration. Additional research into the performance of discretionary tasks must be conducted before confident conclusions can be reached concerning the effects of homogeneity-heterogeneity on process losses.

Divisible tasks. When tasks can advantageously be divided into two or more discretely different subtasks (or must be so divided), potential productivity depends upon the adequacy with which the resources of the available individuals meet the demands of the resulting division of labor. Potential productivity will obviously be highest when the group contains a sufficient number of persons who are strongly qualified to perform each of the specialized work roles. How many such persons are required in order to achieve sufficiency will, of course, depend upon whether the subtasks are disjunctive (one highly qualified person for each subtask is enough), conjunctive (two or more persons may be needed), or additive (the required number of individuals depends upon the specific demands of the subtask, and upon the competence of the highly qualified persons).

If our population consisted entirely of supermen, each of whom could perform any subtask with a high degree of success, all groups would necessarily be homogeneous. Furthermore, homogeneity of this kind would be singularly advantageous, for it would mean that every niche in the work structure would be manned by persons who were eminently qualified to handle their particular jobs. Potential productivity would be maximal, and it would not really matter which person was assigned to perform which function. ("Whoness" would be irrelevant, but high actual productivity might still be obtained only if everyone were highly motivated and if "whatness" and "whenness" were appropriately managed.)

We need not speculate further concerning this imaginary situation; most people are not supermen. Abilities tend to be somewhat specialized, and individuals who are most competent to perform one subtask are likely to be less qualified than their associates to perform another. Unless the total task is extremely easy, each of the subtasks into which it can be divided is likely to call for resources that are not fully available to everyone.

An example will illustrate the advantage of heterogeneity. Golfer A is extremely effective with his woods, but is a poor putter; golfer B excels on the green but is a mediocre driver. If these two persons play as individuals, they may obtain equal scores; although they have very different abilities to perform specific functions, they may be homogeneous with respect to total golf-playing ability. When paired as a team in a tournament that makes success depend upon the sum of the two participants' scores (an "inversely" additive task, since low scores are desirable in golf), no specialization of labor is permitted, and no advantage can accrue to the participants as a consequence of their heterogeneous talents. However, if the rules are changed to permit a team to play only one ball, each member taking those shots he and his partner decide he should execute, heterogeneity becomes an asset. Under these circumstances, a team consisting of persons with complementary strengths and weaknesses will probably defeat a team with equal overall skill whose members are more uniformly competent in all phases of the game, or a team whose members have special skills that are not complementary (e.g., both players are excellent putters but poor drivers). Personnel managers and football coaches obtain the benefits of heterogeneity by deliberately recruiting individuals whose unique skills enable them to play the specialized roles to which they will be assigned.

Group heterogeneity permits high potential productivity when the subtasks that are to be performed call for specialized resources of the kinds possessed by the members. However, heterogeneity necessarily complicates the matching process, and it may have adverse effects on motivation. In order to achieve the beneficial consequences of heterogeneity, members are sometimes required to work permanently on subtasks which they do not find most satisfying, or which seem to carry less prestige than others. Moreover, evidence to be reviewed later suggests that individuals are often most happy when interacting with people like themselves. Thus, although an appropriate pattern of heterogeneity promotes high potential productivity, it may also be responsible for large process losses. The magnitude of such losses is likely to be especially great when individuals' unique qualifications to perform specific functions are not clearly apparent, when prestige systems or time pressures interfere with advantageous matching, or when some subtasks are much less rewarding than others.

Summary: Heterogeneity of abilities. Heterogeneity of abilities tends to establish high levels of potential productivity when tasks are disjunctive. It has the opposite effect when tasks are conjunctive, and is irrelevant to potential productivity when tasks are additive or discretionary. Heterogeneity generally makes prescribed process more difficult to achieve both because it complicates the matching procedure and because it may be responsible for motivational problems.

Heterogeneity of Dispositional Qualities

Few laboratory studies were cited on the previous pages because researchers have shown a strange reluctance to investigate the effects of heterogeneous ability levels on productivity. Perhaps this gap in the empirical literature reflects a feeling that the consequences of diverse abilities on group performance are too obvious to require documentation, or it may reflect psychologists' overriding affinity for studies that examine dispositional variables. Whatever the reason may be, far more attention has been paid to the influence of members' attitudes and personalities than to the effects of their task-relevant abilities. Unfortunately, however, most of the research into the dispositional composition of groups has investigated effects on members' satisfaction or on the ease, efficiency, or volume of interaction in the group. Comparatively little effort has been expended to discover linkages between dispositional qualities and group productivity.

Dispositional qualities and productivity. It is sometimes contended that groups in which members are compatible should function better than those in which members are not compatible. This proposition seems plausible enough, but it is not very meaningful until compatibility is defined and operationalized. According to Schutz (1958), compatibility of personality exists to the degree that one member is inclined to produce the kinds of behaviors another member wants—one person "pulls for" the behaviors the other habitually expresses. For example, a dyad is said to be compatible if one member is inclined to be dominant and the other typically likes to be dominated. Compatibility is also alleged to exist if members' propensities to give and to receive "affection" and "inclusion" are mutually satisfying. According to this view, maximum compatibility occurs when members' inclinations are complementary on all three dimensions, though Schutz acknowledges that, depending on the nature of the situation, compatibility on one dimension may be more critical than on another. Employing paper-and-pencil scales to assess individuals' proclivities to give and receive each of the three kinds of behavior, Schutz assembled compatible and incompatible groups and asked them to work on decision-making and motor assembly tasks. His findings were equivocal and failed to provide very substantial support for the hypothesis that compatibility promotes productivity.

More definitive results were obtained by Moos and Speisman (1962) who assembled dyads consisting of individuals who had obtained very similar or quite dissimilar scores on scales designed to measure dominance. The Schutz instrument and two other tests were employed to evaluate people's propensities to control or to be controlled in social situations, and compatibility was assumed to exist when the dyad contained members who were heterogeneous on these variables. All groups worked on a task that is briefly described by the following exerpt from the experimenter's instructions to his subjects.

> I am interested in how well people can work together. On this table you see three pegs. There are five rings, differing in size, on one of them. The object of this task is to transfer the rings from the peg (designating one peg) to this one (designating another). There are two restrictions in moving the rings: (1) Only one ring may be off the pegs at any one time. (2) You can never put a larger ring on top of a smaller one. You should attempt to complete this task with a minimum number of moves as quickly as you can [p. 192].

Participants were instructed to discuss each move before it was made, and one member was designated by the experimenter to exercise final authority over the decision-making process. Sometimes the individual who had obtained the higher score on dominance was assigned to this role, and sometimes he was not.

The amount of time required to solve the problem was not strongly affected by either the compatibility (heterogeneity) of the dyad or the identity of the person assigned the dominant role. However, the results tended to favor the compatible groups and those in which the more dominant member had been instructed to exercise final authority. The same pattern of outcomes was obtained when the performance criterion was the number of moves. In three of six comparisons, the heterogeneous groups and those in which role and personality were harmonious were found to perform better (fewer moves) than other groups. Although Moos and Speisman's findings are not dramatic or entirely consistent with one another, they suggest that heterogeneity of dominance is sometimes an advantage to the members of a group.

A rather parallel study was conducted by Ghiselli and Lodahl (1958). Groups containing two to four members were randomly assembled from a population of persons who had responded to scales designed to measure self-reliance, general activity, and willingness to take action on the basis of one's own appraisal of situations. Although these characteristics are not perfectly congruent with dominance, they appear to involve somewhat the same social tendencies. Groups worked on a task that has been described earlier in this book; they operated electrical switches that controlled the progress of two toy trains along a circular track. Because the trains were oriented in opposite directions, it was necessary to coordinate their movements, and thus avoid head-on collisions. Groups were urged to run both trains around the track as many times as possible during 12 three-min trials. Nobody was assigned a dominant role in any group.

The findings indicated that although the average "dominance" of the members of a group was unrelated to productivity, the distribution of dominance scores had a marked effect on group success. Specifically, groups in which the discrepancy between the dominance scores earned by the highest and second-highest scoring members was large completed significantly more train trips than other groups. When three or four members were included in a group, the discrepancy between the two top-scoring individuals was critical, but the discrepancy between other pairs of members was not. The results appear to indicate that productivity was highest when the "natural" dominance of the most ascendant person was not contested by anyone else. Heterogeneous groups were more successful than homogeneous ones, but it was only the difference between the top member and all the rest that really mattered.

Further consideration of these two studies suggests reasons why heterogeneity of dominance is sometimes advantageous. Both investigations involved tasks that are unlikely to be performed very well unless all participants submit to the will or direction of a single coordinating agent. The peg-and-ring problem is unlikely to be solved very rapidly by a dyad that attempts to maintain equality of influence by having members alternately decide the next move, or by compromising the conflicting suggestions of the individual participants. The task is essentially unitary in that all steps in its performance are logically interconnected. Unless the total solution is discovered by a single individual, the group will be forced to rely upon ineffective trial-and-error exploration. The two-trains problem also requires a variety of unitary action. Although different electrical switches can advantageously be managed by different persons, it is obvious that effective group performance can occur only if the behaviors of all are guided by a plan of action. Probably any of several different plans will work tolerably well, but a mixture of two or more plans will invite disaster. Consequently, it is important that a single person take charge, and that others do his bidding. To the degree that one member of a group is inclined to be more dominant than others, the desired polarization of planning is likely to occur: One member will enforce his unitary solution to the peg-and-ring problem upon the other, and one person will coordinate the activities by which two trains are sped around a track.

In cases of this kind, the advantage of heterogeneity of dominance should be greatest when members are not officially assigned specialized roles. In the absence of a ready-made role system, members must decide for themselves what kind of work patterns to employ, and whether a single person should be made responsible for the coordination of activities. The presence of a single individual who is inclined to be much more dominant than others should predispose the group to adopt a polarized pattern of authority, which is exactly what is needed to accomplish tasks of the kind under consideration here. However, if an experimenter, an institution, or society at large nominates someone to exercise authority and to manage coordinational problems, a highly ascendent person is not needed in order to assure the emergence of such polarization. Of course, a naturally dominant person may still have a beneficial effect on productivity if he happens to be the member who is assigned the critical role; his natural inclination to dominate others may permit him to perform his assigned function especially well. However, if someone else is arbitrarily matched with the ascendent role, the integrative function is likely to be less forcefully enacted, and the individual for whom dominance is a "way of life" may challenge the authority of the designated office holder. If this occurs, the needed polarization of influence will be threatened and group productivity may suffer.

Some support for these speculations is provided by the Moos and Speisman study which found that dyads in which the more dominant person was assigned the dominant role were more productive than those in which he was not. More convincing evidence is offered by a study conducted by Smelser (1961) which has been reviewed in Chapter 3. When the more dominant members of dyads were assigned responsibility for coordinating the activities by which the two-trains task was performed, productivity was significantly higher than when nobody received any special assignment. Dyads that were not provided with a ready-made role system functioned significantly better than those in which the less dominant member was instructed to exercise authority. Given that members of a group vary in propensity to dominate, they are likely to develop their own polarized pattern, and this emergent role system will probably function better than one that arbitrarily mismatches members and roles.

The foregoing discussion suggests that heterogeneity of dominance should have little or no effect on productivity when members of groups are randomly assigned to specific roles from which they cannot escape. To be sure, heterogeneity will be advantageous in those instances when individuals happen to receive roles for which they are peculiarly qualified by virtue of their unique personalities. Such fortunate arrangements will sometimes occur due to chance factors, but when they do not, heterogeneous groups will experience more serious "mismatches" than will homogeneous groups. Thus the net effect of heterogeneity on the productivity of randomly assigned groups should tend, on the average, to be very slight. Evidence on this point has been provided by Marvin Shaw (1960) who randomly assigned individuals to positions (roles) in communication networks and noted the facility with which they collectively solved the "common symbol" problem. Subsequent analysis of data concerning the personalities of participants revealed no consistent relationship between the heterogeneity of members on a measure of "individual prominence" and their success as a group. Heterogeneity with respect to intelligence and "acceptance of authority" also failed to correlate with group productivity. Heterogeneity of personality can affect productivity either by influencing the way groups divide their task into subtasks, or by affecting the appropriateness with which members are assigned to subtasks. However, when members are randomly matched with predetermined roles, neither of these possibilities can operate, and the impact of heterogeneity is muted.

It should be apparent that the foregoing discussion is predicated on the assumption that the group task is one that can only, or most effectively, be performed when a single individual serves as a coordinating or disagreement-resolving agent. However, some tasks (e.g., envelope stuffing, mountain climbing) are probably best performed by individuals who function as comparatively independent workers operating as equals within a system of constraints imposed by the environment. When this is the case, heterogeneity of dominance may induce participants to weight one another in ways that interfere with productivity. Furthermore, if dominance is negatively correlated with task-relevant skills, as it may be in some instances, heterogeneity is likely to favor a disadvantageous matching of individuals with roles.

We may summarize the arguments and evidence presented above by saying that although heterogeneity of dominance represents "compatibility" of the kind posited by Schutz and others, such heterogeneity should not be expected to have a uniformly facilitative effect on productivity. Depending largely on the nature of the task and the rules under which the task must be performed, we should anticipate that heterogeneity will sometimes impede performance. Available data are sketchy and incomplete, but seem consistent with these conclusions.

A propensity to dominate others is not the only dispositional attribute that has been examined by researchers concerned with the effects of group composition. Hoffman and Maier (1961) used the Guilford-Zimmerman Temperament Survey to measure ten different personality variables, and then assembled groups consisting of four persons whose profiles on these variables were very similar (homogeneous groups) or dissimilar (heterogeneous groups). All groups worked on four discussion tasks that called for creative or integrative solutions to complex problems. For example, one task entailed deciding how the limited funds available for student assistance should be divided among several qualified applicants for financial aid, and another concerned the resolution of disagreements among members of a work team. On three of the four tasks, heterogeneous groups were found to produce more creative solutions than homogeneous groups; on the fourth neither type of group enjoyed an advantage. Homogeneity-heterogeneity appeared to have no effect on participants' satisfaction with the quality of group solutions. In attempting to explain the superiority of their heterogeneous groups, Hoffman and Maier postulated that diversity of personality is associated with diversity of problem-solving perspectives. If the members of a group are very different kinds of people, they will probably possess a wide assortment of views concerning the resolution of complex problems; and when the aim is to produce a highly creative solution, multiple alternatives are desirable. The greater the number of options from which the group may choose, or the larger the number that are available to be integrated into a novel composite, the better the group's product can be.

Hoffman and Maier's interpretation seems plausible, but we do not really know whether (or when) heterogeneity of personality is correlated with heterogeneity of task-relevant views. It is not difficult to imagine that one or more of the ten dispositional variables that served to distinguish heterogeneous from homogeneous groups was associated with problem-solving perspectives, but we do not know which one(s) may have been critical. Our ability to generalize Hoffman and Maier's findings would be greater if information were available concerning the way each of many different personality variables is associated with orientation toward, and competence to work on, each of many kinds of problems.

The second part of Hoffman and Maier's interpretation is not without empirical support. As noted earlier in this chapter, Jenness (1932) found that groups whose members held diverse views concerning an issue were more likely to produce a correct decision than those in which initial impressions were highly homogeneous. Torrance *et al.* (1955) confronted military personnel with hypothetical situations in which survival depended upon the ability of a group to discover ways of avoiding natural and man-made dangers. Groups whose members initially disagreed concerning the best course of action tended to produce better final decisions than those in which agreement was high from the outset. The authors suggest that disagreement provides an increased scale of judgment and thus promotes superior decisions. It may also encourage members of groups to evaluate their premises with considerable care, and thus prevent hasty and inappropriate conclusions.

The foregoing discussion has been focused on the consequences of dispositional heterogeneity when a single coordinating agent is needed to facilitate performance, or when diversity of resources or of individual "prejudices" is an advantage. However, heterogeneity of personality may also be beneficial when a group's success depends primarily upon the quality of its temporal programming. Tasks of this kind have been described earlier in this book. Mintz (1951) asked each of several persons to remove a cone from a jug before it was dampened by an inflowing stream of water. The neck of the jug was large enough to permit only one cone to pass at a time. Kelley *et al.* (1965) told subjects they might escape an impending electrical shock by pressing a switch for three seconds, but this avenue of escape could not be used by two persons simultaneously. In situations of this kind, everyone possesses the resources needed to perform his prescribed act. Furthermore, everyone realizes that interpersonal behaviors must be precisely sequenced. However, task rules do not permit communication of the kind that will allow a single individual to serve as a coordinating agent; participants must evolve their own group solution to the question "who shall act when?" If any two persons insist on being first, no one can succeed, and if everyone waits for everyone else, failure is inevitable. Efficient performance can be achieved only if members of the group somehow arrange themselves in an orderly queue and proceed to "escape" one at a time.

With these considerations in mind, Kelley *et al.* suggested that a group is most likely to be successful if its members hold varying views of the situation—some experiencing greater anxiety and urgency than others. Data obtained by Kelley and his associates did not provide clear support for this contention, but these authors suggest that their procedures may have consituted an inadequate test.

Escape tasks are not the only ones that call for temporal programming. When two or more persons discuss an issue, it is imperative that they take turns expressing their views. If everyone talks at once, nothing very productive can happen, and if everyone waits for everyone else, the outcome is a sterile silence. Perhaps a dyad consisting of two extremely talkative persons will create so many "traffic jams in the mouth of the jug" that its participants will both become inactive, whereas a dyad composed of a talkative and a nontalkative person may proceed with greater alacrity. The necessity to form a queue also exists whenever several members of a group must use the same tool or occupy the same space while performing certain aspects of their task. Situations of this kind are generally governed by explicit role systems that provide the necessary temporal coordination, but when they are not, heterogeneity of dispositional qualities may be advantageous.

It should not be concluded that heterogeneity of dispositional qualities is always a boon. Triandis (1960) seated the two members of his *ad hoc* groups at opposite sides of a table; a cardboard screen prevented them from seeing one another. Each person was given two sketches that depicted emotional expressions. One of the sketches was the same for both members of the dyad, and the assigned task was to discover which picture was the shared one. Communication was limited to an exchange of "messages" consisting of checkmarks on 7-step graphic scales. Thus, for example, a subject might tell his partner that one of his sketches deserved a rating of 6 on a continuum that ranged from intelligent to unintelligent, or a rating of 3 on a scale labeled depressed-excited. Participants were encouraged to communicate in this fashion for 12 min and then attempted to identify the shared sketch. Each group had six trials each of which involved a different set of three sketches.

Triandis was interested in the effect of heterogeneity of members' cognitive dispositions upon their success when functioning as dyads. Consequently, in an earlier individual session he had asked each participant to describe the differences between several sketches similar to those used in the experimental sessions. Pairs of subjects who had spontaneously employed the same descriptive dimensions (e.g., happy-sad) when working alone were categorized as having high "attribute similarity," whereas pairs that had used very different dimensions when performing the preliminary exercise were said to possess low "attribute similarity." When working as a group, the former were found to be more successful in identifying the shared sketches. Thus, given the particular demands imposed by Triandis' task, homogeneity of cognitive propensities was a distinct advantage.

Similar findings have been reported by Runkel (1956) who noted that college students who stressed the same underlying dimension as did their instructor when making judgments tended to obtain better grades in the course than did students who emphasized other dimensions. This result was obtained even when the student and instructor assigned phenomena to very different positions on the dimensions they chose to employ; thus the critical consideration was not homogeneity of judgments, but homogeneity of criteria for making judgments. Apparently two people can communicate most effectively with one another if they characteristically emphasize the same cognitive dimensions.

It is not difficult to reconcile the two seemingly contradictory sets of studies cited previously. Heterogeneity of dispositional qualities should promote productivity when it encourages a felicitous distribution of labor and an appropriate sequencing of actions. It may also have a beneficial effect if the dispositional variable on which members are heterogeneous is correlated with task relevant resources. When this is the case, the most competent members of heterogeneous groups will be more resourceful than the most able members of homogeneous groups. Consequently, the former groups have higher potential to perform disjunctive tasks than do the latter. On the other hand, heterogeneity will inhibit actual productivity to the degree that it seriously impairs communication processes or lowers members' motivation to perform as a group. The former effect is likely to be especially serious when, as in the case of the Triandis and Runkel studies, the need for unique resources and specialized role performances is minimal, but the task requires accurate interpersonal communication. Under these circumstances, the possible advantages of heterogeneity are muted, while the detrimental consequences are free to occur. The impact of heterogeneity on motivation will be discussed on subsequent pages.

Dispositional qualities and motivation. It is sometimes alleged that "birds of a feather flock together," and that homogeneous groups should therefore be expected to command a higher level of motivation from their members than heterogeneous groups. Evidence bearing on these contentions has been obtained by examining the reported satisfaction of individuals who have participated in social interaction with persons who are similar (or dissimilar) to themselves.

Many researchers have investigated the marital satifaction of individuals who resemble their spouses on one or another dispositional or sociological variable. Although the findings of such inquiries are not unequivocal, they appear to indicate that marriages are more likely to be happy if spouses have similar interests, attitudes, and values than if they do not. Results bearing on personality needs have been notably inconsistent, some studies supporting the hypothesis that "opposites attract" and others contradicting that view.

Homogeneity of attitudes and values has also been found to promote interpersonal attraction in other settings. Newcomb (1961) elicited expressions of "life values" from 17 male college students at the time they occupied a rooming house, and then observed the formation of sociometric preferences among members of the group. Friendships were found to develop most readily among persons who had expressed similar values. Research by Izard (1960), Byrne (1961) and many others has revealed a positive relationship between actual (or perceived) agreement with associates and liking for them. However, the effect of "complementary personality needs" (e.g., dominance-submission) on interpersonal attraction has been less thoroughly documented.

The bulk of the available evidence suggests that similar individuals tend to seek one another's company. This conclusion should not be construed to mean that homogeneous groups manifest greater task motivation than heterogeneous ones. People who flock together because they find one another attractive may or may not be inclined to work hard on a joint task. Perhaps they will be content merely to savor the joys of intimate companionship, or be reluctant to mix business with pleasure. Sociability does not necessarily breed productivity. Evidence bearing on this issue is mixed.

Husband (1940) noted that pairs of friends did slightly better than pairs of nonfriends on six of seven experimental tasks, and Van Zelst (1952) reported that construction workers who chose to work together were more productive than those who had been assigned to work teams by management. In the former study, the superiority of friendship pairs may not have been a consequence of greater task motivation; it may instead have reflected the speed and ease with which friends can resolve organizational problems when asked to cooperate for very brief periods of time on tasks that are unlikely to endanger their friendship. In the case of Van Zelst study, it is unclear whether the construction workers chose one another for reasons of congeniality or because their previous contacts had demonstrated that they could work well together. Findings that are more directly relevant to the issue of task motivation have been reported by Scofield (1960) who found that groups of adolescent girls who were nonfriends performed more persistently on an imposed task than did groups of friends. Parallel results have been published by McGrath (1962) who observed the performance of rifle teams over a period of several weeks and noted that groups in which interpersonal attraction was a matter of great concern showed smaller improvements in performance than did those in which task orientation was more typical.

Because research comparing the performance of friends and nonfriends has rarely focused directly upon the events that transpire in task-oriented groups (who does what when?), it is unclear whether friendship affects the solution of organizational problems, the level of task motivation, or both. However, it is apparent that people sometimes prefer to work with nonfriends. Jennings (1943) asked the female inmates of a corrective institution to list the names of associates with whom they preferred to participate in intimate, friendly, nonwork situations. Inmates were also asked to specify acquaintances with whom they liked to work on assigned jobs within the institutional setting. The two lists were not the same; associates who were especially desirable as confidants or as intimate friends were not universally chosen as work partners. Jennings suggested that dispositional qualities strongly affect acceptability in intimate, "psyche groups," but that membership in task-oriented "socio-groups" is influenced by collective impersonal criteria.

Homogeneity of dispositional qualities seems to promote friendship, but we may surmise that it sometimes has adverse effects on task motivation, particularly when work activities are extended over long periods of time.

Summary: Heterogeneity of dispositional qualities. Although dispositional qualities affect members' ratings of their satisfaction with group experiences and outcomes (see the reviews by Mann, 1959, and Heslin, 1964), evidence concerning the impact of such variables on actual productivity is sparse and contradictory. The effect of dispositional heterogeneity on performance may be expected to depend upon task demands. When an adequate role system is available to guide collective action, dispositional qualities may have little effect on outcomes. In the absence of a role system, heterogeneity may either promote or inhibit task motivation and the solution of organizational problems.

Group Size and Composition

As was noted in the last chapter, the effect of group size on productivity often reflects a relationship between size and the ability of the group's most (or least) competent member, or between size and the resources of the persons who are available to be matched with specific subtasks. When this is the case, it is the competence of specific members, rather than the number of members, that is the critical determinant of potential productivity. In other instances, size is a disadvantage because it means that the "weakest link in the chain" is likely to be very weak. In the paragraphs that follow, we will examine relationships between size and composition more carefully, and attempt to infer some consequences of such relationships.

Everyday experience suggests that the members of large groups are generally less similar to one another than the members of small groups. Perhaps, as students of clique formation have sometimes noted, very small groups tend to be highly selective and to admit only like-minded individuals to membership. If this is true, small groups may be small because only a few like-minded recruits are available; a preference for homogeneity limits group size. But it is also possible that small groups are homogeneous *because they are small,* rather than small because they are homogeneous.

Consider what will happen if we randomly assemble groups of varying sizes from a population in which an attribute is normally distributed. As noted earlier (see pp. 70), a single, randomly selected individual will, on the average, fall at the middle of the population distribution. Members of two-person groups will tend to occupy position at the 33rd and 67th percentiles, and members of triads will, on the average, cluster at the 25th, 50th, and 75th percentiles. When four persons are included in the group, they will tend to fall at the 20th, 40th, 60th, and 80th percentiles. Although these statements express statistical tendencies rather than immutable facts about every group of a given size, they reveal an important relationship between size and composition. Large groups are likely to include a more heterogeneous assortment of members than are small groups. By chance alone, the highest and lowest scoring individuals will resemble one another less as group size increases.

The second column of Table 5.2 reports the expected discrepancies between the extreme members of groups containing two to eight persons. Differences are expressed in standard score units rather than percentiles because the former provide a more accurate basis for comparison. It is apparent that

TABLE 5.2

Group Size and the Heterogeneity of Members [a]

Group size	Difference between highest and lowest scoring members	Difference between highest and second-highest scoring members	Average difference between adjacently ranked members
2	.88	.88	.88
3	1.35	.67	.67
4	1.68	.59	.56
5	1.94	.54	.48
6	2.14	.51	.43
7	2.30	.48	.38
8	2.44	.46	.35

[a]All differences are expressed in standard score units, and represent averages that should be obtained when many groups of a specified size are randomly assembled from a population in which the measured attribute is normally distributed.

discrepancies increase (but at a decelerating rate) as group size increases, and that eight-person groups are likely to contain a range of "talent" or "disposition" that is almost three times as great as that of dyads. Unless steps are taken to negate this trend, an increase in group size will generate an increase in heterogeneity. Consequently, the coordination problems of large groups are likely to be especially complex both because there are many persons whose behaviors must be coordinated and because the many persons have highly diverse resources and dispositional qualities.

The third column of Table 5.2 reports expected discrepancies between the highest and second-highest ranking members of groups. The larger the group, the more similar these two individuals will tend to be. Thus the most competent or the most "dispositionally qualified" person is likely to be less unique in large groups than in small ones. Competition for dominance or status should therefore tend to be more acute in large groups, for no single individual will clearly surpass all others in requisite skills or personal propensities. The coordination problems that may follow from such a rivalry have already been noted in our discussion of Ghiselli and Lodahl's (1958) research; groups were more successful in running toy trains around a track if one member had scored much higher than anyone else on a measure of propensity to dominate.

The last column of Table 5.2 indicates the average discrepancies between adjacently ranked members of groups of varying sizes. In an eight-person group, members will tend to differ from their most similar associates by only .35 standard score units, whereas in a three-person group the comparable difference will be almost twice as large (.67 standard score units). The more members there are, the more similar any member will be to someone else in the group. Thus, although large groups are heterogeneous in the sense that they contain a diverse assortment of individuals (see the second column of Table 5.2), they are homogeneous in the sense that any participant is likely to find a few associates who share his skills, attitudes, or general orientation. This combination of heterogeneity and homogeneity should expose large groups to the danger of splintering or clique formation. Research has in fact documented the tendency of such groups to break into smaller parts. Thus, for example, Hare (1952) found that when discussing the relative importance of various pieces of camping equipment, small groups of boy scouts had little difficulty achieving consensus, but groups of a dozen boys generally broke into two or three subgroups and often failed to reach agreement. Similarity in the midst of diversity sometimes permits a high level of potential productivity, but it is likely to be responsible for large process losses.

The previous analysis suggests that, by chance alone, large groups will tend to be more heterogeneous than small ones, though the individual members of large groups will be less unique than those of smaller groups. Of course policies may be instituted to reduce these effects of size, but they are unlikely to eliminate them. In a survey of 500 real-life groups, Hemphill (1949) obtained a correlation of .31 between size and heterogeneity on a variety of sociological variables. Similarly, Hollingshead (1949) noted that high school cliques tend to be both very small and much more homogeneous than larger groups or the population from which they are drawn. In studies of this kind, it is not entirely clear whether size is the cause or the effect of homogeneity-heterogeneity, but free-forming groups appear to manifest relationships that parallel those suggested by Table 5.2.

Summary

Members of groups may be heterogeneous with respect to task-relevant resources and/or dispositional qualities. Relationships among various abilities and dispositional qualities are not yet very clearly established, and a group that is known to be heterogeneous with respect to one variable may also be heterogeneous on several others as well. Consequently, the impact of any specific type of heterogeneity may be subject to a variety of interpretations.

Heterogeneity of task-relevant abilities tends to establish high levels of potential productivity when the task is disjunctive. It has the opposite effect when tasks are conjunctive, and is irrelevant to potential productivity when the task is additive. Heterogeneity of abilities generally makes prescribed process more difficult to achieve because it complicates the weighting or matching procedure and because it may be responsible for motivational problems.

The effect of heterogeneity of dispositional qualities on performance should depend upon task demands. If no role system is available, heterogeneity may encourage the development of needed specialization of function and polarization of work activities. It may also facilitate (or inhibit) the matching of persons with subtasks they are most qualified to perform. Evidence concerning such effects is very sparse and inconclusive.

Large groups tend to be more heterogeneous than small ones, though individual members of the former are typically less uniquely different from their associates than are their counterparts in small groups.

Chapter 6

Motivation

How well a group *can* perform a task depends upon the adequacy with which members' resources meet task demands. How well the group *actually* performs depends, in addition, upon the willingness of members to contribute their resources to the collective effort, and upon the success with which members coordinate their individual activities. Actual productivity equals potential productivity when there are no losses due to nonoptimal motivation or coordination. This chapter examines some of the variables that affect motivation and which, therefore, may be expected to influence the productivity of groups.

Motivation is, of course, an exceedingly complex matter—one which has commanded the interest of scholars since the time of the ancient Greeks. It has been an issue of central concern to psychologists from Freud to the present day. In this book, we can do no more than examine a few issues that bear most directly upon group performance. Attention will be focused upon two questions: How are the motivations of an individual affected by the presence of other people, and how should rewards be allocated to group members in order to minimize process losses?

The Presence of Observers or Co-Workers

Social Facilitation and Inhibition

Participation in group activity exposes the individual to innumerable stimuli that do not impinge upon the solitary worker. Ordinarily, the individual is aware of the presence of his associates, and he observes their behaviors as he goes about his work. Furthermore, he knows that his colleagues may be monitoring and evaluating his performance. Does the presence of other members affect his motivation and task behavior?

Since the turn of the century, researchers have repeatedly noted that the performance of certain tasks appears to be facilitated by the real or imagined presence of co-workers or passive spectators. When in the presence of others, human subjects have been found to turn fishing reels more rapidly, to pull more vigorously on an apparatus designed to measure finger strength, and to solve simple arithmetic problems more rapidly. These and similar findings led Allport (1924) to suggest that the sight and sound of others working on the same problem somehow augment the individual's motivation and prompt him to perform more effectively. However, the validity of Allport's argument was undermined by the subsequent discovery that performance is sometimes facilitated by the presence of associates who are not working on the same task but are merely observing the individual's behaviors.

Although social facilitation is a common phenomenon, social inhibition also occurs. People who work in the company of others tend to learn nonsense syllables less rapidly than people who work alone; they are also *less accurate* in solving arithmetic problems, less successful in learning finger mazes, and more prone to err when working on syllogistic reasoning tasks. The effects of co-workers and spectators on individual performance are comparatively easy to detect, but difficult to explain.

The mere presence of others. Many of the troublesome inconsistencies in the research findings are resolved by a theory proposed by Zajonc (1966). According to this view, performance is facilitated when the task requires the individual to produce *well-learned* behaviors; it is inhibited when the task involves *learning new responses* or the performance of behaviors that are not yet well learned. Seen in this light, facilitation and inhibition reflect essentially the same motivational principle: individuals who work in the presence of others are more highly "aroused" than those who work alone. High arousal prompts people to produce behaviors that rank high in their "response hierarchy." Thus when the "correct" reaction is one that has been very well learned, high arousal facilitates performance, but when the task requires responses that are new or only poorly learned, arousal has an inhibitory effect.

Zajonc's theory is consistent with a wide array of research findings. People who are asked to do fairly routine, "easy" tasks generally seem to be more productive if they work under arousal-provoking circumstances (e.g., time pressures, instructions to outproduce rivals, the prospect of receiving an attractive reward for their proficiency or a noxious punishment for their inefficiency). And when the task involves complex or poorly learned behaviors, such circumstances are sometimes found to inhibit performance. Furthermore, the great majority of the findings generated by research dealing with social facilitation-inhibition seem, at least by hindsight, to fit the pattern specified by Zajonc: The presence of others tends to facilitate the performance of well-learned responses and to inhibit the learning and performance of new responses. Of course, there are limitations on the applicability of this generalization; a person who is totally unmotivated to learn a new behavior when alone may be sufficiently aroused to do the job when in the company of others, and a well-learned speech that can be delivered flawlessly in private may be incoherently rendered when the speaker confronts his audience. Apparently, either too much or too little arousal inhibits performance; what constitutes the ideal level of motivation seems to depend upon the degree to which the individual has already learned and rehearsed the appropriate response.

Two aspects of Zajonc's theory are open to serious question: The arousal which is responsible for social facilitation or inhibition may not be the blind, directionless surge of energy which Zajonc pictured it to be, and the *mere presence* of others may not be sufficient to instigate it. Although unchanneled drive states may occur (see Schachter, 1964), the conditions that provoke arousal usually prejudice the individual's behavior in one direction or another. People are generally aroused to perform specific tasks, to obtain specific outcomes, or to avoid discriminable noxious stimuli. Whether the arousal that powers one course of action is the same as that which prompts another is not entirely clear. The physiological processes associated with the hunger drive are different, at least in detail, from those implicated in the sex drive, but we cannot be so confident about differences between the arousal states that favor one thought or perception over another. When the facts about arousal are eventually known they may indicate that blind, indiscriminate mobilization of energy is a rare occurrence among adult human beings, and that most instances of arousal entail the kind of directional commitment implied by the concept of motivation.

Recent evidence suggests that the presence of others is arousing only (or primarily) when the others who are present are believed to be in a position to affect one's outcomes. This is the case when others are expected to evaluate one's performance (perhaps adversely), to demonstrate by their own superior proficiency that one's performance is inferior, or to deprive one of desired goals. Cottrell, Wack, Sekerak, and Rittle, (1968) discovered that the presence of blindfolded "spectators" failed to enhance the emission of behaviors that ranked high in people's response hierarchies, and Henchy and Glass (1968) found that dominant responses were given more frequently by subjects who believed that an audience was evaluating their performance than by subjects who worked alone or before a "nonevaluating" audience. Together these two studies suggest that *mere presence* is not sufficient to produce social facilitation or inhibition. However, even if mere presence does have arousal qualities, we may doubt that it is a very important determinant of everyday behavior. In real-life settings, the people who are present almost invariably are in a position to evaluate, excell, compete, or otherwise shape the individual's behaviors—mere presence is a rare phenomenon.

Evaluation apprehension. If mere presence is unlikely to account for much variation in people's motivations, what is it about the presence of others that matters? As already noted, arousal seems to occur when the others who are present are in a position to evaluate one's performance. This is especially likely to be the case when the others are performing the same task as the individual himself; each persons's own level of performance serves as a convenient baseline against which to evaluate the work of others, and ego-defensive motives are likely to encourage comparisons. However, others need not be working on the same task in order to prompt evaluation apprehension. If they have worked on the task in the past, or have observed someone else work on it, they have a frame of reference for evaluation. Men who have never played basketball can and do judge the skill of professional players, and women who are unable to knit often evaluate the quality of knitted garments. Unless an activity is extremely esoteric, an observer is a potential evaluator.

Needless to say, evaluation apprehension may have either an adverse or favorable effect on performance. Which will occur appears to depend in part upon the degree to which the task has been mastered; a skilled athlete is likely to perform best before an audience, whereas a rank amateur is not. However, evaluation apprehension is not a blind, unprejudiced energizer. It steers behavior as well as propelling it. It motivates people to do those acts which are likely to elicit favorable evaluations and to neglect those which will not be evaluated. Thus Allport's (1924) subjects produced *many* word associations when in the presence of coactors who were potential evaluators; this is what they had been told to do and, therefore, what they needed to do in order to be evaluated favorably. On the other hand, their word associations were not very unusual or imaginative; quantity, the dimension on which evaluation was likely to be based, was facilitated, but quality was inhibited.

In some settings, evaluation apprehension clearly inhibits task performance. Studies of factory work have repeatedly revealed the effect of informal rules concerning what constitutes a proper day's work. Employees who are entirely capable of exceeding the informal standard often yield to evaluative pressures even when they could earn additional income by being more productive. Similarly, college students sometimes settle for the "gentleman's grade" of B (or C) because to do otherwise would invite adverse evaluations from peers. Research on conformity pressures has repeatedly demonstrated that many people, on hearing the manifestly incorrect judgments of co-workers, endorse their associates' views rather than become targets of criticism. Evaluation apprehension is a powerful motive which may either facilitate or inhibit task performance. It is likely to have a facilitating effect when task behaviors have been well learned and are expected to evoke favorable appraisals. Inhibiting effects may be anticipated when task behaviors have been poorly learned or are likely to elicit adverse appraisals.

Competition. A detailed discussion of competition occurs in a subsequent section of this chapter where competition is compared to cooperation. Here it is sufficient to note that people often realize they are contriently interdependent with respect to desired payoffs. When the supply of a desired commodity is fixed or limited, one person's success increases the likelihood that another will fail or, at best, obtain only a meager reward. The payoff in question may, of course, be a favorable evaluation which can be obtained only by performing at least as well as one's co-workers. When evaluations are distributed in this manner, an individual who works in the presence of his competitors may be more highly motivated to do whatever is required than one who works alone and does not even realize that his productivity will be compared with that of others. Thus, Dashiell (1930) repeated some of Allport's work on social facilitation, modifying the procedures slightly and taking special care to control subjects' beliefs about the way their performances would be evaluated. His data led him to conclude that competitive attitudes were primarily responsible for the faster, but less accurate task behaviors of subjects who worked in the presence of others. Comparison and differential evaluation become especially salient possibilities when one works in the presence of others who are doing the same task.

Allport realized that people seek favorable evaluations when participating in coacting groups, and one of his studies appears to have demonstrated that fact in a dramatic way. Subjects who either worked alone or in the presence of co-workers judged the pleasantness-unpleasantness of odors, some of which were extremely disagreeable while others were very pleasing. The important finding was that bad odors were judged less obnoxious, and good ones less pleasant, by subjects who worked in the coacting situation. Allport concluded that the presence of others accentuates the salience of comparison and thus motivates the individual to avoid expressing judgments that might deviate substantially from those of other persons. Consequently, the individual tempers his inclination to give extreme ratings to stimuli. ("Others can disagree with me only by feeling that an odor is less extreme than I do: I can protect myself against adverse comparison and evaluation by rating extreme odors a little more moderately than I otherwise would.") Of course, the effect of anticipated comparison and evaluation need not always be an increase in moderation; if an individual believes that others prefer extreme positions (or regard fast work as better than slow work), evaluation apprehension may motivate him to compete by espousing extreme positions (or by working fast).

Modeling. Whenever an individual can observe the task-relevant behaviors of his co-workers, he may model his own activities after theirs. Research (see, for example, Bandura and Walters, 1964) had indicated that this is most likely to happen when co-workers are observed to be making progress or to be receiving rewards for their efforts. However, modeling also occurs when there is no clear indication that the model is succeeding. The observed behaviors of associates suggest ways of proceeding which might not otherwise be apparent to the individual, and the fact that associates are pursuing a particular course of action tends to legitimize or endorse its use as a tactic for solving the problem at hand.

Modeling may do more than influence the direction an individual's actions will take. It may also affect the intensity of the individual's motivation. Kelley *et al.* (1965) in a study described earlier (see Chapter 4) noted that one person's fear-provoked behaviors may intensify the fear experienced by another. People who are extremely frightened are likely to rush for the exit of a burning theater. Others who are not initially so frightened can scarcely avoid noticing this behavior, and are likely to construe it as evidence that the situation is indeed perilous. Because the actions of the most frightened people are more readily observed than those of persons who remain calm, the modeling process tends to intensify fears and to encourage unrestrained escape behaviors. When Kelley *et al.* arranged their experimental situation so that subjects would be certain to observe that some of their co-workers were behaving calmly, the tendency of the group to stampede was significantly reduced.

Whether modeling will have a facilitating or inhibiting effect on performance obviously depends upon whether the model performs in accordance with task demands. Presumably it also depends upon the degree to which the modeled responses have already been learned, and upon the intensity of the motivation experienced by individuals in the absence of the model.

Summary: The Presence of Observers or Co-Workers

When people work in the presence of an audience or of co-workers who are doing the same task, their performance may be either facilitated or inhibited. Evaluation apprehension, competition, and modeling tend to intensify arousal and steer behavior along specific channels. Depending upon the complexity of the prescribed task, and upon the skill of the individual, increased arousal may have either a beneficial or deleterious effect upon performance. The steering effects of evaluation apprehension, competition, and modeling may also be either helpful or harmful; they should facilitate performance when they guide behaviors in directions demanded by the task, but inhibit it when they channel behavior in other directions.

Members of groups are seldom passive observers of one another's performance, or co-workers who merely function in one another's presence. Usually each member interacts with others, and has the capacity to exert a fairly direct influence on their performance and rewards. When this is the case, the subtle effects discussed previously are likely to be overshadowed by the impact of the group's system for allocating payoffs.

Payoff Systems

One of the most widely verified psychological principles maintains that people do that for which they are rewarded—or believe they will be rewarded. It is sometimes difficult to specify in advance the kinds of payoffs for which a particular individual will work, or even to identify them after he has acted, for human beings are motivated to gain and retain a much wider assortment of rewards than are rats or chimpanzees. However, the basic principle is valid: If you want John Doe to perform act X, make it seem worthwhile for him to do so.

When John Doe works alone, it may be comparatively easy to manipulate the amount and kind of payoffs that are available to him. A teacher or experimenter may control his receipt of money, praise, or status-bestowing feedback, and make these rewards contingent upon his task performance. However, when John Doe operates as a member of a group, the group itself is likely to exercise partial control of his payoffs. He may be rewarded for task-irrelevant behaviors, or offered payoffs that are too small to induce him to do his best. Groups sometimes reinforce members for clowning, being sociable, or working slowly rather than for contributing to task performance.

Even when rewards are contingent upon the quality of task performance, an individual's payoffs may depend upon the quality of his associates' behaviors as well as his own. This is the case when the amount of reward available to the group is determined by the effectiveness of its collective action, or when each members's share of the available payoff is a function of his contribution relative to that of other members. Game theorists have explored the ways in which an individual's rewards may be linked to the behaviors of an associate.

Game Studies

Two prisoners have been taken into custody and accused of a joint crime. Each realizes that if neither turns State's evidence, burglary charges will be

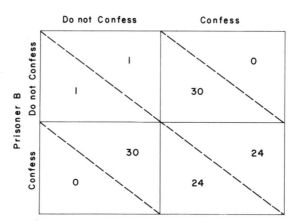

Fig. 6.1. The prisoner's dilemma. Entries above the diagonals represent months of incarceration for Prisoner A. Entries below the diagonals represent months of punishment for Prisoner B.

dropped and a short sentence for disturbing the peace will be imposed. The district attorney propositions each prisoner separately, offering to free either if he alone confesses, but promising heavy sentences if both confess. Each prisoner's predicament is complicated by uncertainty as to whether or not his accomplice will confess, and by the fact that his own fate depends on his colleague's behaviors as well as his own. If both elect to seek maximum payoff (avoidance of punishment) by confessing, the consequences will be jointly disastrous. Fig. 6.1 reports the alternatives that are open to prisoners A and B, and the (negative) payoffs associated with each of four possible patterns of response. The numbers in the cells may be regarded as representing months of imprisonment. Payoffs for prisoner A are reported by the numbers above the diagonals while the payoffs for prisoner B are indicated below the diagonals.

Figure 6.1 illustrates qualities which are common to many payoff schemes: One person's outcomes depend in part upon the actions of other persons, some combinations of actions yield greater returns than other combinations, and co-participants often receive unequal payoffs. These features of the prisoner's dilemma make it an interesting research tool for social psychologists who study collective action. Subjects are given copies of a payoff matrix and asked to play the "game" many times in succession, each time electing one of the two available courses of action and learning into which cell their joint actions have placed them. For experimental purposes, it has generally been convenient to employ payoff schemes with positive rather than negative rewards, and to use payoffs that are less variable than those shown in Fig. 6.1.

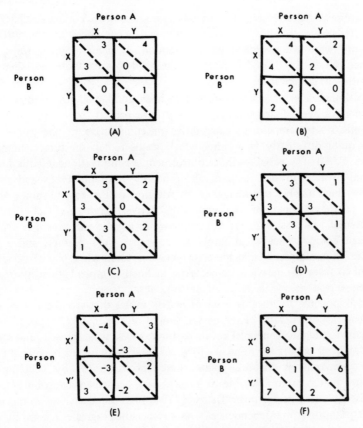

Fig. 6.2. Illustrative payoff matrices. (A) Modified prisoner's dilemma matrix. (B) Promotive matrix—equal payoffs. (C) Promotive matrix—unequal payoffs. (D) Independence matrix. (E) Contrient matrix—zero sum. (F) Contrient matrix—constant sum.

Following each "trial," subjects are typically rewarded with the number of "points" (or pennies, dimes, or quarters) indicated in the cell designated by their joint actions. Matrix A of Fig. 6.2 is a payoff scheme that retains the major features of the prisoner's dilemma.

Such a matrix is said to create a "mixed motive" situation. If participants wish to maximize their combined earnings, both should always choose alternative X, but if one wishes to outdo the other he should select alternative Y because it guarantees that he will never be beaten and may yield a margin of four points in his favor. Depending upon which of these two strategies a subject tends to follow he is said to be cooperatively or competitively motivated. In attempting to identify factors that favor one or the other motive, researchers have manipulated discrepancies among the payoffs offered by the cells of the matrix, observed the responses of friends versus strangers, compared the effects of points versus monetary rewards, employed accomplices or computerized opponents who are programmed to respond in predetermined ways, and examined the effects of oral instructions designed to accentuate the salience of cooperation or competition.

Although a great many studies have been conducted, the results of the research have been disappointing. Findings have proven to be rather unstable, and subjects who are clearly cooperative or competitive in one game often behave quite differently in another which seems to tap the same parameters (Sermat, 1970). The variables that control people's motivations in situations of the kind created in the research are probably both numerous and subtle; certainly they involve considerations in addition to the payoff values of the matrix. Perhaps some of the confusion derives from the fact that the experimental task has many of the trappings of a game and thus may tend to encourage competitiveness, attempts to outsmart one's partner, and a high incidence of exploratory, trial-and-error behavior. Even when payoff values are designed to favor cooperation, subjects are inclined to mix a high proportion of competitive responses with their cooperative ones.

It is possible to imagine a set of matrix values that are likely to prompt individuals to "cooperate." Each person should receive maximum payoff when his behavior is highly beneficial to his partner as well as to himself, and should receive reduced payoff (or none at all) when his actions are less beneficial to his partner. Matrix B in Fig. 6.2 meets these specifications. By selecting the alternative that is more favorable to himself, each participant contributes to the best possible outcome for both. Deutsch (1949) has called such an arrangement one of "promotive interdependence": As any person progresses toward his own goal, he necessarily promotes goal achievement by his associate as well. In the extreme case, such as that depicted by Matrix B, the payoffs of participants are perfectly and positively correlated, and there is no way that one person can succeed at the expense of the other. To be sure, an obstreperous game-player might occasionally elect to "cut off his own nose" by choosing alternative Y, but such a masochistic maneuver should be a rare occurrence.

Matrix C preserves the essential features of Matrix B, but depicts a case in which two participants receive correlated but unequal payoffs. Outside the laboratory or the game room people are rarely rewarded for merely choosing an alternative; generally they must work for what they get. The contributions of some workers may be judged to be more essential and worthy of reward than those of other workers. Matrix C may be seen as a case in which worker A is on a higher pay schedule than worker B whose alternatives are labeled X' and Y' in recognition of the fact that his job is probably different from that of worker A.

Promotive matrices have rarely been used in game research. Payoff systems that neither invite nor permit the expression of competitive desires are of little use to investigators whose major aim is to learn how and why people compete. Nor are promotive matrices very helpful in revealing the dynamics of cooperative motivations; they induce people to act "cooperatively" but do not reveal whether such behavior is prompted by a desire to help oneself or to help one's partner. Self interest is completely confounded with partner interest, leaving the nature of participants' motivations in doubt. However, because such matrices channel collective action in predictable directions, they are of interest to anyone who wishes to understand or guide group behaviors. If prescribed process calls for person A to produce act X, and for person B to produce act X', a promotive payoff system is likely to shape actual process to fit that prescription.

Matrix D of Fig. 6.2 should also encourage the occurrence of acts X and X'. Here each person's payoffs are unaffected by the behavior of his partner, but each receives more reward for producing one act rather than another. There is no way in which participants can either compete or cooperate, for each individual's payoffs are determined by himself alone. Self interest is independent of partner interest, the former sufficing to assure the occurrence of a specific pattern of collective action.

Although independence matrices are of little use in the examination of cooperative and competitive motivations, they are widely employed in industry, business, schools, and other institutions to assure the performance of necessary functions. Each of many participants is assigned a role, the payoff of each being contingent upon his role performance. Such a system can be responsible for an intricately organized pattern of collection action, though each person strives to obtain his own personal payoff. Workers in an automobile factory may be apathetic about producing cars and uninterested in helping or hindering their neighbors on the assembly line, but they fasten rivets and tighten bolts because these are the actions that earn a weekly paycheck. Needless to say, workers sometimes receive a variety of incidental payoffs in addition to their weekly wage, and role enactment is not always entirely satisfactory. However, the major and necessary inducements that keep most large organizations moving are those encompassed by an independence matrix. When prescribed process entails prolonged and delicate interlocking of the behaviors of many persons, harmony of self interest and prescribed process may be essential.

Matrices E and F in Fig. 6.2 are called "contrient" because participants exert contrary effects upon one another's payoffs. To the extent that person A succeeds, B fails. Payoffs are negatively correlated and there is no way in which both persons can prosper simultaneously or one can prosper without depriving the other. Matrix E depicts a situation in which the "winner takes all"; such an arrangement is said to create a zero-sum game because no matter what actions players follow, gains and losses cancel one another—each of the four cells sums to zero. Matrix F is exactly like E except that all entries have been increased by a value of four. The sum of the entries in each cell becomes eight, and, although one person's gains still come at the expense of the other's losses, even the loser generally receives a small payoff. Both matrices inhibit the expression of cooperative motives.

Game theorists have proposed rules which should be followed by an individual in order to maximize his gains, or, at least, minimize his losses (the so-called minimax strategy). In both Matrix E and F, the lower right-hand cell is called a saddlepoint. Such a cell contains entries that are the smallest in their column, but the largest in their row. Whenever a saddlepoint exists (and sometimes there is none) a prudent strategy is said to entail always choosing the alternative that involves that cell. If both persons follow this strategy, each will at least minimize his losses, and if one's partner pursues a different course, positive gains will be forthcoming. Much of the attention of game theorists has been focused on the maneuvers that players employ in an effort to emerge victorious over their opponents.

In the context of this chapter, contrient matrices deserve attention not because they provide a setting for the enactment of subtle strategies or the use of exploitative chicanery, but because they have implications for task motivation. When group members are contriently interdependent, they ordinarily do much more than select one of two alternatives; their activities entail the performance of task-relevant behaviors, and the cell of the matrix into which they fall depends upon *who does what how well*. Each participant's payoffs reflect not only what he and his opponent do but also how well each performs. Consequently, it is reasonable to surmise that contrient matrices sometimes induce very intense motivations. Athletes are reported to try harder when competing against opponents than when merely practicing their craft, and students are alleged to study most assiduously when a competitive exam is imminent. Murphy, Murphy, and Newcomb (1937) analyzed 15 different studies dealing with the impact of contrient situations and concluded that competition generally leads to intensified effort.

There are several reasons why this might be so. When payoffs are contriently distributed, the disparity between the rewards obtained by the winner and loser is typically rather large; unless a participant surpasses the performance of his opponent, he obtains little or nothing for his effort. Furthermore, there is often a wide margin of uncertainty about how well one's opponent will do. Unlike situations in which the criterion of success is stable and familiar, a contrient arrangement generally requires the individual to exceed a flexible and unknown standard which is likely to be high because it is established by an opponent who is presumably trying to be maximally proficient. Under these circumstances, neither participant can afford to do only enough to win; enough is an undefined quantity which may require one's utmost effort. Even if the opponent's performance can be accurately gauged, a contrient matrix may encourage the individual to do better than the bare minimum that will assure success. Contrient matrices almost certainly accentuate the salience of social comparison and thus add personal prestige to the payoffs one must take into account. Winning big confers rewards in addition to those directly controlled by the matrix, and losing big entails costs that are not adequately described as failure to receive the larger of two proffered payoffs.

However, there are obvious limits beyond which contrient interdependence cannot be expected to intensify effort. If one's opponent is believed to be a very weak performer, one need not work very hard to be successful. Moreover, victory over such a contender bestows little honor or prestige. There is evidence suggesting that exceedingly able opponents may also fail to elicit a maximum effort. When the probability of success is extremely low, people may resign themselves to failure (Atkinson, 1957; Bakis, 1952; Dreyer, 1954) or decide that unachievable payoffs are not, after all, very attractive (Cohen, 1955; Hyman, 1953). Furthermore, individuals tend not to compare themselves with others whose abilities are thought to be vastly greater than their own (Festinger, 1954); consequently, their prestige may not be endangered when they vie against clearly superior opponents.

The findings of game research have been too diverse to be concisely summarized. Mixed-motive matrices have received most attention and appear to generate both competitive and cooperative behaviors. The variables that favor one versus the other outcome have not yet been very clearly identified. Contrient games sometimes provoke strong rivalry and stimulate intense task motivation, but these consequences have not been very uniformly noted. Promotive and independent matrices have been studied less frequently, perhaps because their effects are too predictable. Games that compel or strongly encourage everyone to win equally are not very exciting or informative.

For our purposes, the findings of game research are less important than the matrices that have been used. The findings tend to be unstable, to account for only small portions of the observed behaviors, and to represent reactions to mixed-motive matrices which are not especially typical of group payoff systems. The competitive atmosphere created by the game-like qualities of the experimental setting, subjects' limited freedom to communicate with one another, and their essentially effortless capacity to place themselves into the column of their choice are features of the situation which are unlikely to be duplicated when real-life groups work on tasks.

However, the matrices clearly depict the ways group members may be linked to one another in their pursuit of goals. On subsequent pages, we will speak of promotive, contrient, and independent payoff systems, using these terms to designate interdependencies of the kinds explored by game theorists. The research we are about to examine explores people's behaviors in nongame situations, where there are few restraints on communication and where the individual's effortful behavior places him (and sometimes his associates) in one or another cell of a payoff matrix. Examination of such research will require us to consider not only the payoff relationships *within the group,* but also *interdependencies among groups.*

Allocation of Payoffs within and among Groups

In 1949, Deutsch reported a study comparing the effects of promotive and contrient payoff systems on group behavior. Instead of attending regular lecture sections, students enrolled in an introductory psychology course met once each week in five-member groups. An important part of each 3-hr session was the examination of a human relations problem for which participants were urged to suggest solutions. Each week 50 min were devoted to discussion of a different problem and to the preparation of written recommendations for action. Students' grades for the 5-week period were primarily determined by the quality of their own, or their group's performance on these tasks.

Members of half the groups were told that each would receive the same grade for the period, that grade being determined by a comparison of their group's performance with that of other groups. Thus payoffs were to be allocated equally within any group, but unequally among groups. This system for distributing rewards was designed to establish promotive interdependence. The other half of the groups were informed that members would be ranked with respect to their contributions to task success, and that each member's grade would reflect his rank within his own group. These instructions imposed contrient interdependence upon participants since one person's success necessarily limited the success of others. As discussion proceeded, four observers recorded pertinent aspects of the ongoing process, and at the conclusion of each session observers rated the group on a number of dimensions.

Promotive groups were found to differ from contrient ones in a number of ways. Their members were less homogeneous with respect to both the kind and quantity of contributions, perhaps because the total performance of the group determined payoffs and no member needed to duplicate or repeat the contributions of another in order to demonstrate that he was at least as productive as anyone else. Members of promotive groups were judged to be more attentive to one another's suggestions and to experience fewer communication problems. They were also credited with manifesting greater "we-feeling" and being more friendly toward one another.

When the written recommendations of groups were examined, those produced by promotive groups were found to contain more words and were judged to be of higher quality. However, these findings must be interpreted with caution because members of contrient groups probably saw little opportunity to gain payoffs by contributing to the creation of a good written product; for them the critical concern was undoubtedly their own performance during the discussion which preceded the writing of the report. Deutsch noted that members of contrient groups usually permitted one conscientious individual to do the entire write-up; others showed no interest in it, never examined it, and directed their attention solely to the discussion itself. Had contrient members believed that they would be rewarded for having their own ideas incorporated into the report or for personally contributing to its adequacy, the quality of the report might have been substantially increased.

In 1961, Hammond and Goldman suggested that Deutsch's research might be regarded as having compared groups that were internally contrient with groups that were externally contrient. Although all members of Deutsch's "promotive" groups received the same payoff, the groups themselves were contriently related to one another. Should the behavior of such groups be construed as reflecting their promotive internal payoff system or their contrient external relationship? To answer this question, Hammond and Goldman compared the performance of four kinds of groups.

Students in psychology classes were offered the opportunity to earn extra course credit by participating in discussion groups which met one hour per week for four weeks. During each session the groups, most of which contained five members, discussed a human relations problem and prepared a written report of their recommendations for action. To establish promotive internal relationships, half of the groups were told that all members would receive the same amount of payoff, but Hammond and Goldman varied the manner in which the magnitude of this joint payoff would be determined. Some internally promotive groups were informed that the amount of extra credit each member would receive depended upon how well the group performed relative to other groups. This combination of instructions closely paralleled Deutsch's "promotive" treatment; it made the group internally promotive, but externally contrient to other groups. Other groups that were assured all members would receive the same payoff were told that the amount of extra credit each person would receive depended entirely upon how well the group's performance satisfied previously established criteria. Thus any number of groups might conceivably receive maximum payoffs, and no group's performance could affect the payoff of any other group. This experimental treatment made the group internally promotive but externally independent of other groups.

Some of Hammond and Goldman's groups were informed that each member's performance would be evaluated against that of every other member of his group, and that the amount of extra credit received by any individual would depend upon his rank in the group. This treatment made the group internally contrient but externally independent of other groups.

Finally, some of the groups were told that each member's payoff depended solely upon how well his own performance satisfied previously established criteria; consequently, any number of members could obtain high

TABLE 6.1

Combinations of Internal and External Interdependence Examined by Several Investigators

External (group-to-group) interdependence	Internal (member-to-member) interdependence		
	Promotive	Independent	Contrient
Promotive	—	—	—
Independent	Hammond & Goldman (1961) Julian & Perry (1967) Myers (1962) Rosenthal & Cofer (1948)	Hammond & Goldman (1961)	Deutsch (1949) Hammond & Goldman (1961)
Contrient	Deutsch (1949) Hammond & Goldman (1961) Julian & Perry (1967) Myers (1962) Schachter *et al.* (1954)	—	Julian & Perry (1967) —

payoffs if they performed well. The group was both internally and externally independent.

Table 6.1 locates the four treatments employed by Hammond and Goldman in an arrangement that depicts the nine possible ways payoffs may be allocated to groups and their members. Deutsch's two treatments are also entered in appropriate positions in the table, as are the payoff systems examined by other researchers whose work will be described later. The reader will note that no entries are contained in the top row of Table 6.1. Within a business or military organization two or more departments, work units, or squads may, of course, be promotively interdependent. But examination of literature dealing with large organizations would expand our task to unmanageable proportions.

Hammond and Goldman's major findings are summarized in Table 6.2, columns 4 and 5 of which report data for groups of the kinds Deutsch called "contrient" and "promotive." Examination of the entries in these two columns reveals little support for Deutsch's conclusions. To be sure, internally contrient groups produced more comments than did internally promotive groups. However, judges' ratings of coordination, communication, and attentiveness do not concur with Deutsch's findings. There appears to be no obvious reason why

TABLE 6.2

Summary of Findings Concerning the Effects of Four Payoff Systems[a]

	Internally independent, externally independent.	Internally promotive, externally independent.	Internally contrient, externally independent. (Deutsch's contrient treatment)	Internally promotive, externally contrient. (Deutsch's promotive treatment)
Mean number of remarks per session	148	152	151	129
Percentage of all remarks that are task oriented	96	87	84	85
Rank order of judges' ratings on:				
Coordination	2[b]	1	3	4
Orientation of effort	1	2	4	3
Communication	1	2	3	4
Involvement and atten- tiveness	1	2	3	4
Recognition of relevant factors	2	1	4	3

[a]Adapted from Hammond and Goldman (1961).

[b]Judges rated groups on five-point scales at the conclusion of each session. After all sessions had been completed, ratings for each type of group were summed across sessions, and the four kinds of groups were ranked with respect to their total rating on each variable. A rank of 1 indicates that groups of a specified type were rated higher on a variable than were any other type of group.

Hammond and Goldman's data should not have paralleled those of the earlier investigation. The two studies are alike in important ways, but, of course, they also differ with respect to many details such as the amount of payoff subjects could earn (greater in Deutsch's study), length of the special sessions, identity of experimenters, and the university from which subjects were drawn. Differences such as these may account for the disparities between findings, but if seemingly minor departures from an original research procedure are sufficient to cancel or greatly alter experimental outcomes, one may doubt that the findings have very wide applicability to real-life situations.

There is another way of evaluating the outcomes of the two studies. Columns 4 and 5 of Table 6.2 represent different external relationships as well as different internal ones. A more appropriate test of the impact of promotive versus contrient internal interdependence is provided by an inspection of columns 3 and 4, both of which involve external independence. This comparison suggests that promotive and contrient internal payoff systems do not differentially affect the number of remarks made by a group, or the percentage of all remarks that are task oriented. However, internally promotive groups rank consistently higher than contrient ones on process variables. Thus when external group relations are "held constant," Hammond and Goldman's data support Deutsch's contention that promotive internal relationships encourage coordination of effort, effective communication, and attentiveness.

It should be noted that groups which were both internally and externally independent tended to rank higher on process variables than did any other type, though their superiority over internally promotive groups was too small to be of any consequence. Internal independence appears to have been fully as effective as promotive interdependence in motivating members to make task contributions; indeed, 96 percent of all remarks by members of internally independent groups were task relevant in character. If a person's payoff depends entirely upon his personally meeting an established standard of task performance, he is likely to be strongly motivated to do what is required to meet it.

Perhaps the reader is surprised to learn that Hammond and Goldman's internally promotive groups did not produce more and better task contributions than groups that were internally independent. When each member's payoffs depend upon the performance of his associates as well as on his own behaviors, is it not reasonable to believe that every member will work especially hard in order to avoid "letting others down?" Will participants not be unusually helpful to one another because none can succeed alone? If any member is prone to slack his duty, will not others exert pressure upon him to improve his performance? The answer to each of these questions appears to be "yes, sometimes."

Promotive interdependence represents a quasi-conjunctive arrangement. Nobody can succeed unless everyone succeeds, so any incompetent or recalcitrant person can substantially impair everyone else's prospects of goal achievement. Under these circumstances, the poor performer may indeed be assisted and pressured, but such measures may not be sufficient to make him an equal partner. If two or three members of a group have little ability or enthusiasm for work, others may be compelled to conclude that there is little chance the group can achieve a prescribed standard of performance or hold its own in competition with other groups. As prospects of success fade, even those who are willing and able may decide that further effort is futile. Football coaches realize that a desire to win is of little motivational significance unless it is accompanied by a belief that winning is possible.

Some of the *advantageous* effects of promotive interdependence have been documented by Thomas (1957) in a study cited in Chapter 3. Five women sat at a round table and constructed cardboard houses, each participant either performing all phases of the job or performing only a part of the total process and passing the product to her colleagues for completion. All groups were told the task was a measure of "general work intelligence," but some were informed that they would be scored as a group and others that each individual would receive a score. It was not clear whether individual scores would reflect comparative performance within the group or the degree to which the individual satisfied a predetermined criterion. However, it is probably safe to assume that subjects interpreted the individual scoring system as imposing contrient interdependence. Relationships among groups were so vaguely specified that no assumption about external interdependence seems justified.

Regardless of whether individual members performed specialized functions or all aspects of house construction, they reported a greater feeling of responsibility to associates when payoffs were promotive than when they were (presumably) contrient. Members of promotive groups also indicated greater willingness to help others, though this difference was extremely small when subjects performed specialized functions. Promotively interdependent groups produced more cardboard houses than did contrient groups, but this finding was not statistically significant. In general, Thomas' data support the contention that promotive interdependence motivates group members to help one another and to perform well so that nobody else's progress will be impeded.

However, we may doubt that Thomas' findings are valid for all kinds of groups and tasks. His subjects were comparative strangers working on easy tasks which any mature female should have been able to perform rather well. Furthermore, the proffered payoff entailed "intelligence" and was probably sufficient to induce all subjects to work hard. Consequently, people should have had little reason for believing that anyone's performance would seriously impair the group's progress, or that the group had a low probability of success. The impact of promotive payoff systems is likely to be mediated by participants' appraisals of the probability that their group will receive the desired payoff; in Thomas' study the probability of success should have seemed high.

When success is unlikely, members of promotive groups may forsake their helpful, harmonious ways and seek individual gains. Myers (1962) staged a rifle tournament for R.O.T.C. trainees. Randomly assembled three-man teams either participated in a 25-bout round robin competition with other teams or attempted to meet prescribed team standards of proficiency during 25 sessions. In neither case did subjects ever learn their individual scores, but after each bout competitive teams were made aware of their standing in the league, and noncompetitive teams were quietly informed whether or not they had met the established criterion. Trophies were promised to members of winning competitive teams and to members of any noncompetitive team that "qualified." Thus the competitive teams were internally promotive and externally contrient while the noncompetitive ones were internally promotive and externally independent.

At the end of the second and fifth weeks, members of all teams rated one another on a variety of scales designed to measure interpersonal esteem. Successful teams of both types manifested increasing amounts of intermember acceptance and approval, while unsuccessful teams of both kinds experienced decreasing member acceptance. On the average, interpersonal esteem remained higher in externally contrient groups, a finding that Myers interpreted as indicating that external competition has the effect of drawing teammates together. While there can be no doubt that groups sometimes become more harmonious when confronting a common enemy, it should be remembered that this reaction occurred only in the case of rifle teams that were successfully coping with the challenge.

A single, indifferent or inept member may be enough to threaten the harmony and cooperation of internally promotive groups. Rosenthal and Cofer (1948) had small groups of college students throw darts at a target, each group receiving a score that was the sum of the members' scores. Student groups did not compete against one another, but were urged to surpass a standard allegedly established by groups of government workers who had performed the same task. Therefore, the payoff system was internally promotive and, depending upon how participants interpreted the criterion of performance, either externally independent or contrient. An experimental accomplice who assumed an attitude of open indifference and neglect, but who performed at the level of the average individual, was planted in some groups but not others. Groups that included such a confederate tended to lose confidence in goal attainability, and members became more concerned about their own personal performance than about group success. In another study Schachter, Nuttin, de Monchaux, Maucorps, Osmer, Duijker, Rommetveit, and Israel, (1954) organized boys' clubs in several countries. The first task of each group was to build a model airplane, competing under strong incentives with other clubs. Thus groups were internally promotive and externally contrient. An experimental accomplice in each group steadfastly advocated the construction of an obviously inferior model. This deviant individual was rejected in all clubs, but rejection was more severe when members anticipated that their group would fail in the competition than when they believed that it might still be successful.

The evidence summarized previously suggests that promotive payoff systems intensify task motivation, stimulate mutual helpfulness, and encourage interpersonal acceptance and coordination *provided a strong joint effort is thought necessary and likely to be successful.* However, if the collective efforts of such a group hold little promise of success, participants conclude that they are yoked with unsatisfactory partners. Hostility is engendered, and members tend to pursue individual outcomes which may or may not contribute to performance of the collective task. Needless to say, if promotive payoffs seem virtually guaranteed regardless of the quality of the group's performance (because other groups are thought to be exceedingly inept, or because the criterion of success is very easily met), some or all members of the group may not be motivated to work very hard. Internally promotive relationships appear to have their salutory effects only when success is neither completely guaranteed nor highly unlikely. Perhaps Deutsch's promotive groups worked harmoniously and effectively in competition with other groups because members felt that a strong collective performance was both necessary and sufficient to assure group success; perhaps Hammond and Goldman's promotive groups were rather disorganized and ineffectual because members believed that the competition was weak (high payoffs were assured), or because members felt their group had little chance of winning.

A final study will complete our survey of research exploring issues raised by Deutsch. Julian and Perry (1967) assigned the students enrolled in an experimental psychology course to four-person teams. Team members were instructed to work together on a laboratory exercise, though each was required to prepare his own written report. Some teams were told that the reports submitted by their group would be scored against predetermined criteria, and that all members would receive the same grade (internally promotive, externally independent). Others were informed that each member's report would be compared with those of his teammates, the best being graded A, second best B, etc. (internally contrient, externally independent). Finally, some groups were told that all reports would be competitively evaluated against all others, each student receiving a grade that reflected the quality of his own report regardless of the team in which he had worked. This treatment cannot be very confidently categorized. According to the payoff rules, all participants were contriently related to their teammates *and* to everyone else. However, the members of any team might have regarded the situation as one in which the success of each was tied somewhat promotively to the success of others in the same team—by helping one another, each might write a report that would compete successfully against those of outsiders. Although this possibility existed, we accept Julian and Perry's judgment that their payoff instructions induced contrient internal relationships. However, unlike Julian and Perry, who conceived each of these groups to be independent of the others, we regard them as externally contrient; if members of one group succeed, they automatically impeded the success of persons working in other groups.

Members of groups that were internally promotive and externally independent submitted poorer written reports than did members of either of the other two kinds of groups. However, members of these internally promotive groups were judged by themselves and by an observer to have maintained the most harmonious interpersonal relations; members described their groups as especially warm, happy, and active. The other two types of groups did not differ substantially from one another either with respect to productivity or group atmosphere. Julian and Perry concluded that a group may need to be either internally or externally contrient in order for its members to be highly motivated to perform task functions. Although "pure cooperation" (promotive internal relationships with independent external ones) appeared to generate harmony and favor shared responsibility, Julian and Perry suggested that it also induced lower individual task involvement and lower task motivation.

Both the study by Julian and Perry and the one by Hammond and Goldman indicate that groups that are internally promotive and externally independent tend to be harmonious. Deutsch did not observe groups working under this combination of conditions. Like Deutsch, Hammond and Goldman noted that internally contrient groups prepare poor written reports, but Julian and Perry found the opposite to be true. This contradiction probably reflects the differential importance of the written reports in the three studies. For Julian and Perry's subjects, the report was the sole determinant of payoffs, whereas for subjects in the earlier investigations it was, at most, only one of several determinants. Indeed, in the case of contriently interdependent subjects it probably seemed almost irrelevant. People are likely to do that for which they expect to be rewarded, and Julian and Perry's contrient subjects apparently worked hard on their individual reports.

Although it is apparent that payoff systems affect motivation, their impact is likely to be mediated by expectations and perceptions that are only loosely controlled by external or internal interdependencies. Payoff systems may favor the expectation that outcomes are dependent upon individual effort, on assisting others, or are largely beyond the control of the individual. They sometimes identify specific responses that will be rewarded, but more often leave the individual with a troublesome margin of uncertainty concerning what he should do to maximize his returns. When payoffs depend both on the individual's own performance in his group and on the group's overall performance, or on the group's success *vis à vis* other groups, uncertainty is compounded. Neither the amount of earnings available for distribution within the group nor the individual's share of those earnings is established. In the face of such uncertainty, task motivation is likely to reflect situational or personality variables that are not directly manipulated by the payoff system.

Consequently, it is not surprising that the line of research initiated by Deutsch has yielded seemingly inconsistent findings. Most of these inconsistencies are probably more apparent than real, for different investigators have tended to compare the effects of different combinations of payoff conditions. When treatments are assigned to appropriate cells of Table 6.1, and allowance is made for other factors noted previously, complexity rather than inconsistency characterizes the findings. Perhaps this complexity can be reduced by a more systematic examination of task demands.

Payoff Systems and Task Demands

A major difficulty in interpreting research dealing with promotive, contrient, and independent payoff systems is that they are generally imposed without regard for the nature of the task that is to be performed. Within a single study, major features of the task are held constant, and the investigator compares the effects of two or more different payoff systems on group process, member happiness, or productivity. However, the nature of the task is a matter of minor concern, and little effort is expended to determine whether the findings obtained when groups work on one task are replicated when a different job is to be performed. Furthermore, the imposed system usually links everyone's rewards to the performance of the same globally defined activity. The payoff received by any individual or any group depends on how well he or it performs the same functions that every other individual or group is performing. Such an arrangement may be appropriate when tasks are unitary and no real specialization of function is possible. However, many tasks, including some of those employed in the research cited earlier, are not unitary, and can best be attacked through a division of labor. When this is the case, the critical issue is not how much payoff should be given for how much performance, but *who* should receive how much for doing *what*.

It should be recalled that the game theorist explores the impact of payoff matrices in a setting which requires his experimental subjects to do nothing more than select one of two options. The subject need not earn his way into the category of his choice, he merely wills himself into it. Studies that impose promotive, contrient or independent payoff systems on *ad hoc* groups take an important step beyond the game theorist; they require the individual to place himself in a payoff slot by performing task-relevant activities. However, the character of the required behaviors is usually of incidental importance because the experimenter's primary goal is to demonstrate the pervasive effects of payoff systems rather than to identify the kind of system that will induce the right persons to do the right things.

Two studies have reflected more than a casual interest in task demands. In research earlier cited, Thomas (1957) had women build cardboard houses. Each woman either performed all phases of the task or only part of the total process. Participants worked under promotive or contrient payoff systems, the former arrangement resulting in greater feelings of mutual responsibility and slightly higher levels of productivity. However, there was little evidence that the impact of the payoff systems depended upon whether specialization of function was required. It should be noted, however, that specialization was arbitrarily manipulated by experimental fiat and had no obvious relevance to the abilities and preferences of the participants or to other aspects of the task.

Miller and Hamblin (1963) assigned 3-person groups the task of deciding which of 13 numbers the experimenter had selected. Each subject was privately informed of 4 numbers the experimenter had *not* chosen, so the task could readily be performed by employing electrical signals to exchange information. However, in half of the groups, subjects were permitted to guess without penalty and thus could obtain the correct solution without communication with their associates. When guessing was not permitted, members were functionally interdependent, but when guessing was allowed each could perform the task without any assistance. Payoffs were "points" awarded to the group as a whole for rapid completion of the work. The group's points were distributed to members in three different ways. In some groups, all members received an equal number of points regardless of who solved the problem first. In other groups, the member who finished first received two-thirds of the points and the second person to complete the task received one-third. Finally, in some groups, members who finished first, second, and third received one-half, one-third, and one-sixth of the group's points.

All of Miller and Hamblin's groups were externally independent; the magnitude of a group's payoff depended only on the speed with which its members solved the problem. Internally, some groups were promotively interdependent (equal rewards) and others were contriently interdependent. Promotive groups were found to perform better than contrient ones when members were functionally interdependent (exchange of information was essential), but the payoff systems did not differ significantly in their effects on productivity when each person was free to work as an individual (guessing was not penalized). Miller and Hamblin review a number of other studies that seem to support their conclusion. However, in many cases, the external relationships of experimental groups have been so vaguely defined, and payoffs have been so small or intangible, that comparison across studies is difficult. In spite of these obscurities, it seems safe to conclude that promotive interdependence within a group tends to facilitate performance when the task demands that all members assist one another.

A continued effort to identify the kinds of tasks that are best served by promotive, contrient, or independent payoff systems might prove fruitful. However, a case can be made for pursuing a different approach. In theory, even if not always in fact, we should be able to evaluate the resources available to group members, and identify the demands that are imposed by the task that is to be performed. In earlier chapters we have seen that such an analysis sometimes permits fairly precise statements to be made about "prescribed process"—about who *should* do what, when, in order to maximize productivity. Once these critical questions are answered, it may be possible to tailor a payoff system to fit the resources of the personnel and the demands of the task. Presumably, the most effective system will be one that motivates each member of the group to do whatever it is he is most qualified to do. Sometimes the most appropriate payoff system will motivate certain members to do nothing at all.

The following pages describe in rough outline the kinds of payoff systems that may be appropriate when tasks are additive, disjunctive, conjunctive, discretionary, or complementary. The analysis and conclusions are necessarily speculative because very little relevant research has been conducted.

Additive tasks. When potential productivity equals the sum of the contributions individual members of the group *can* make, it is desirable to motivate each member to do his best. But if rewards depend entirely upon individual performances, inter-member coordination may be neglected and actual productivity may suffer. Thus in the case of Ringelmann's rope-pulling groups a strong effort by each member resulted in a good group showing only if all members pulled at the same time and in the same direction. An appropriate payoff system will reward participants for doing the right thing at the right time and in proper relationship to the activities of other persons. Of course, when an additive task entails shoveling snow or stuffing envelopes, comparatively little interpersonal coordination is needed; a "piece rate" payoff system that makes the group internally independent may stimulate very good collective action.

When coordination is critical, a special functionary may be needed to guide and reward the behaviors of group members. Thus Ringelmann's task might be performed under the surveillance of electronic equipment which evaluates the simultaneity and directionality as well as the strength of each person's pull, and which allocates rewards on the basis of all three criteria. Although such an apparatus could certainly be developed for the management of rope-pulling groups, in real-life situations a contrivance of this kind is not ordinarily available. Instead, a single member may function as a coordination specialist, monitoring the performance of all others and endeavoring through the use of instructions, signaling systems, feedback processes, and differential rewards to induce everyone to perform well and in concert with everyone else. The person who handles some or all of these functions is likely to be called a leader, foreman, or supervisor.

The use of a coordination specialist has certain disadvantages. The person who fills this role cannot ordinarily contribute directly to the performance of the task; thus the group's fund of usable task-relevant resources is reduced. More important, no human monitor is likely to perform the coordination function with the precision of a computer, or be regarded by those he supervises as a thoroughly insightful and impartial coordinating and rewarding agent. When the required pattern of coordination is extremely complex, and is not reducible to a set of clearly definable, interlocking roles, a single human "manager" is likely to be only partially effective and to generate feelings of discontent among those whose payoffs he controls.

In such cases, a promotive system may be more effective than one which links each individual's rewards to the "appraised" value of his contribution. An individual is unlikely to strive very hard to obtain payoffs that are contingent upon his personal contribution to processes that cannot be described or evaluated very objectively. However, if his payoff is dependent upon the performance of the group as a whole, he may be motivated to do whatever is needed to augment the group's success. Perhaps he will not know just what he should do in order to be maximally helpful, but he will at least feel that doing the right thing at the right time is important. In this connection, it is instructive to recall that Mintz's (1951) subjects were much more successful in withdrawing cones from a jug when winning depended upon everyone's getting his cone out than when each individual who withdrew his cone was said to be a winner. A promotive payoff system may be advantageous when the task requires interpersonal coordination that is not readily achievable through a system of individual payoffs; people are rewarded for coordinating as well as performing.

Disjunctive tasks. When potential productivity is established by the resources of the group's most competent member, prescribed process requires that particular person to do his best, and all other members to accept his performance as the group's product. If the identity of the most able person is clear to all, a promotive payoff system may encourage the proper matching since it permits everyone to profit from the superior performance of the most resourceful individual. However, if the task requires a large expenditure of time, effort, or other resources, a somewhat larger than average share of the total reward may have to be earmarked for the member who does the work. Very large inequalities should presumably be avoided lest they stimulate less resourceful persons to usurp the responsibility of performing in the group's behalf.

In many cases, the identity of the most able person is not known, and can be discovered only through an examination of individual performances. Consequently, an appropriate payoff system may need to serve three purposes: (a) induce all members of the group to produce the best individual products they can; (b) motivate everyone to evaluate individual products in an impartial fashion; and (c) encourage acceptance of the best individual product. These three essential activities roughly parallel three stages of a group discussion which Bales (1950) has called orientation, evaluation, and control. It is reasonable to anticipate that a payoff system that facilitates one activity may inhibit another.

The ease and objectivity with which individual contributions can be evaluated determines whether members' payoffs can be made contingent upon the quality of their personal products. If appraisal is easy, maximum effort is likely to be elicited by a reward system that makes each person's remuneration depend upon the merit of his individual contribution. Promotive and contrient internal systems have the disadvantage of diluting the relationship between quality and reward, the former by permitting the individual to feel that he need not attempt what others will probably do better than he anyhow, and the latter by creating circumstances under which individual members feel they have little chance of "winning." [It is to be recalled that Deutsch's internally promotive groups manifested great inequality of participation, and that Kelley *et al.* (1965) reported data suggesting that members of large groups do not try very hard to escape impending electrical shock when the contrient nature of the situation makes sucess seem improbable.] When payoffs are independently allocated, each person is likely to realize that his reward depends upon the quality of his individual contribution, and that he need not perform better than everyone else in order to receive a desirable payoff. Such a pattern of incentives should tend to maximize the number and quality of individual products.

When the quality of individual outputs cannot be readily evaluated, a payoff system that promises a reward for contributing a product (regardless of its quality) should have the effect of increasing the number of alternatives among which the group may choose. Such a payoff system will create conditions resembling those established in the "brainstorming" studies cited earlier in this book.

Regardless of how individual contributions are elicited, they must sooner or later be examined and appraised. If evaluation is easy (as in the case of a eureka task) this stage of the process is routine and calls for no special allocation of rewards; presumably members will readily identify the best available product. However, when evaluation is difficult, some payoff schemes are more likely than others to favor an impartial comparison of alternatives. Objectivity will be inhibited by a scheme that rewards the individual for having his own personal product evaluated favorably, and facilitated by one that reinforces people for expressing many insightful comments concerning all available options. In this connection, it is pertinent to note that Hoffman and Maier (1967) found that groups tend to accept whichever of several alternatives first receives a moderate amount of support from discussants. Consequently, it is probably advantageous to reward participants for delaying a decision until all options have been carefully examined.

We may surmise that the most highly evaluated individual contribution will ordinarily be selected as the group's product; evaluation will usually dictate acceptance. However, a less attractive option may gain endorsement when individual payoffs depend upon having one's own contribution chosen by the group. Consequently, it is important that both self-interest and group-interest be served by selection of the best available alternative. A promotive payoff system provides the needed congruence of goals and thus should tend to favor acceptance of the most highly evaluated product.

In our earlier discussion of disjunctive tasks, we noted that solutions offered by high status persons have a better than average chance of acceptance even when they are not meritorious. Status is a deserved or undeserved "weighting" of individuals which carries the implication that some people's activities are more worthy of attention and acceptance than others'. Status may also decree that rewards should be unequal and thus may nullify the equalitarian impact of a promotive payoff system.

Conjunctive tasks. If the group can do no better than its most inept member permits it to do, serious motivational problems are almost inevitable. Unless members are rather homogeneous, the more competent will be severely restricted by the least able, and the latter is likely to be clearly identified as the one who is responsible for everyone else's limited progress. Under such circumstances, members may attempt to desert the group or to expel the least competent person from it.

Under strictly conjunctive conditions, there is little that anyone can do to increase the competence of the least able member, but steps may be taken to keep him properly motivated and to reward others for their forbearance. No system of payoffs is likely to be entirely satisfactory, but a promotive arrangement probably has the greatest chance of maintaining tolerable internal relationships. It offers the least able person rewards that are contingent upon the goodness of his own performance, and it provides others with an incentive for encouraging him to do his best.

Needless to say, groups that are conjunctive with respect to one criterion of performance are usually additive, disjunctive, or complementary with respect to other criteria. If the group is to endure very long, major payoffs must ordinarily be linked to the latter criteria; mountain climbers may be contented to work with a slow colleague so long as the important consideration is safety rather than speed.

Discretionary tasks. When success depends upon the manner in which the contributions of individual members are weighted and assembled, a promotive payoff system has the merit of making self-interest parallel group-interest. No member is rewarded for having his own contribution weighted more heavily than anyone else's, so each can afford to be as objective as possible. Of course, if previous experience has demonstrated that some members are clearly more qualified than others to perform the task at hand, slightly unequal rewards may be appropriate.

Complementary tasks. Most real-life tasks are divisible. Prescribed process requires each participant to concentrate on those phases of the total task which he is most qualified to perform. An ideal payoff system will reward different people for doing different things. However, this ideal is sometimes difficult to achieve.

It is often the case that a task can be divided in several different ways, and the best way of dividing it depends on how resources are distributed among group members. The idiosyncratic abilities of Jack Sprat and his wife left little room for doubt about the most effective way of apportioning meat-eating responsibilities, but if the platter had contained a more varied assortment of foods a different pattern of specialization might have been in order. Furthermore, the special abilities and limitations of available personnel are seldom as apparent as were those described in the nursery rhyme. Often they become evident only after task activities have begun. When neither the preferred pattern of subtasks nor the best matching of persons with subtasks is obvious, a promotive payoff system has the merit of at least permitting an appropriate pattern of specialization to emerge. Independent and contrient reward schemes require everyone to perform all aspects of the task, or necessitate an arbitrary division of the task into subparts; when rewards are obtained through individual performance, people need to know what it is they are expected to do in order to qualify for them.

Sometimes the identity of subtasks is obvious from the outset, and the problem is one of stimulating individuals to match themselves with subtasks they are especially qualified to perform. Here again a promotive payoff system seems most appropriate because it dictates that nobody will receive very much reward unless all subtasks are adequately performed, and it permits members of the group to experiment with a variety of matching arrangements.

People are often required by an authority figure, or by their colleagues, to perform specific subtasks. This kind of arrangement is commonplace in industry, on athletic teams, and wherever collective action is guided by a thoroughly developed role system. Assuming that people are appropriately matched with subtasks, it is probably advisable to make each person's rewards contingent upon the adequacy with which he enacts his assigned role. Thus a baseball pitcher who wins twenty games should be more highly rewarded than one who wins only five, and a brick mason who is very productive should receive a larger paycheck than one who is not. Either an independent or contrient payoff system will establish the desired relationship between performance and rewards, but it is generally important that "losers" under a contrient arrangement receive substantial reinforcement for their participation. The pitcher with a bad earned-run average may do little more than watch from the sidelines, but he must be rewarded for being available and for providing the regulars with competition. The mediocre brick mason may be needed to complete the job on time. When the contributions of both the "losers" and the "winners" are essential to group success, an independent payoff system is likely to function better than one that is contrient.

Of course, the previous discussion implies that the quality of role enactment can be objectively evaluated. When such is not the case, or when individual performance cannot be very adequately monitored, equity considerations may make a system of equal rewards more appropriate.

Also neglected in the previous discussion is the problem of allocating payoffs to persons who enact different roles. Is a good pitcher more deserving than a good shortstop? There appears to be no universally valid answer to questions of this kind. It is often essential that every subtask be performed well, and the total task therefore assumes a quasi-conjunctive character. When this is true, the critical consideration is likely to be the ease with which the "weakest link in the chain" can be replaced by a stronger one. If good pitchers are abundant and good shortstops are not, market conditions rather than the importance of the role tend to determine required payoffs. Of course, the availability of competent replacements is usually influenced by the amount of training (as well as talent) demanded by the role. This is a major reason why the going wage for skilled tradesmen is higher than that for unskilled labor, and why airline pilots receive higher incomes than bus drivers.

Humanitarian considerations have also been ignored in our examination of payoff systems. We have focused upon factors that may be expected to influence group productivity, and have said nothing about the desirability of providing everyone with an assortment of payoffs that will maintain dignity, self-respect, health, and general well-being. Needless to say, group productivity, though it often promotes these ends, is not a suitable guarantee that important human needs will be met.

Summary: Payoff Systems

People tend to do those things for which they expect to be rewarded, and are more intensely motivated to gain valuable rewards than to achieve insignificant ones. Humans strive to obtain many kinds of payoffs, some of which are contingent upon their contributing to the task performance of groups. In many cases the payoffs of one individual are linked to those of other members of the same group, and indirectly to the payoffs of persons in other groups that compete or cooperate with his own.

Game theorists have described the kinds of goal interdependencies that may prevail among members of a group, and have explored the strategies people employ when the payoff system permits them either to cooperate or compete with one another. However, the findings of this research have been rather inconsistent and appear to have limited applicability to most real-life situations.

Social psychologists have applied the game theorist's notions to situations in which individuals do not merely will themselves into a payoff category but must work to be eligible for rewards. Groups are assigned tasks that have important consequences, and the effects of imposed payoff systems on members' effortful behaviors are examined. Early attempts to employ this research paradigm concentrated on the impact of internal (member-to-member) payoff relationships, but it soon became apparent that external (group-to-group) interdependencies could not be neglected. The latter often determine the fund of rewards available to the group, and thus influence the magnitude of the payoffs individual members may receive.

Evidence accumulated through this type of research is not yet complete enough to justify categorical conclusions. However, promotive internal goal relationships appear to encourage greater specialization of function, and more mutual attentiveness and helpfulness than do contrient or independent arrangements. When the criterion of performance is an individualistic one, independent payoff systems may generate a high level of productivity, and when task performance requires the coordination of specialized functions, promotive interdependence may be the superior pattern. However, quality of performance has not been very thoroughly evaluated. Productivity is probably highest when internal and external payoff systems combine to convince members of the group that their rewards can be maximized by working hard and in the manner dictated by task demands.

Unfortunately, the mediating effects of task demands have not yet received very much attention. However, it is apparent that prescribed process depends upon whether the task is additive, disjunctive, conjunctive, discretionary, or complementary. If we wish to minimize "process losses," our payoff system should be tailored to match the task; it should induce the right person to do the right thing at the right time.

A Note on Cohesion

Webster defines cohesion as the tendency to stick together. A true test of a group's cohesion would entail observation of its members' reactions to disruptive influences. However, no one is completely sure he can specify the kinds of situations that are disruptive, and there are ethical and practical restraints on our freedom to expose groups to environments we believe to be divisive. Consequently, although cohesion is widely discussed, it is almost never subjected to direct experimental examination. Researchers create conditions that are believed to make a group attractive or unattractive to its members, and they note the effects of group experiences on interpersonal attractions, but they rarely conduct experiments that evaluate the "sticking-togetherness" of members.

Although interpersonal attraction is an important basis for cohesion, it is certainly not the only one. Work groups sometimes persist in the face of adversity even though members have little affection for one another, and industrial psychologists often obtain low or even zero correlations between inter-member esteem and measures of the success with which groups cope with their environments. People obviously remain in groups for a variety of reasons: they enjoy the activities, desire the wages or other tangible payoffs they hope to receive, wish to satisfy ego needs, avoid boredom, alleviate uncertainty and fear, or escape the more oppressive social restrictions imposed by other groups. Perhaps all of the reasons people remain in groups can be subsumed under the term "attraction," but an abstract label should not obscure the fact that many different bonds may be holding members together.

It is also important to recognize that attraction is not entirely a matter of liking the outcomes one receives, or expects to receive, from participation in the group. Even minimal membership requires the individual to incur costs: he must expend time, energy, or perhaps money. Affiliation often entails the requirement that certain alternative payoffs be sacrificed, that the individual subordinate some of his personal preferences to those of other members, or that he risk entanglement in unpleasant social situations from which it will be difficult to extricate himself. Except in rare instances involving the application of brute force, we may conclude that such costs are incurred because the individual anticipates receiving payoffs which outweigh his investment. He is "attracted" to the group because the valence of the expected rewards exceeds the costs he feels he must accept. Desired payoffs generate attraction only if they permit the member to anticipate a "net gain" from his participation.

However, net gain is not solely a function of anticipated costs and payoffs. Even when expected rewards are high and costs are moderate, an individual's enthusiasm will be tempered if he feels that desired rewards may not actually be delivered. Many of the payoffs that make a group attractive are somewhat probabilistic; whether or not they will become available for distribution to members depends upon the group's success, or upon factors over which neither the individual nor the group has very much control. Other payoffs, such as the satisfaction of ego needs or escape from boredom, are likely to be more readily available for allocation to members, but the group may or may not bestow such benefits upon a particular individual. When outcomes are uncertain, their incentive value may be assumed to be a multiplicative function of their valence and the subjective probability that they will be delivered when proper costs are incurred (Lawler, 1968; Vroom, 1964). If either valence or subjective probability falls to zero, the individual has no incentive to incur the costs of group membership. If both are high, the group offers an attractive "expected payoff." However, expected gain, rather than expected payoff, should mediate attraction. An individual should find a group attractive to the extent that the expected payoff (i.e., Valence × Subjective Probability) exceeds the costs he believes he must incur.

Attraction $= f \Sigma$ [(valence × subjective probability) − cost].

The summation symbol in the previous formula indicates that attraction is a positive function of all expected gains; the symbol is necessary because groups frequently offer their members several different kinds of payoffs.

People are sometimes attracted to a group, but find another still more attractive. Each group offers substantial net gains, but one promises rewards with higher valences or subjective probabilities, or entails lower costs. Whenever an individual's limited resources compel him to choose among alternative payoffs, or among alternative means of obtaining payoffs (e.g., among groups), we assume he will attempt to maximize his net gain (Thibaut & Kelley, 1959). He will choose to affiliate with the group which seems to meet his needs most adequately, and will decline (perhaps reluctantly) to participate in other groups that are also attractive. Thus, although a cohesive group is presumably attractive to its members, attraction does not guarantee cohesion; to survive a group needs to be more attractive than others that compete for its members' scarce resources.

Of course, it would be unreasonable to contend that people are always aware of every alternative open to them, or that they self-consciously "compute" the expected gains offered by each. However, there can be little doubt that people scan their repertories of familiar options in search of superior opportunities (March & Simon, 1958), and that this process involves a comparison of valences, subjective probabilities, and required costs. Like bettors at the race track, each of us surveys the prizes, the chances, and the prices when choosing among alternatives. Our decisions may be based on fanciful premises, but they reflect our appraisals of the gains and losses offered by available options.

There is another sense in which attraction is not synonymous with cohesion. Certain members of a group are usually more critical to its success and permanence than are others. Such persons may perform onerous duties, assume special responsibilities, or contribute unique resources. Their departure from the group might well signal the end of its existence, whereas the loss of other members would not endanger its survival. Consequently, cohesion depends upon *who* is attracted how much to the group, rather than upon the average level of attraction. To ensure that members stick together in the face of adversity, payoff systems must maintain a favorable distribution of attraction.

Summary

The presence of others may affect the dedication with which an individual works and/or the direction his efforts take. Evaluation apprehension, competition, and modeling often induce individuals to behave differently in a group than they do alone. When the presence of others brings behavior into increased harmony with task demands, social facilitation is said to occur. When the effect entails reduced harmony of behavior and task demands, it is called social inhibition.

In most real-life groups, people are not merely passive observers of one another's performance, nor are people's activities limited to those of co-workers engaged in parallel action. Members of groups usually participate in complex behavioral interchanges, each to some degree complementing, assisting, hindering, or inspiring others. Prescribed process calls for an intricate arrangement of who, what, when; and each individual's outcomes are likely to depend upon the adequacy with which that arrangement is realized. Payoff systems that link one person's rewards to those of another are often employed to induce people to participate in collective, rather than merely parallel, action. To the degree that a payoff system brings actual process into accord with prescribed process, it has the effect of increasing group productivity.

An ideal payoff system will motivate each member of the group to do whatever prescribed process indicates he should do. If unambiguous answers to the who, what, when questions are available, each individual may be rewarded for good performance of his designated function. However, prescribed process is not ordinarily so evident, and payoffs must be allocated in a fashion that encourages an advantageous matching of persons with subtasks, and a felicitous interlocking of each individual's actions with those of his associates.

Research does not yet permit us to reach unequivocal conclusions concerning the merits of promotive, contrient, and independent payoff systems. The effectiveness of each appears to depend upon the nature of task demands and the clarity with which those demands reveal the intricacies of prescribed process. It is important to distinguish between external and internal payoff arrangements, for the character of the former may determine the relative effectiveness of internally promotive, contrient, and independent reward systems.

Cohesion is the "sticking-togetherness" of group members. A group is cohesive to the degree that its members (and especially those who perform critical functions) are more highly attracted to it than to other available groups. Attraction reflects members' appraisals of the payoffs they may receive, the subjective probability that the desired payoffs will actually be delivered, and the costs of membership. Cohesion is a consequence of motivation, and thus may be expected to vary as a function of the payoff system that guides group activity.

Chapter 7

System and Process

Process has been a recurrent theme of this book. We have inferred the processes that are "prescribed" by task demands, group size, and composition. We have also noted some of the factors that are responsible for "process losses." Our concern has been to explain why actual process often differs from prescribed process, and we have suggested that payoff schemes are sometimes instrumental in bringing the former into closer accord with the latter.

Process is not merely a prerequisite to productivity; it is also the adhesive by which the members of a group are bonded to one another. Without process, the whole would be nothing but the sum of its parts, and the group could be relegated to the realm of metaphor or illusion. However, the group is an active enterprise in which members reciprocally shape one another's actions. Collective process transforms an assortment of individuals into a social system.

The Group as a System

Observable and Unobservable Events

The great astronomer, Johann Kepler, had very bad eyesight. As a consequence, he spent little time observing the celestial bodies that were his major interest. Instead, he studied data accumulated by fellow astronomers, and noted that their observations revealed regularities in the changing character of the firmament. What happened to one star was closely correlated with the movement of another, or with the successive locations of the sun or moon. After lengthy examination of recurrent patterns in the data, Kepler announced his discovery of the solar system; the sun, the earth, and several planets constituted a cluster of highly interrelated parts, each responding to the others, the entire set somehow maintaining itself as a distinguishable whole in spite of incessant internal change. In an effort to strip Kepler's discovery of its mystery, Sir Isaac Newton propounded his famous laws of gravitation, which were also employed to account for falling apples and the erosion of riverbanks. Much later other investigators, noting that certain planetary movements were not entirely consistent with Kepler's description of the solar system, postulated the existence of additional parts that had not yet been observed, but which would explain the seemingly aberrant behaviors of recognized parts. With the help of mathematicians, astronomers directed their telescopes toward Neptune and Pluto which were discovered in locations "demanded" by the system.

This sequence of scientific developments illustrates several important principles. Discovery starts with observation; all science depends upon sense data concerning what can be seen, heard, felt, or smelled. To be sure, our frail receptor organs may be assisted by mechanical contrivances such as telescopes, microscopes, or tape measures, but these instruments aid, rather than replace, observation. Having noted what he can about a realm of phenomena, the investigator, or a Johann Kepler who works with the data of others, attempts to organize the findings into understandable patterns. The search for understanding may take many forms, but it usually entails assumptions about unobservable events, processes, or entities. As Francis Bacon said, the subtlety of nature is greater many times over than the subtlety of the human senses. Consequently, researchers often presume their data to reflect only small fragments of a larger whole, much of which is not directly accessible to observation. Kepler's solar system was visible only to the "mind's eye" because its essence lay in the patterned interrelationships of the parts rather than in the parts themselves. Although the system was largely intangible and could not be seen or felt, it was an invaluable aid to understanding the actions of observable planets. Kepler "assembled" parts into a larger whole, and then explained the behavior of the parts as consequences of the whole.

Scientists often move in the opposite direction. Biologists, chemists, and physicists usually regard observable entities as wholes which they explain as consequences of the actions of smaller and sometimes unobservable parts. Thus the structure of a cell and the density of a metal are said to be established by the nature and movements of subatomic particles that are no more accessible to human sense organs than Kepler's solar system. Moving from observable wholes to unobservable parts has proven to be a very productive strategy; it has been responsible for many of the major discoveries of modern science. However, the reverse procedure has also demonstrated its worth, and neither approach can be judged inherently superior to the other.

Regardless of whether observables are too large and diffuse to be seen, or too small and fleeting, they elude our sense organs. Thus their "reality" cannot be confirmed by consensual validation; we cannot say that their authenticity is affirmed by the direct experience of many competent observers. Instead, we must rely upon more roundabout tests of their genuineness. If a postulated unobservable permits us to order our sense data in a meaningful way, if it implies no consequences that contradict carefully accumulated observations, and if it allows us to predict phenomena that are subsequently proven to occur, we conclude that it is real. Genes, subatomic particles, and the solar system have passed these tests.

Though we often feel more confident of phenomena we can see, hear, feel, or smell, there is no assurance that observables deserve great trust. The human senses are tuned to receive a limited range of stimuli, and fail to register events, such as X rays and high-frequency sounds, that fall outside that range. Perhaps the evolutionary process through which our sense apparatus was developed favored a sensitivity to medium-sized events. Ability to detect the presence of predators, food objects, streams, and stones had survival value, but our ancestors could have done little about genes, subatominc particles, or solar systems even if they had been able to see them. In any case, only a portion of the universe appears to be recorded in our direct experience, and this selectivity may reveal more about our own perceptual inadequacy than about the reality of events.

The Nature of Systems

Whether an observer will perceive a group as an entity, or only as a collection of separate individuals, depends in part upon the distance from which he views it. When seen from a mile away, a column of marching soldiers may seem to be a single unit, but a dozen persons assembled around a table are likely to see one another as discrete individuals. Like the forest that becomes only trees when it surrounds us, or the sponge that is transformed into a mass of visually distinct organisms under the microscope, the group loses its apparent solidarity when seen up close.

Recognizing that human sensitivities are tuned to middle-sized entities and may fail to register the wholeness of aggregatès that are too large or too small, Campbell (1958) proposed a number of tests of group "entativity:" we should look for the clues that impart a Gestalt-like quality to middle-sized objects, and employ these clues in our evaluation of social aggregates. Thus a group will be seen as an entity to the degree that its parts are in close proximity to one another, are similar in character, move together in space and thus share a common fate, and form a spatial organization or pattern. Campbell concluded that although some social aggregates meet these criteria moderately well, the legitimacy of the group as an object of scientific inquiry is not yet thoroughly established.

Three decades earlier, F. H. Allport (1924) had declared groups to be illusory phenomena, residing only in the heads of those who were victims of the "group fallacy." Allport concluded the group was unacceptable as an object of scientific investigation because it was not denotable: it could not be identified except by pointing to its members. One could not stumble over a group or detect its existence after its members had departed the scene. Moreover, its parts were not in close physical contact with one another and had the disconcerting habit of becoming disengaged for long periods of time.

The arguments of Campbell and Allport explain why groups are not experienced the same way organisms are. However, some of their objections are as damaging to molecules and solar systems as they are to human groups. If science were restricted to an examination of denotable phenomena, or to the investigation of configurations that form strong perceptual Gestalts, it would be a very impoverished enterprise.

How groups are experienced by observers is less critical than the interdependencies that link members to one another. For it is the latter that determine whether a group can or must be regarded as a system: A set of interacting components that are more directly responsive to one another than to components outside the set. Because the components of such a set tend to react to outside events by influencing and reacting to one another, the impact of environmental events is diffused throughout the system. In most cases, systems appear to maintain a "homeostatic" balance, but the "favored equilibrium" is likely to be somewhat flexible and to change over time. Some systems are intermittent, their parts engaging and subsequently disengaging one another in epidosic fashion. Others remain substantially intact while old parts are replaced by new ones; for example, many of the cells of the human body live only a short time, but the system may persist for three score and ten years.

Some writers, called general systems theorists, suggest that knowledge gained about one system can be generalized to another, for all systems are alike in important respects. The merits of this contention remain to be evaluated. To be sure, all systems are *by definition* alike with respect to the criteria by which they are classified as systems, just as all animals share the features by which they are identified as animals. However, similarities at a very abstract level of analysis do not guarantee the presence of similarities at more concrete levels. All systems entail mutual responsiveness of parts, but molecules, organisms, groups, and galaxies are manifestly different kinds of systems. Perhaps facts discovered about one of them may be regarded as hypotheses about the others, but proof will require diligent research.

What is both important and true about all systems is that the behavior of any part is strongly influenced by the behavior of other parts. Consequently, a piece-by-piece examination of a system is not likely to be entirely fruitful; when together the pieces behave differently than when apart. The capabilities of a system depend upon the distribution of characteristics among the parts, and the system survives as a consequence of coaction rather than individual action. The whole is more than the sum of its parts; it is, in addition, the relationships among its parts. To the extent that a group functions as a system, individualistic approaches to the explanation of collective behavior can never be completely satisfactory.

Is the Group a System?

When we look at a group we see individuals and their behaviors. If the group is a system, that fact is not ordinarily apparent. To see the system, we must permit the "mind's eye" to supplement our sense data. In some respects, our task is easier than was Kepler's, for we can observe what happens when we manipulate a group, take it apart, and put it back together again. On the other hand, our perceptions may be more subject to bias than were his; he was not a part of the system he studied; there was no "individualistic" astronomy to contend that each planet behaves in accordance with its own dispositions and learning experiences; and his eyesight was so poor that neither the parts nor the whole enjoyed perceptual primacy. Our persistent membership in groups may make us insensitive to their character—we may resemble the goldfish that is reputed to be unaware of the water because he is always in it. Our "first-hand knowledge" of human behavior, and our ability to perceive individuals but not groups, may lead us to resist the notion that we are ever parts of a system. If planets were endowed with human eyes and brains, perhaps they too would proclaim their independence.

Several lines of evidence suggest that groups may legitimately be regarded as systems. When participating in groups, individuals often behave quite differently than when alone. Personality measures generally do a poor job predicting how people will behave in groups, and there are many reasons for saying that the actions of individuals are shaped by the interdependencies that prevail in groups. Finally, analysis of collective action reveals the systematic patterning of members' behaviors.

Social influence. Early studies of real-life groups (Durkheim, 1938; LeBon, 1914) revealed that mob behavior is dramatically different from the behaviors individuals are prone to produce when acting alone, and studies of social influence have disclosed striking effects within the confines of the laboratory. Thus, for example, Asch (1951) demonstrated that many people support the judgments expressed by their associates even when those judgments are blatantly inconsistent with sense data. Milgram (1963) found that, when urged to do so, well-meaning adults almost uniformly administered "painful electric shocks" to an experimental accomplice who pleaded inability to bear further anguish, and asserted that he had a bad heart. Lewin (1953) showed that individuals whose attitudes are highly resistant to individual appeals are sometimes susceptible to group persuasion, and Orne and Evans (1965) noted that a long series of experiments had failed to identify any task so onerous that college students would refuse to perform it when asked to do so.

Less dramatic evidence of social effects on individuals' behaviors has been reported earlier in our discussion of social facilitation and inhibition, and our examination of weighting and matching processes. A central theme of this book has concerned the role of interpersonal influence as a determinant of who will do what, when. Our limited ability to predict group outcomes stems from uncertainty about the course such influences will take. It is usually much easier to deduce what a group *can* do than to predict what it *will* do.

Another line of evidence involves the data of many studies designed to identify personality variables that predict how individuals will behave in groups. A Harvard report (Solomon & Lemann, 1951) on 5 years of investigation concluded that such research has had little success because members of a group constitute a system. Mann (1959) examined several hundred studies published between 1900 and 1957. The obtained correlations between specific personality variables and behavior in a group varied greatly from one study to another, but in no case was the median correlation for a relationship higher than .25. When a person functions as a member of a group, his behavioral predispositions are likely to be less critical than the demands of the social system.

The coercive effect of a group is especially apparent when a new member is introduced into an ongoing social unit. Merei (1958) observed the behaviors of children on the playground, noting the frequency with which each copied the actions of others or complied with their demands. Special play groups were then assembled, each consisting of from three to six children who had been submissive on the playground. Groups met for about 40 min per day in a room equipped with appropriate furniture and toys. After three to six meetings, the behaviors of children had become rather standardized.

> The children formed traditions such as permanent seating order (who should sit where); permanent division of objects (who plays with what);

group ownership of certain objects, ceremonies connected with their use, expressions of belonging together; returning to certain activities; rituals; sequences of games; forming a group jargon out of expressions accidentally uttered, etc.*

At this point, each child's freedom to behave in an individualistic manner had been severely curtailed. Each was subject to implicit rules and regulations which he and others had collectively formulated.

Merei then introduced another child into the group. This new "member" was an individual who had been highly dominant on the playground; in most cases he was a year or two older than other members. In every case, the newcomer attempted to impose his own preferences upon the group, and in every case but one he failed. To be sure, he sometimes seemed to become the most influential member, but he achieved this effect by first learning the rules which governed the group's actions, and by then commanding others to do what they would have done even if he had not been present. Or he usurped nominal ownership of the toys, but permitted them to be used as they had been before he arrived on the scene. In the single instance in which the newcomer succeeded in reorganizing the behavior of the group, three previous newcomers had failed. Merei suggests that the cumulative impact of four dominant individuals, introduced into the group on four successive days, had reduced the group to a collection of children who played side by side rather than together. In other groups, the new child was assimilated into the existing social system without appreciable changes being made in the existing pattern of behavior.

Norms and roles. What Merei called traditions, others have called norms and roles. In order to minimize conflict and disorder, members of groups tend to reach implicit or explicit agreements about rights and obligations. Normative prescriptions apply equally to everyone who encounters a given type of situation; norms specify *what* must, or must not, be done *when*. Roles are more complex in that they entail different sets of rules for different categories of people; a role system specifies *who* must, or must not, do *what, when*. Etiquette books and army manuals describe norms and roles that are alleged to govern behaviors in certain settings.

Norms and roles are convenient mechanisms for ensuring the stability of the group. Roles, because they almost invariably require individuals to produce behaviors that are geared to those of their associates, give the group a systematic quality. Participants are rewarded for reacting to one another in ways that have seemed in the past to promote collective achievement and to minimize interpersonal discord.

*From Merei, F. Group leadership and institutionalization. *Human Relations,* 1949, **2,** page 24. Reprinted by permission of Plenum Publishing Corp.

If a novice enters a group without having learned its norms and roles, he is likely to have a disruptive effect on established routines. Consequently, many highly structured groups expose new members to a training program that teaches the fundamentals that must be mastered before full participation can be undertaken. Other groups accomplish the necessary indoctrination in less formal ways. Regardless of the character of the initiation process, the new member learns what to do; he also discovers that rewards and punishments are associated with proper and improper behavior. The group is a reactive enterprise; its parts respond to one another in ways that promote mutual accommodation.

Norms and roles are not so apparent in very small groups or in groups that are newly formed. However, as Goffman (1959) had indicated, even the interaction of a pair of strangers is likely to be guided by expectations concerning what is proper, necessary, or fair. Anthropologists often discover socially enforced regularities in the behaviors of preliterate people, even when the people themselves are unaware of them. The commonplace tends to go unnoticed by those who are thoroughly indoctrinated.

Shared fate and functional interdependence. The components of a system often wax and wane together. Thus an injury to one part of an organism may have adverse effects throughout the body, or necessitate compensating changes by other parts. Groups are not organisms, but their parts sometimes manifest similar interdependencies.

Members of a group have a "shared fate" whenever either the internal or external payoff system is promotive. Members are functionally interdependent when the goal activity of one cannot succeed without the assistance of others. The most capable member of a group cannot provide the solution to a disjunctive task unless his associates are willing to let him do so, and when tasks are divisible, behavioral interdependence is almost inevitable. Throughout this book, we have noted that successful task performance is likely to entail a combination of wise action and prudent inaction; members are matched with subtasks, or are enjoined to do nothing but accept the outcomes generated by others.

Shared fate is sometimes forced upon a group by the environment in which it operates. Nonmembers respond to the group as though it were an undifferentiated entity. The public at large is inclined to treat all members of a streetcorner gang as equivalent individuals, and gang members are likely to overlook differences between one policeman and another. Feedback, like more tangible reinforcements, is commonly allocated to all even when it is prompted by a few. Allport (1924) was right: We treat people as members of a group, and by so doing we encourage them to act as members. Shared fate promotes functional interdependence.

Shared fate and functional interdependence are ubiquitous phenomena. Although they are more typical of some aggregations than others, they are almost universal concomitants of prolonged social interchange. Deutsch (1949) suggests that promotive interdependence is the critical criterion by which a sociological group can be identified, while Cattell (1951) contends that ". . . a group is a collection of organisms in which the existence of all is necessary to the satisfaction of certain individual needs of each." The former view emphasizes shared fate, whereas the latter stresses functional interdependence. Both imply that groups have the qualities of a system.

Lessons from leadership research. When social scientists turned their attention to the group as a task-performing unit, they looked for a single individual whose presence or behaviors somehow determined the actions of others. Groups, it was assumed, succeeded or failed because they had good or bad leaders. Social scientists might therefore make a commendable contribution by identifying the qualities that enable an individual to be a good leader, and by describing the behavior by which the leader increases group productivity and member satisfaction. Leadership research has been voluminous, but the "great man" has escaped detection and no satisfactory recipe for good leadership has been devised.

Early investigations compared the personality traits of leaders and followers, popular and unpopular leaders, and leaders of productive and unproductive groups. Although individual studies sometimes yielded encouraging leads, subsequent work seemed always to cast doubt upon the generality of the findings. No specific kind of person was a successful leader of all sorts of groups. In 1939, Lewin, Lippitt, and White explored the impact of authoritarian, democratic, and laissez-faire styles of leadership on the "social climates" of boys' clubs. The results of this inquiry received widespread attention, but proved to have limited applicability to other types of groups.

Frustrated in their search for all-purpose leaders, investigators altered their tactics. The essential thrust of the new approach was set forth by Hemphill (1949) who contended that "there are no absolute leaders, since successful leadership must always take into account the specific requirements imposed by the nature of the group which is to be led, requirements as diverse in nature and degree as are the organizations in which persons band together [p. 225]." Guided by this view, researchers explored the mediating effects of group size and composition, and the role of task and situational demands on the success of specific leaders or leadership styles. The situational approach demonstrated that the situation mattered, but it did not progress very far toward the goal of identifying the kinds of persons or behaviors that are successful in specific settings. It usually left the *process* of leadership unattended, neglected the needs and actions of followers, and treated the leader as a semiautonomous agent.

Before examining more recent developments, it is well to note two troublesome qualities of the early research. Investigators never achieved much agreement concerning the criteria by which a leader should be identified, and they tended to conceive the group as an entity in which influence flowed primarily in one direction.

The following are some of the ways theorists and researchers identified leaders:

Leaders are persons assigned to the leader role by an experimenter, either with or without the enumeration of special duties and functions.

Leaders are persons identified as such by observers, or by group members, either with or without the delineation of criteria for identification.

Leaders are persons whose presence and/or behaviors in the group strongly influence the group's activities or products.

Leaders are persons who are highly chosen by other members as friends, confidants, or co-workers.

Leaders are persons whose suggestions, commands, or example are regularly accepted and followed by other group members.

Leaders are persons who occupy certain positions within an institutionalized role structure—foremen, lieutenants, company presidents.

Leaders are persons with whom others identify, and who therefore inspire and channel the activities of group members.

Leaders are persons who are observed to perform certain specified functions.

It is obvious that investigators bestowed the mantle of leadership upon an extremely diverse assortment of people. It became increasingly apparent that the various selection criteria were not all identifying the same persons as leaders. People told by an experimenter that they were "the leader" did not necessarily win the endorsement of followers, perform special functions, or even have much effect on group process. Differently phrased sociometric questions sometimes identified different leaders, and the person with whom others identified was not always the one who occupied the dominant position within the role structure. It is not surprising that studies appeared to contradict one another, and that no single set of qualities was found to typify the good or bad leader.

Efforts to locate and analyze the leader were prompted by a hierarchical conception of the group. If a single member tends to shape the behaviors of a group, we should identify that person and determine how and why he exercises such irresistable power. However, if a group is a system, we must anticipate that no single person is likely to dominate its actions, that each member adjusts to others, and that hierarchical arrangements often conceal mutual interdependencies that are essential to the group's continuance. The "dominant" child in Merei's play groups acquired apparent authority by subjecting himself to the will of others; dominance was purchased at the cost of submission, and we are not sure who exerted the greater influence over whom.

To be sure, there are groups in which a single person overshadows others. The teacher commands the classroom and the foreman manages his workers. However, cases of this kind usually reflect the impact of a larger social unit. The teacher is the agent of the community and the foreman expresses the dictates of the organization; both derive their clout from the larger system to which they are subordinate. Within the groups they "lead," each must adjust to the whims and foibles of the led. In moments of candor, teachers and foremen confess that they sometimes feel helpless in the midst of their charges. The army sargeant who is given autocratic power over his squad may nevertheless find that he is dominated by it (Merton, 1957).

Leadership theorists were not totally unaware of the reciprocal nature of leader-follower relationships. They often asserted that a leader must have "membership character," win the approval or at least the grudging consent of the followers, and remain sensitive to followers' needs. However, an individual who met such requirements was apparently licensed to manage the group's affairs. The leader was a semi-insulated director of group processes, rather than a full-scale participant in those processes. Furthermore, his hegemony was usually conceived to be very broad; he might not be a "great man" outside his group, but his influence shaped almost everything of importance that happened inside it.

When the group is conceived as a system, a member's influence depends upon the character of his participation in the group's processes. His actions are responses to others' behaviors as well as stimuli that evoke reactions in others. It is most unlikely that a single individual is the chief determinant of all phases of the group's activities. He may be a coordination specialist who, more than anyone else, regulates the group's processes by controlling who may do what, when. Or he may be a motivating agent who stimulates others to contribute their resources and keeps interpersonal conflicts from developing. In some groups, a single individual possesses a larger fund of task-relevant resources than anyone else and functions as an "expert leader." In most cases, resources are more uniformly distributed, and a majority of members specialize in doing whatever they are qualified to do, and in reacting to the behavior of others. Specialization can take many forms, and research (Slater, 1955) suggests that rather stable role differentiations sometimes emerge within the first few hours of a group's existence. There is no apparent reason however, for asserting that one specialty is inherently more important than another, or more worthy of being called leadership. Each is likely to entail the performance of functions that are essential. Moreover, it should be remembered that specialization is a collective matter; a specialty can exist only if other specialties also exist. If one person concentrates on certain functions, someone else must attend to the chores he neglects. Members of a group become specialists with the tacit or explicit consent and cooperation of their associates. Systems permit specialization to occur, and often become more cohesive as a consequence of it (Durkheim, 1947); specialized parts are even more dependent upon the system than are those that are not so specialized.

Two trends are discernible in very recent literature. The first is an increased tendency to recognize that the leader, however he may be identified, is a product of, and a participant in, group processes. He functions within a system that is shaped by others as well as himself. Like his associates, he adjusts to the demands of the system.

The second trend is a notable decrease in the use of the word "leader." All parts of a system are important; each effects others and contributes to the ongoing process; and the specialized activities of one part are likely to be no more critical than those of others. To call any member of a group a leader is to imply greater inequality of contribution and more asymmetry of influence than observation justifies. Furthermore, the leadership label usually carries too many meanings to be very useful. As Thibaut and Kelley (1959) have noted, "In virtually all cases, leadership seems to be analyzable in terms of other, simpler concepts."

By its failures, leadership research encouraged acceptance of the notion that the group is a system; once that notion was accepted, a revised view of leadership was inevitable.

Process

The components of a system interact. Although living systems are never completely closed to outside influences, their parts are especially responsive to one another. Action by one part stimulates a flow of events in other parts, and an enduring (though sometimes evolving) pattern of interrelationships is preserved. If the parts cease to interact, the system dies—or is at least recessed until interaction is resumed.

The events by which a group maintains itself as a system are, of course, the actions of individual human beings. However, man's capacity for communication links one person to another, and the actions of each may become elements in a continuing process.

Webster defines "process" as a series of actions or operations definitely conducing to an end. In Chapter 1 of this book, we described group process as a series of behaviors, one following after another, each to some degree determined by those which have gone before and each, in turn, influencing those that will come later. Perhaps it is true that all process "conduces" to an end, but the end is sometimes not achieved; often it is not identifiable at the time the events are occurring; and frequently it is not "intended" or "sought" by the agents participating in the actions. Furthermore, some of the events in a contingent series may inhibit achievement of the end toward which other events are moving; one muscle opposes another, and members of a group sometimes attempt to move in opposite directions. To exclude those actions that mar the consistency of the sequence would require that we ignore the vicissitudes of process.

It is probably impossible to produce a complete description of any group process. Such a document would contain not only a detailed account of who is observed to do what, when, but also a precise report of unobserved events transpiring inside the individual members. Person A's overt act stimulates a chain of events within person B whose observable response is more directly prompted by his own internal behaviors than by the action of A. What we see in a group are the tops of the icebergs; what happens below the water affects what we see, but is generally hidden from sight. We describe what we can see and make educated guesses about the rest. Of course, it is possible to explore some of the actions that occur below the water line; many branches of psychology attempt to infer unseen processes by manipulating and observing what happens in plain view, and some examine the internal workings of rats as a way of deducing information about man's hidden behaviors. These procedures usually focus upon one iceberg at a time and thus do not reveal very much about the lengthy sequences of events that are group process.

The predicament of the group theorist is not unlike that of persons who study other systems. The physiologist may describe the interaction of parts within an organism, but the parts are themselves composed of still smaller, interacting parts. A complete description of organic processes might entail an account of the behaviors of particles within atoms that are components of molecules which are, in turn, the units of which cells are built. When systems are composed of subsystems, description usually cannot deal with a large portion of the total assembly. Generally, we know too little about the connections between layers, and lack the concepts by which knowledge about one level can be linked to information about the next. In theory, it may be desirable that a description of group process tell us what every molecule in every member is doing, but such an ideal is unattainable. Fortunately, much can be learned by dealing with the observable behaviors of the human parts, and by seasoning our observations with an occasional dash of inference drawn from the work of those who specialize in reaching conclusions about man's internal transactions.

Group Process

If the group is a system, its processes should be orderly. The uninstructed eye may see only the actions of parts, but the thoughtful vision of a Johann Kepler should discover a collective tidiness.

Who acts how often? In 1952, Stephan and Mishler reported a lengthy investigation of discussion groups. Observers counted the number of oral contributions made by each of several college students during very informal class meetings. Any uninterrupted utterance was regarded as a contribution, and tallies were made during most of a 1-hr session. The groups contained from 4 to 12 members and at least 4 sessions of each size were studied. After all data had been collected, members of each group were rank-ordered with respect to the frequency of their participation. Thus, for example, the individuals in a four-person group were ranked 1 through 4. The data for all sessions of the same size were combined by adding the tallies for members with the same rank. This procedure produced a single participation score for all top-ranked members of four-person groups, another score for all second-ranked members, etc. The important findings concern the relationships among these measures of partici-pation.

Figure 7.1 reports data for 15 seven-member sessions. The percentages of all contributions made by persons at each of the 7 ranks are indicated by the dots, while the dashed line identifies the percentages that are estimated for each rank by an exponential model. The model asserts that there will be a constant ratio of speaking frequencies across adjacently ranked pairs of participants. Thus, if second-ranked persons speak .661 as often as first-ranked persons, third-ranked individuals will participate .661 as frequently as those who are second-ranked, etc. The model does not specify the magnitude of the ratio—only that it will be constant from one pair of ranks to another within a single group. The dashed line in Fig. 7.1 is empirically derived to minimize discrepancies between the obtained data and the estimates generated by the constant-ratio model. The fit appears to be very close: Each rank produced about .661 as many contributions as the next higher rank.

The model was equally successful in estimating participation rates for sessions of other sizes. Altogether, Stephan and Mishler "predicted" a total of 72 values (one for each rank in groups ranging in size from 4 to 12). The largest error occurred in four-person sessions where second-ranked persons were estimated to produce 17.5 percent of all contributions, but were actually responsible for 20.5 percent. Only 9 of 72 obtained values deviated by as much as 1 percent from the estimated values. The "constant ratio" was not constant across different sized sessions, nor did the model contend that it should be. The ratio varied from .589 for 4-person sessions to .727 for those involving 12 members. Each increase in group size added an increment to the ratio. Thus the slope of the estimation curve (i.e., the dashed line in Fig. 7.1) was somewhat steeper for smaller groups and flatter for larger ones.

Some of Stephan and Mishler's findings suggest that the ratio is not completely independent of the dispositions of the people who compose the group. Two new 7-person groups were formed, all members being persons who had ranked in the top one-third of groups observed earlier. Two other groups were assembled from individuals who had ranked in the bottom two-thirds

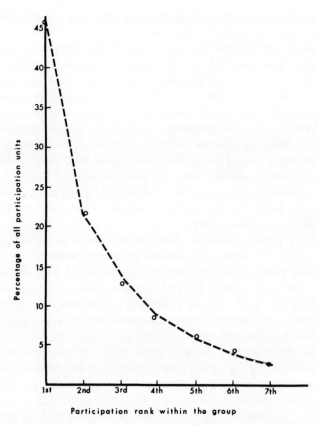

Fig. 7.1. The percentage of all units of participation produced by persons at each rank with seven-person groups. From data reported by Stephan and Mishler (1952).

during earlier sessions. The constant-ratio model estimated the participation rates of these newly constituted groups with about the same precision as before, but the ratios were different. As might be expected, groups containing only persons who had previously been observed to be high participators yielded a high ratio (.799 instead of .661 as had been the case for the earlier, unselected 7-member groups). However, the new groups composed of low participators had a ratio of only .567. It is not at all clear why a collection of "nontalkative" persons should manifest greater inequality of participation than an unselected group. Perhaps such persons compete for the privilege of *not* talking, the result being that a few individuals who are especially sensitive to task demands make whatever contributions seem essential while others joyfully participate only to the extent of expressing necessary civilities and encouraging George to do it. By contrast, groups composed of talkative persons presumably induce severe competition for scarce talking time, the result being that everyone demands, and is somehow accorded, a share of the limelight.

Stephan and Mishler did not contend that all groups abide by the constant-ratio principle. Indeed, they noted several circumstances that might prevent such a pattern from emerging. A role system might prescribe equal or grossly unequal participation rates; differences among members might divide them into two or more distinct categories with markedly different participation relationships; or the free competitive expression of participation potentials might be inhibited by coercive restraints. However, acknowledging that one's findings are not universal truths does not explain why those findings are the truth about certain groups. Why are participations so neatly patterned in relatively unstructured groups of the kind studied by Stephan and Mishler? Why this particular pattern rather than another one? These questions have not yet been answered very satisfactorily.

Horvath (1965) proposed that members of a group are guided by a "pecking order" that allows an individual to act only when no one above him is talking. If all persons have the same inclination to act when the opportunity presents itself (i.e., when no higher-ranking person is speaking), actual participations will be distributed as Stephan and Mishler observed them to be. Social systems often enforce a "pecking order," but Horvath's assumption that everyone has the same inclination to act seems unacceptable.

Other theorists (e.g., Coleman, 1960; Leik, 1967) have advanced alternative explanations built on assumptions concerning the distribution of participation potentials among group members, the propensity to react when spoken to, the operation of chance factors, etc. It is difficult to evaluate such theories because they propose a complex interplay of variables that are not ordinarily subject to direct observation. For our purposes, it is sufficient to note that they entail assumptions about differences among parts, and about the manner in which the actions of one part are conditioned by the actions of other parts. In this respect, they are theories that attempt to explain the behaviors of a system; they are loosely analogous to the gravitational theory by which Francis Bacon explained the actions of the solar system.

It is most unlikely that Stephan and Mishler's subjects were simply participating at rates they personally found congenial. By employing the logic of sampling theory (see Chapter 2), it can be demonstrated that randomly chosen members of a group would behave in accordance with the "constant ratio" principle only if "participation potentials" were distributed in a highly skewed fashion in the parent population. Since the inclination to act seems to be more or less normally distributed among people, something must happen in the group to shape the participation of its members. The processes of the system reveal regularities that reflect the mutual effects of parts upon one another.

The impact of an environmental event that impinges upon one part of a system may be "absorbed" or negated by the actions of other parts. Bavelas, Hastorf, Gross, and Kite, (1965) demonstrated that operant procedures could be used successfully to increase an individual's rate of participation in his group *provided other members were negatively reinforced for speaking*. However, positive reinforcement had no appreciable effect on the individual's behavior when it was not accompanied by negative reinforcement to the rest of the group. The investigators concluded that it is not enough to encourage a quiet person to participate more; "room" must be provided for his increased verbal output. As Lewin (1953) discovered in his research on attitude change, it is sometimes easier to change the entire group than to change a single member.

To whom are acts directed? Many of the acts that occur within groups are directed toward elements of the environment, or toward the group as a whole. However, others can be identified as having been directed to specific members of the group.

In the research that has already been described, Stephan and Mishler noted not only the originators of assertions but also the target persons for whom assertions were intended. After all data had been collected, members of groups were ranked with respect to the frequency with which they had been targets, and the "constant ratio" model was employed to estimate the percentages of times acts had been directed toward first-ranked persons, second-ranked persons, etc. These estimates matched the obtained percentages rather well; only 13 of 72 "predictions" erred by as much as 1 percent. The ratios for receipt of acts were slightly lower than those for performance of acts, indicating that group members tended to be more unequal as targets than as originators. However, persons who produced many acts tended also to be the targets of many acts.

Bales (1950) has also reported a strong relationship between the sending and receiving of acts. Stephan (1952) applied the "constant ratio" model to Bales' published data and obtained a good fit. Although Bales' groups were engaged in discussion, as Stephan and Mishler's were, his unit of observation was the smallest vocal or expressive act observers could assign to any of 12 content categories. The fact that the model successfully estimated percentages of acts originated and received within Bales' groups indicates that its applicability is not limited to data in the form of uninterrupted utterances.

If a part of a system behaves in ways that endanger the progress of other parts, or that threaten the continuance of the system, action may be taken to correct the errant conduct of the malfunctioning part. In the case of a human group, such action is likely to involve communication. Schachter (1951) connived to have experimental accomplices included in the membership of newly formed clubs on a college campus. At the first meeting, one accomplice steadfastly maintained an extremely deviant position on an issue, whereas another accomplice initially advocated the same deviant position, but subsequently brought his view into harmony with that of the group. In all clubs, both deviants were targets of many communicative acts during the first few minutes of the discussion period. However, communication to the compliant accomplice decreased as he yielded to the blandishments of others, while the persistent deviant tended in most cases, to receive a steadily increasing flow of messages. The exception to this trend occurred in clubs for which the issue was especially important; in such groups communication to the persistent deviate increased until the final moments by which time it was probably apparent to all that no amount of argument would produce a conversion. In all clubs except those for which the issue was of little importance, the persistent deviate was rejected at the conclusion of the session. He was most strongly rejected by clubs for which the issue was highly important.

Communication is the major ingredient by which groups are held together. When a part of the system fails to function appropriately, it becomes the target of messages from others. If communication fails to induce the desired adjustments, the recalcitrant member may be punished or expelled from the system.

What and when? The most ambitious attempt to chart the flow of group process has been made by R. F. Bales and his students. After several years of preliminary work, Bales proposed a set of 12 content categories into which the actions of a discussion group might be said to fall.

Social-emotional area: positive reactions

    1. Shows solidarity, raises other's status, gives help, reward.
    2. Shows tension release, jokes, laughs, shows satisfaction.
    3. Agrees, shows passive acceptance, understands, concurs, complies.

Task area: attempted answers

    4. Gives suggestion, direction, implying autonomy for other.
    5. Gives opinion, evaluation, analysis, expresses feeling, wish.
    6. Gives orientation, information, repeats, clarifies, confirms.

Task area: questions

    7. Asks for orientation, information, repetition, confirmation.
    8. Asks for opinions, evaluation, analysis, expression of feeling.
    9. Asks for suggestion, direction, possible ways of action.

Social-emotional area: negative reactions

    10. Disagrees, shows passive rejection, formality, withholds help.
    11. Shows tension, asks for help, withdraws out of field.
    12. Shows antagonism, deflates other's status, defends or asserts self.

When used in research, the 12 categories are listed as columns on a paper tape that moves slowly under an aperture in a console. Two or more observers record ongoing process by making pencil marks on the tape. Each codable act is assigned to the appropriate category, and symbols are employed to identify the source and target of every event. Because the tape moves at a constant speed, the completed record reveals the temporal relationships among events. The technique produces data concerning who, what, when, and to whom.

Bales's procedure is not very appropriate when the group's behavior is largely nonvocal, and its general applicability is restricted by the fact that very extensive training is required to enable observers to achieve a satisfactory level of reliability. In spite of these limitations, the technique has been widely used. In the paragraphs that follow, we will note only a few of many findings.

Bales's (1953) data suggest that the content of a group discussion tends to be fairly stable; about 25 percent of all acts are positive reactions, 57 percent are attempted answers, 7 percent are questions, and 11 percent are negative reactions. While these figures are only approximations and are not alleged to be accurate for all kinds of groups, they are assumed to reflect equilibrium-producing processes that operate in many social systems. They are seen as ". . . the final result of a repetitive series of cycles, each of which consists of: (1) an initial disturbance of the system (precipitated by the introduction of a new idea, or opinion, or suggestion into the group) followed by (2) a 'dwindling series of feedbacks' and corrections as the disturbance is terminated, equilibrated, or assimilated by other parts or members of the system [p. 117]."* What Bales means by an equilibrium becomes apparent when one imagines what would happen if an accomplice were planted in a group and instructed to upset the 25-57-7-11 distribution of acts. No matter which class of events the accomplice might try to push out of proportion, his behaviors would undoubtedly stimulate other members to behave in ways that would restore the balance: Questions prompt answers, answers evoke positive or negative reactions, positive reactions lead to a new cycle of suggestions and feedbacks, etc. If our accomplice were obstreperous enough to endanger the pattern, he would probably be physically or psychologically exiled from the group.

In other analyses, Bales has looked more closely at the temporal arrangement of acts. Do certain types of events characteristically follow other types? If the first of two acts is produced by person A and the second by person B, are the contingencies different than they would be if both were produced by person A? The data indicate that temporal clustering does indeed occur, and that its character depends upon whether the acts are produced by one or by more than one person. When only one person is involved, Bales speaks of "proaction," but when "action changes hands" he employs the label "reaction."

*From R. F. Bales, *Working Papers in the Theory of Action* (T. Parsons, R. F. Bales, and E. A. Shils, Eds.) Glencoe, Illinois: Free Press, 1953. Used by permission of the copyright owner, Macmillan Co., New York.

When a single individual is responsible for two successive acts, an expression of disagreement is twice as likely to be followed by opinion giving as is the case when successive acts are produced by different people (51 percent versus 25 percent of the observed instances). Proaction involves many fewer instances in which tension release follows itself (37 percent) than does reaction (68 percent). A single individual is less likely to produce two antagonistic acts in a row (22 percent) than are two persons who act in tandem (36 percent). Like a language in which certain words tend to occur together, group process manifests a clustering of events. Whether two acts have an affinity for one another depends in part upon whether they are both generated by the same person. However, the collective behaviors of two or more interacting persons appear to be no less patterned than the actions of a single individual.

Fragments of Process

The previous discussion has been focused on relationships among observable behaviors of group members. We have looked at the tops of the icebergs and discovered that their actions reveal the regularities of a system. However, we have not attempted to probe the underwater events that are almost certainly implicated in what goes on in clear view. We have treated group process as a continuing sequence of observable acts, and have not worried about the critical events that occur inside the people who produce those acts. A complete description of group process would deal with internal events as well as with person-to-person transactions.

Our approach has not been very typical of the times. During the past decade, researchers have tended to deal with the single individual in a highly controlled setting. The environment is manipulated, the individual receives messages from real or imaginary persons, and his reactions are observed. However, the individual has little opportunity to affect anyone else, to establish two-way relationships with others, or to participate in anything that very closely resembles collective action. The aim of such research is to discover how individuals process incoming stimulation and how they learn to cope with changing situations. The strategy is that of traditional psychology which Sears (1951) has called monadic. "In spite of their long prepossessions with social influences on the individual, psychologists think monadically. That is, they choose the behavior of one person as their scientific subject matter. For them, the universe is composed of individuals. These individuals are acted upon by external events, to be sure, and in turn the external world is modified by the individual's behaviors. However, the universal laws sought by the psychologist almost always relate to a single body. They are monadic laws and are stated with reference to a monadic unit of behavior [pp. 478-479]."

There is nothing inherently wrong with a monadic approach, so long as one remembers that it involves a piece-by-piece examination of the parts of a system. The pieces may behave differently when reassembled, but there may be no better way to learn about internal events that mediate between stimulus and response. Many fragments of process are embedded within the boundaries of the single individual, and they must be discovered or inferred in whatever manner is feasible. However, we can agree with Sears' contention that the monadic unit must sooner or later be expanded into a dyadic one that encompasses the combined actions of two or more persons. The research efforts of recent years suggest that most investigators are in no hurry to accomplish the expansion Sears had in mind.

The study of icebergs will not be complete until events that occur below the water line are linked to those that occur above. Much can be learned without getting wet, or without bothering to consider the impact of one iceberg upon another. However, each of these convenient ploys generates knowledge about fragments of a larger whole. Group process is also individual process, and much of individual process is imbedded in group process.

A Brief Summation

Early in this book, we considered the notion of prescribed process: a series of acts which, if they occur, permit the group to be maximally effective in the performance of a task. We suggested that prescribed process is a matter of the right person doing the right thing at the right time, and we noted that actual process often deviates from that which is prescribed. When this is the case, process losses cause the group's actual productivity to fall below its potential productivity.

Prescribed process depends upon the nature of the task and the size and composition of the group. A careful analysis of these factors sometimes permits us to specify who *should* do what, when, in order to maximize productivity. However, members of a group may not know how their efforts can best be expended. Even when the details of prescribed process are evident to all, members may not be motivated to do what is demanded of them. For this reason, it is often advantageous to devise payoff systems that reward each participant for performing his portion of the prescribed process.

Finally, the chapter we are now concluding has focused on the group as a system, and has viewed process as the essential bond by which members are held together in relationships that impart a quality of wholeness to the group. A group cannot be productive for very long unless it survives as a system, and survival requires that the group cope with its environment. In this respect, all groups must be productive in order to endure.

Humans have the capacity to evaluate and reorganize their collective behaviors. Perhaps the human group is the only system in which the parts can reflect on the success of the arrangement within which they function, and can institute deliberate changes. This ability permits the group to be far more flexible than a herd of musk oxen or a colony of ants. If a task must be performed, human ingenuity can probably discover the kind of process that will do it; man can engineer the system in which he operates. Though our knowledge of collective process is still rather primitive, the most troublesome unanswered questions concern the goals toward which group action *should* be directed rather than the manner in which it *can* be directed. Achieving productivity will probably be easier than deciding what should be produced.

References

Allport, F. H. *Social psychology.* Boston: Houghton, 1924.

Anderson, N. H. Group performance in an anagram task. *Journal of Social Psychology,* 1961, **55**, 67-75.

Asch, S. E. Effects of group pressure upon the modification and distortion of judgments. In H. Guetzkow (Ed.), *Groups, leadership, and men.* Pittsburgh, Pennsylvania: Carnegie Press, 1951. Pp. 171-190.

Asch, S. E. Studies of independence and conformity: A minority of one against a unanimous majority. *Psychological Monographs,* 1956, **70** (9, Whole No. 416).

Atkinson, J. W. Motivational determinants of risk-taking behavior. *Psychological Review,* 1957, **64**, 359-372.

Bakis, E. The so-called DP-apathy in Germany's DP camps. *Transactions of Kansas Academy of Sciences,* 1952, **55**, 62-68.

Bales, R. F. *Interaction process analysis: A method for the study of small groups.* Cambridge, Massachusetts: Addison-Wesley, 1950.

Bales, R. F. The equilibrium problem in small groups. In T. Parsons, R. F. Bales and E. A. Shils (Eds.), *Working papers in the theory of action.* New York: Macmillan (Free Press, Glencoe, Ill.), 1953.

Bales, R. F. and Borgatta, E. F. Size of group as a factor in the interaction profile. In A. P. Hare, E. F. Borgatta, and R. F. Bales (Eds.), *Small groups: Studies in social interaction.* New York: Knopf, 1955. Pp. 396-413.

Bales, R. F., Strodtbeck, F. L., Mills, T. M., and Rosenborough, M. E. Channels of communication in small groups. *American Sociological Review,* 1951, **16**, 461-468.

Bandura, A. and Walters, R. H. *Social learning and personality development*. New York: Holt, 1964.

Barker, R. G. Ecology and motivation. *Nebraska symposium on motivation*, 1960, **8**, 1-50.

Barker, R. G. *Ecological psychology: Concepts and methods for studying the environment of human behavior*. Stanford, California: Stanford Univ. Press, 1968.

Barnlund, D. C. A comparative study of individual, majority, and group judgment. *Journal of Abnormal and Social Psychology*, 1959, **58**, 55-60.

Bavelas, A. A mathematical model for group structures. *Applied Anthropology*, 1948, **7**, 16-30.

Bavelas, A., Hastorf, A. H., Gross, A. E., and Kite, W. R. Experiments on the alteration of group structure. *Journal of Experimental Social Psychology*, 1965, **1**, 55-70.

Byrne, D. Interpersonal attraction and attitude similarity. *Journal of Abnormal and Social Psychology*, 1961, **62**, 713-715.

Campbell, D. T. Common fate, similarity, and other indices of the status of aggregates of persons as social entities. *Behavioral Science*, 1958, **3**, 14-25.

Campbell, J. P. and Dunnette, M. D. Effectiveness of T-group experiences in managerial training and development. *Psychological Bulletin*, 1968, **70**, 73-104.

Cartwright, D. and Zander, A. *Group dynamics: Research and theory*. New York: Harper, 1968.

Castore, G. F. Number of verbal interrelationships as a determinant of group size. *Journal of Abnormal and Social Psychology*, 1962, **64**, 456-458.

Cattell, R. B. New concepts for measuring leadership, in terms of group syntality. *Human Relations*, 1951, **4**, 161-184.

Cohen, A. *Delinquent boys*. Glencoe, Illinois: Free Press, 1955.

Coleman, J. S. The mathematical study of small groups. In H. Solomon (Ed.), *Mathematical thinking in the measurement of behavior*. Glencoe, Illinois: Free Press, 1960. Pp. 46-69.

Comrey, A. L. Group performance in a manual dexterity task. *Journal of Applied Psychology*, 1953, **37**, 207-210.

Comrey, A. L. and Deskin, G. Further results on group manual dexterity in men. *Journal of Applied Psychology*, 1954a, **38**, 116-118.

Comrey, A. L. and Deskin, G. Group manual dexterity in women. *Journal of Applied Psychology*, 1954b, **38**, 178-180.

Comrey, A. L. and Staats, C. K. Group performance in a cognitive task. *Journal of Applied Psychology*, 1955, **39**, 354-356.

Cottrell, N. B., Wack, D. L., Sekerak, G. J., and Rittle, R. H. Social facilitation of dominant responses by the presence of an audience and the mere presence of others. *Journal of Personality and Social Psychology*, 1968, **9**, 245-250.

Darley, J. M. and Latané, B. Bystander intervention in emergencies: Diffusion of responsibility. *Journal of Personality and Social Psychology*, 1968a, **8**, 377-383.

Darley, J. M. and Latané, B. When will people help in a crises? *Psychology Today*, 1968b, **2**, 54-57.

Dashiell, J. F. An experimental analysis of some group effects. *Journal of Abnormal and Social Psychology*, 1930, **25**, 190-199.

Dashiell, J. F. Experimental studies of the influence of social situations on the behavior of individual human adults. In C. Murchison (Ed.), *Handbook of Social Psychology*. Worcester, Massachusetts: Clark Univ. Press, 1935. Pp. 1097-1158.

Davis, J. *Group performance*. Reading, Massachusetts: Addison-Wesley, 1969.

Deutsch, M. The effects of cooperation and competition upon group process. *Human Relations*, 1949, **2**, 129-152 and 199-231.

Dreyer, A. S. Aspiration behavior as influenced by expectation and group comparison. *Human Relations,* 1954, **7**, 175-190.

Durkheim, E. *The rules of sociological method.* New York: Free Press, 1938.

Durkheim, E. *The division of labor in society.* (G. Simpson, Tran). Glencoe, Illinois: Free Press, 1947.

Farnsworth, P. and Williams, W. F. The accuracy of the median and the mean of a group of judges. *Journal of Social Psychology,* 1936, **7**, 237-239.

Faust, W. L. Group versus individual problem-solving. *Journal of Abnormal and Social Psychology,* 1959, **59**, 68-72.

Festinger, L. A theory of social comparison processes. *Human Relations,* 1954, **7**, 117-140.

Festinger, L. and Thibaut, J. Interpersonal communication in small groups. *Journal of Abnormal and Social Psychology,* 1951, **46**, 92-99.

Gamson, W. A. Experimental studies of coalition formation. In L. Berkowitz (Ed.), *Advances in experimental social psychology,* Vol. 1. New York: Academic Press, 1964. Pp. 81-110.

Ghiselli, E. E. and Lodahl, T. M. Patterns of managerial traits and group effectiveness. *Journal of Abnormal and Social Psychology,* 1958, **57**, 61-66.

Gibb, J. R. The effects of group size and of threat reduction upon creativity in a problem solving situation. *American Psychologist,* 1951, **6**, 324. (Abstract)

Goffman, E. *The presentation of self in everyday life.* Garden City, New York: Doubleday Anchor, 1959.

Goldman, M., McGlynn, A., and Toledo, A. Comparison of individual and group performance of size three and five with various initially right and wrong tendencies. *Journal of Personality and Social Psychology,* 1967, **7**, 222-226.

Golembiewski, R. T. *The small group: An analysis of research concepts and operations.* Chicago: Univ. of Chicago Press, 1962.

Guetzkow, H. Differentiation of roles in task-oriented groups. In D. Cartwright and A. Zander (Eds.), *Group dynamics: Research and theory.* Evanston, Illinois: Row, Peterson, 1960. Pp. 683-704.

Gurnee, H. Maze learning in the collective situation. *Journal of Psychology,* 1937, **3**, 437-443.

Hammond, L. K. and Goldman, M. Competition and non-competition and its relationship to individual and group productivity. *Sociometry,* 1961, **24**, 46-60.

Handyside, J. D. An estimate of the size of primary working groups in British industry. *Occupational Psychology,* 1952, **26**, 106-107.

Hare, A. P. A study of interaction and consensus in different sized groups. *American Sociological Review,* 1952, **17**, 261-267.

Hare, A. P. *Handbook of small group research.* Glencoe, Illinois: Free Press, 1962.

Hemphill, J. K. The leader and his group. *Education Research Bulletin,* 1949, **28**, 225-229.

Henchy, T. and Glass, D. C. Evaluation apprehension and the social facilitation of dominant and subordinate responses. *Journal of Personality and Social Psychology,* 1968, **10**, 446-454.

Heslin, R. Predicting group task effectiveness from member characteristics. *Psychological Bulletin,* 1964, **62**, 248-256.

Hoffman, L. R. and Maier, N. R. F. Quality and acceptance of problem solutions by members of homogeneous and heterogeneous groups. *Journal of Abnormal and Social Psychology,* 1961, **62**, 401-407.

Hoffman, L. R. and Maier, N. R. F. Valence in the adoption of solutions by problem-solving groups: Quality and acceptance as goals of leaders and members. *Journal of Personality and Social Psychology,* 1967, **6**, 175-182.

Hollingshead, A. B. *Elmtown's youth: The impact of social classes on adolescents.* New York: Wiley, 1949.

Homans, C. G. *The human group.* New York: Harcourt, 1950.

Homans, C. G. Social behavior as exchange. *American Journal of Sociology,* 1958, **63**, 597-606.

Horvath, W. J. A mathematical model of participation in small group discussions. *Behavioral Science,* 1965, **10**, 164-166.

Hovland, C. I., Janis, I. L., and Kelley, H. H. *Communication and persuasion.* New Haven, Connecticut: Yale Univ. Press, 1953.

Husband, R. W. Cooperative versus solitary problem solution. *Journal of Social Psychology,* 1940, **11**, 405-409.

Hyman, H. The value systems of different classes: A social psychological contribution to the analysis of stratification. In R. Bendix and S. M. Lipset (Eds.), *Class, status, and power.* Glencoe, Illinois: Free Press, 1953. Pp. 426-442.

Izard, C. E. Personality similarity and friendship. *Journal of Abnormal and Social Psychology,* 1960, **61**, 47-51.

James, J. A preliminary study of the size determinant in small group interaction. *American Sociological Review,* 1951, **16**, 474-477.

Jenness, A. The role of discussion in changing opinion regarding a matter of fact. *Journal of Abnormal and Social Psychology,* 1932, **27**, 279-296.

Jennings, H. H. *Leadership and isolation.* New York: Longmans, Green, 1943.

Johnson, H. H. and Torcivia, J. M. Group and individual performance on a single-stage task as a function of distribution of individual performance. *Journal of Experimental Social Psychology,* 1967, **3**, 266-273.

Julian, J. W. and Perry, F. A. Cooperation contrasted with intragroup and inter-group competition. *Sociometry,* 1967, **30**, 79-90.

Kelley, H. H., Condry, J. C., Jr., Dahlke, A. E., and Hill, A. H. Collective behavior in a simulated panic situation. *Journal of Experimental Social Psychology,* 1965, **1**, 20-54.

Klugman, S. F. Group and individual judgments for anticipated events. *Journal of Social Psychology,* 1947, **26**, 21-33.

Lanzetta, J. T. and Roby, T. B. Effects of work group structure and certain task variables on group performance. *Journal of Abnormal and Social Psychology,* 1956, **53**, 307-314.

Latané, B. and Rodin, J. A lady in distress: The effects of friends and strangers on bystander intervention. *Journal of Experimental Social Psychology,* 1969, **5**, 189-202.

Lawler, E. E., III. Effects of hourly overpayment on productivity and work quality. *Journal of Personality and Social Psychology,* 1968, **10**, 306-313.

Leavitt, H. J. Some effects of certain communication patterns on group performance. *Journal of Abnormal and Social Psychology,* 1951, **46**, 38-50.

LeBon, G. *The crowd.* London: T. Fisher Unwin, 1914.

Leik, R. K. The distribution of acts in small groups. *Sociometry,* 1967, **30**, 280-299.

Lewin, K. *Field theory in social science.* New York: Harper, 1951.

Lewin, K. Studies in group decision. In D. Cartwright and A. Zander (Eds.), *Group dynamics: Research and theory.* Evanston, Illinois: Row, Peterson, 1953. Pp. 287-301.

Lewin, K., Lippitt, R., and White, R. K. Patterns of aggressive behavior in experimentally created "social climates." *Journal of Social Psychology,* 1939, **10**, 271-299.

Lorge, I. and Solomon, H. Two models of group behavior in the solution of eureka-type problems. *Psychometrika,* 1955, **20**, 139-148.

Maier, N. R. F. and Solem, A. R. The contribution of a discussion leader to the quality of group thinking: The effective use of minority opinions. *Human Relations,* 1952, **5**, 277-288.

Mann, R. D. A review of the relationships between personality and performance in small groups. *Psychological Bulletin,* 1959, **56,** 241-270.

March, J. G. and Simon, H. A. *Organizations.* New York: Wiley, 1958.

Marquart, D. I. Group problem solving. *Journal of Social Psychology,* 1955, **41,** 103-113.

McCurdy, H. G. and Lambert, W. E. The efficiency of small human groups in the solution of problems requiring genuine cooperation. *Journal of Personality,* 1952, **20,** 478-494.

McGrath, J. E. The influence of positive interpersonal relations on adjustment and effectiveness in rifle teams. *Journal of Abnormal and Social Psychology,* 1962, **65,** 365-375.

McGrath, J. E. and Altman, I. *Small group research.* New York: Holt, 1966.

Merei, F. Group leadership and institutionalization. In E. E. Maccoby, T. M. Newcomb, and E. L. Hartley (Eds.), *Readings in social psychology.* New York: Holt, 1958. Pp. 522-532.

Merton, R. K. *Social theory and social structure.* Glencoe, Illinois: Free Press, 1957.

Milgram, S. Behavioral study of obedience. *Journal of Abnormal and Social Psychology,* 1963, **67,** 371-378.

Miller, L. K. and Hamblin, R. L. Interdependence, differential rewarding, and productivity. *American Sociological Review,* 1963, **28,** 768-778.

Mintz, A. Nonadaptive group behavior. *Journal of Abnormal and Social Psychology,* 1951, **46,** 150-159.

Mohanna, A. and Argyle, M. A cross-cultural study of structured groups with unpopular central members. *Journal of Abnormal and Social Psychology,* 1960, **60,** 139-140.

Moos, R. H. and Speisman, J. C. Group compatibility and productivity. *Journal of Abnormal and Social Psychology,* 1962, **65,** 190-196.

Murphy, G., Murphy, L. B. and Newcomb, T. M. *Experimental social psychology.* New York: Harper, 1937.

Myers, A. Team competition, success, and the adjustment of group members. *Journal of Abnormal and Social Psychology,* 1962, **65,** 325-332.

Newcomb, T. M. *The acquaintance process.* New York: Holt, 1961.

Orne, M. T. and Evans, F. J. Social control in the psychological experiment. *Journal of Personality and Social Psychology,* 1965, **1,** 189-200.

Roby, T. B. and Lanzetta, J. T. Work group structure, communication and group performance. *Sociometry,* 1956, **19,** 105-113.

Rosenthal, D. and Cofer, C. N. The effect on group performance of an indifferent and neglectful attitude shown by one group member. *Journal of Experimental Psychology,* 1948, **38,** 568-577.

Runkel, P. J. Cognitive similarity in facilitating communication. *Sociometry,* 1956, **19,** 178-191.

Ryack, B. L. A comparison of individual and group learning of nonsense syllables. *Journal of Personality and Social Psychology,* 1965, **2,** 296-299.

Schachter, S. Deviation, rejection, and communication. *Journal of Abnormal and Social Psychology,* 1951, **46,** 190-207.

Schachter, S. The interaction of cognitive and physiological determinants of emotional state. In P. H. Leiderman and D. Shapiro (Eds.), *Psychobiological approaches to social behavior.* Stanford, California: Stanford Univ. Press, 1964. Pp. 138-173.

Schachter, S., Nuttin, J., de Monchaux, C., Maucorps, P. H., Osmer, D., Duijker, H., Rommetveit, R., and Israel, J. Cross-cultural experiments on threat and rejection. *Human Relations,* 1954, **7,** 403-439.

Schutz, W. C. *FIRO: A three-dimensional theory of interpersonal behavior.* New York: Holt, 1958.

Scofield, R. W. Task productivity of groups of friends and nonfriends. *Psychological Reports*, 1960, **6**, 459-460.

Sears, R. R. A theoretical framework for social behavior and personality development. *American Psychologist*, 1951, 6, 476-482.

Sermat, V. Is game behavior related to behavior in other situations? *Journal of Personality and Social Psychology*, 1970, **16**, 92-109.

Shaw, D. M. Size of share in task and motivation in work groups. *Sociometry*, 1960, **23**, 203-208.

Shaw, Marjorie E. A comparison of individuals and small groups in the rational solution of complex problems. *American Journal of Psychology*, 1932, **44**, 491-504.

Shaw, Marvin E. Acceptance of authority, group structure, and effectiveness of small groups. *Journal of Personality*, 1959, **27**, 196-210.

Shaw, Marvin E. A note concerning homogeneity of membership and group problem solving. *Journal of Abnormal and Social Psychology*, 1960, **60**, 448-450.

Sherif, M. *The psychology of social norms.* New York: Harper, 1936.

Simmel, G. *The sociology of Georg Simmel.* (Trans, by K. H. Wolff). Glencoe, Illinois: Free Press, 1950.

Slater, P. E. Role differentiation in small groups. *American Sociological Review*, 1955, **20**, 300-310.

Slater, P. E. Contrasting correlates of group size. *Sociometry*, 1958, **21**, 129-139.

Smelser, W. T. Personality influences in social situations. *Journal of Abnormal and Social Psychology*, 1961, **62**, 535-542.

Solomon, R. L. and Lemann, T. N. *Report of the first five years, 1946-1951.* Cambridge, Massachusetts: Harvard Laboratory of Social Relations, 1951.

Steiner, I. D. Interpersonal behavior as influenced by accuracy of social perception. *Psychological Review*, 1955, **62**, 268-274.

Steiner, I. D. Models for inferring relationships between group size and potential group productivity. *Behavioral Science*, 1966, **11**, 273-283.

Steiner, I. D. and Rajaratnam, N. A model for the comparison of individual and group performance scores. *Behavioral Science*, 1961, **6**, 142-147.

Stephan, F. F. The relative rate of communication between members of small groups. *American Sociological Review*, 1972, 17, 482-486.

Stephan, F. F. and Mishler, E. G. The distribution of participation in small groups: An exponential approximation. *American Sociological Review*, 1952, **17**, 598-608.

Taylor, D. W. Problem solving by groups. In *Proceedings of the XIV International Congress of Psychology*, 1954. Amsterdam: North Holland Publ., 1954.

Taylor, D. W., Berry, P. C., and Block, C. H. Does group participation when using brainstorming facilitate or inhibit creative thinking? *Administrative Science Quarterly*, 1958, **3**, 23-47.

Taylor, D. W. and Faust, W. L. Twenty questions: Efficiency in problem solving as a function of size of group. *Journal of Experimental Psychology*, 1952, **44**, 360-368.

Taylor, F. W. *Principles and methods of scientific management.* New York: Harper, 1911.

Thelen, H. A. Group dynamics in instruction: Principles of least group size. *School Review*, 1949, **57**, 139-148.

Theodorson, G. A. Elements in the progressive development of small groups. *Social Forum*, 1953, **31**, 311-320.

Thibaut, J. W. and Kelley, H. H. *The social psychology of groups.* New York: Wiley, 1959.

Thomas, E. J. Effects of facilitative role interdependence on group functioning. *Human Relations*, 1957, **10**, 347-366.

Thomas, E. J. and Fink, C. F. Models of group problem solving. *Journal of Abnormal and Social Psychology,* 1961, **63,** 53-63.

Thomas, E. J. and Fink, C. F. Effects of group size. *Psychological Bulletin,* 1963, **60,** 371-384.

Thorndike, R. L. On what type of task will a group do well? *Journal of Abnormal and Social Psychology,* 1938, **33,** 409-413.

Torrance, E. P. Some consequences of power differences on decision making in permanent and temporary three-man groups. *Research Studies, State College of Washington,* 1954, **22,** 130-140.

Torrance, E. P. and Staff, Survival Research. A report of the fourth year of development. CRL Field Unit No. 2, Stead Air Force Base, Reno, Nevada, 1955.

Triandis, H. C. Cognitive similarity and communication in a dyad. *Human Relations,* 1960, **13,** 175-183.

Van Zelst, R. H. Validation of a sociometric regrouping procedure. *Journal of Abnormal and Social Psychology,* 1952, **47,** 299-301.

Vroom, V. H. *Work and motivation.* New York: Wiley, 1964.

Watson, G. B. Do groups think more efficiently than individuals? *Journal of Abnormal and Social Psychology,* 1928, **23,** 328-336.

Wegner, Norma and Zeaman, D. Team and individual performances on a motor learning task. *Journal of General Psychology,* 1956, **55,** 127-142.

Wicker, A. W. Size of church membership and members' support of church behavior settings. *Journal of Personality and Social Psychology,* 1969, **13,** 278-288.

Wiest, W. M., Porter, L. W., and Ghiselli, E. E. Relationship between individual proficiency and team performance and efficiency. *Journal of Applied Psychology,* 1961, **45,** 435-440.

Zajonc, R. B. *Social psychology: An experimental approach.* Belmont, California: Brooks/Cole, 1966.

Ziller, R. C. Group size: A determinant of the quality and stability of group decisions. *Sociometry,* 1957, **20,** 165-173.

Ziller, R. C. and Behringer, R. D. Assimilation of the knowledgeable newcomer under conditions of group success and failure. *Journal of Abnormal and Social Psychology,* 1960, **60,** 288-291.

Author Index

Subject Index